INFLATION,
THE QUANTITY THEORY,
AND RATIONAL EXPECTATIONS

Studies in Monetary Economics

Editor

KARL BRUNNER

Associate Editors

RUDIGER DORNBUSCH
PIETER KORTEWEG
THOMAS MAYER

Volume 5

NORTH-HOLLAND PUBLISHING COMPANY
AMSTERDAM • NEW YORK • OXFORD

Inflation,
the Quantity Theory,
and Rational Expectations

EDUARD JAN BOMHOFF

Erasmus University
Rotterdam
The Netherlands

NORTH-HOLLAND PUBLISHING COMPANY
AMSTERDAM • NEW YORK • OXFORD

ISBN: 0 444 85472 x ✓
First edition 1980
1st reprint 1983

ISBN: 0 444 85472 x

Publishers:
NORTH-HOLLAND PUBLISHING COMPANY
AMSTERDAM ● NEW YORK ● OXFORD

Sole distributors for the U.S.A. and Canada:
ELSEVIER NORTH-HOLLAND, INC.
52 VANDERBILT AVENUE
NEW YORK, N.Y. 10017

Library of Congress Cataloging in Publication Data

Bomhoff, Eduard Jan, 1944-
  Inflation, the quantity theory, and rational
expectations.

  (Studies in monetary economics ; v. 5)
  Bibliography: p.
  Includes index.
  1. Inflation (Finance) 2. Quantity theory of
money. 3. Inflation (Finance)--United States--
Mathematical models. 4. Inflation (Finance)--
Netherlands--Mathematical models. I. Title.
HG229.B593   332.4'1'051   80-11133
ISBN 0-444-85472-X

PRINTED IN THE NETHERLANDS

INTRODUCTION TO THE SERIES

This series publishes books of interest to students and researchers working in the fields of macro-economics, monetary theory and policy, banking and the operation of financial markets. It is intended that works of empirical emphasis will be included in the series along with theoretical contributions. Publications will include research monographs and the proceedings of significant conferences. The editor welcomes submissions of manuscripts for inclusion in the series.

to Janneke

'Wage rates, productivity, profits; that is what we should be discussing instead of all this nonsense about money supply.'

Roy Harrod

'Inflation is always and everywhere a monetary phenomenon.'

Milton Friedman

'You can reconstruct macro-models by paying a little more attention to the supply side and get a reasonable account of the 1970s.'

Robert Solow

'Existing Keynesian macroeconometric models are incapable of providing reliable guidance in formulating monetary, fiscal and other types of policy ...there is no hope that minor or even major modifications of these models will lead to significant improvement in their reliability.'

Robert Lucas
Thomas Sargent

. . .

CONTENTS

ACKNOWLEDGMENTS

I am greatly indebted to Pieter Korteweg for many discussions over a number of years. His continuing interest could not be more appreciated. Arnold Merkies read the complete manuscript and suggested many improvements, particularly in section 2.1, for which I am very grateful. Helpful comments were also received from participants at the ninth Konstanz Seminar on Monetary Theory and Monetary Policy where an early version of chapter 2 was presented.

I would also like to express my sincere appreciation to Jacqueline Rijsdijk, Fred Bär, Cees Bangma and Jan Ooms for computational assistance, to Albany Brown for patiently indicating a number of stylistic improvements, and to Liesbeth Knulst for checking the references. Lilian Becks-v.d. Ackerveken, Ciska Glerum, Marleen Koffijberg and Fransje Wels typed the manuscript quickly and efficiently. I thank them all.

Eduard J. Bomhoff

Chapter 1

AN ECONOMIC THEORY OF INFLATION

1.1. INTRODUCTION

Not so long ago, inflation was simply regarded as the
consequence of too much money chasing too few goods. Economists
in the 1920's generally accepted the quantity theory of money
(Maier, 1978), and the single term "inflation" was used both
to describe a persistent rise in the general level of prices
and to denote increases in the volume of money in circulation:

> "When I began studying economics at the University of
> Vienna, immediately after the First World War, we were
> having a rapid increase of prices in Austria and, when
> asked what the cause was, we said it was inflation!
> By inflation we meant the increase in that thing which
> many are now are afraid to mention -- the quantity of
> money."
>
> (Machlup, 1972, p. 26).

The present study fits in that old tradition. It reaches
the same conclusion as Machlup and his fellow-students half
a century ago: a continuous rise in prices is caused by
a similar increase in the quantity of money. However, the
argumentation is different and is based on recent advances in
economic theory and statistical methodology.

The whole corpus of economic theory and econometric
practice is currently being overhauled as economists try, with
more consistency than before, to apply one of the basic
principles of their science, that of economic rationality.
The assumption that people behave rationally has always been

1

"economics' main export commodity to the other social sciences" (Simon, 1978a, p. 4). At the same time, the profession itself has often violated the rationality postulate, particularly in the field of modelling expectations. Not as a matter of principle, but for statistical and analytical convenience (Nerlove, 1967, p. 128), economists preferred adaptive expectations or other simple forecasting schemes that were selected on a priori grounds without considering whether these mechanical formulas provided rational predictions. A much-needed innovation has been provided by the time-series techniques of Box and Jenkins (1970), so that modern theoretical insights, for example in the relation between money and prices under rational expectations (Brock, 1972, 1974), can now be implemented empirically.

It is sometimes claimed that quantity theorists hold an extreme view about price flexibility because they assume that a change in one relative price, e.g. the price of coffee, will lead to a decrease in real balances, and thus to a fall in other prices, so that an aggregate price index does not necessarily have to go up. In the models of chapters 2 - 4, however, we shall postulate proportionality, not between the stock of money and the price level, but only between the expected rate of money growth and the expected rate of inflation. Allowance will be made for temporary discrepancies between expected and actual rates of price change, so that relative price changes can have short-term effects on an aggregate price index.

We shall assume that economic agents are rational and capable of distinguishing between changes in the "underlying" rate of inflation on the one hand and accidental one-time changes in the price level on the other. This distinction is lost in models that base expectations of inflation partly or wholly on past rates of price change (for example: Sargent, 1976c, 1977a). In such models, a rise in the price of coffee not only affects the current rate of price change but also the rate of inflation in all future periods. Such an outcome is truly extreme, unless we make particular assumptions about wage-price behaviour and about a completely passive monetary policy. The alternative hypothesis, on which the present study will focus, is that agents know the difference between transitory "blips" in a price index and movements in the sustained rate of inflation. It follows that one cannot model their inflationary expectations by a weighted average of actual past rates of price change. Instead, these inflationary expectations will be based on expectations about future growth of the money stock.

The question of how to calculate inflationary expectations would not arise, of course, with a theory of inflation that does not require expectations at all. Such a theory does indeed exist and is popular with some economists. According to this theory (sometimes called neo-Keynesian), trade unions are sufficiently powerful to determine the rate of wage inflation. Entrepreneurs then try to protect their profits by increasing prices. The monetary authorities accommodate by supplying enough money to finance the necessary increase in nominal demand, because a non-accommodating monetary policy would cause unemployment:

> "Wage rates, productivity, profits; that is what we should
> be discussing around this table instead of all this non-
> sense about money supply."
> (Harrod, 1972b, p. 99).

Such a view of inflation assigns substantial power to trade unions to fix wages and to entrepreneurs to set prices. Changes in the power of these groups then cause changes in the rate of inflation. Problems with the definition and measurement of economic power (Barry, 1976, and Anderson, 1978) and the fact that

> "there is a great deal to suggest that many unions
> normally operate with an unused margin of monopoly power"
> (Brittan, 1978, p. 174),

mean that various untestable ad-hoc hypotheses are usually needed to "explain" why the rate of inflation goes up or down.

The difficulty with this approach is not that it transcends the boundaries of economic science. No explanation of *why* inflation happens can be purely economic; one based on the quantity theory is no exception.

> "Economic factors, and they alone, can explain how
> inflation happens, but economic factors alone cannot
> explain why."
> (Hirsch, 1978, p. 263).

However, the power-theory of inflation also rejects economic
analysis as useless for the question *how* inflation happens.
Its followers stress the new and sociological aspects of the
current inflation as a double excuse for not stating empirically
refutable hypotheses. Harrod claims:

> "This new wage-price explosion is altogether unprecedented,
> and my own opinion is that the causes are sociological."
> (1972a, p. 44).

Wiles states:

> "I incline to put much the larger weight on *less strictly
> economic factors*. It is, surely, the communications
> revolution which, making everyone instantly aware of
> everything, has sharply increased the amount of envy and
> imitation in the world, and reduced the number of things
> that are sacrosanct. We have moved from wage claims based
> on the actual situation in the trade through claims based
> on concessions made elsewhere in the economy to claims
> picked out of the air."
> (1973, p. 378).

The present study is limited to the question *how* inflation
happens, and its aim is to investigate what economic analysis,
founded on the assumption of rational behaviour, can contribute.
Only when choice-theoretic assumptions have failed to account
for the evidence, should the scientist be prepared to resort to
other explanations that are more ad-hoc and thus have lower
predictive power. As far as the post-war inflation in the U.S.
and the Netherlands is concerned, this will not be necessary
since the economic theory that we shall employ will survive
a confrontation with the data.

In the following three sections, we shall take up first
why the assumption of rational behaviour is such a vital one

for the economist (section 1.2.); second, why it should
certainly be applied to the formulation of expectations
(section 1.3.); and third, how the Box-Jenkins technique can
help to calculate empirical proxies for rational expectations
(section 1.4.). An attempt will then be made in chapters 2 - 4,
to revisit the quantity theory with strict application of the
principle of rationality.

1.2. RATIONAL BEHAVIOUR

Throughout this study, we shall assume that economic subjects
act rationally and form their expectations about the future in
a rational manner. Strict application of this principle is still
unusual in economic research and tends to be met with strong
objections. We shall therefore postpone technical comments about
the ways in which rational expectations can be modelled until the
next section, and first try to explain why the assumption of
rationality has been made.

Economic science formulates and tests hypotheses about
individual human action that can be derived from inter-temporal
optimizing processes, under the assumption that the maximand is
given. The use of such optimization techniques is what is meant
by the assumption of economic rationality. The question whether
much or little of man's purposeful behaviour can be fruitfully
studied in this way and with it the question whether man acts
rationally in the economic sense becomes an empirical issue.
Hypothesis testing will show the "coverage" of the rationality
assumption and should guard economists from economistic
solipsism.

Experience so far has indicated that in contemporary
society important aspects of many activities are amenable to
economic analysis (and thus to the automatically implied
assumption of rational behaviour).
According to Godelier (1966):

"The more complex the division of labour, the more do

economic activities acquire relative autonomy in the
social totality and the easier is it to define elementary
economic categories, that is, categories and laws that are
"simply" economic. Contrariwise, the simpler a society is,
the less possible is it to isolate the economic from the
other elements in social life, and the more complex will
be the analysis of an apparently economic mechanism, since
the entire social configuration is directly present at the
heart of this mechanism."
(p. 302 of the English translation).

Also, according to Sahlins (1976, p.p. 212-213):

"Not only is Western civilization characterized by the
structural separation of functional spheres, ... but ....
all are subordinated to the requirements of the economy
...., (whereas) in primitive society, economic, political,
and ritual action are organized by the one generalized
kinship structure ....

     The two cultural orders elevate certain institutional
relations to a position of dominance, as the site from
which the symbolic grid is precipitated and the code
objectified. In bourgeois society, material production is
the dominant locus of symbolic production; in primitive
society it is the set of social (kinship) relations.
.... (C)apitalist production is as much as any other
economic system a cultural specification and not merely
a natural-material activity; for as it is the means of
a total mode of life it is necessarily the production of
symbolic significance. Nevertheless, because it appears to
the producer as a quest for pecuniary gain, and to the
consumer as an acquisition of "useful" goods, the basic
symbolic character of the process goes on entirely behind
the backs of the participants -- and usually of economists
as well, insofar as the meaningful structure of demand is
an exogenous "given" of their analyses .... The reasoning
is simple and *violates no conventional understanding of
the capitalist process* ...." (emphasis added).

The relative autonomy and the predominance of the economic sphere explains why rational means-end analysis is often fruitful in modern market economies. Many human actions in these societies are amenable to economic analysis because the purpose of such action is unambiguously known. Many useful hypotheses about firms, for example, can be formulated on the safe assumption that firms maximize profits. (An assumption about the firm's goal must be made a priori, since one cannot use the same observations both to determine the purpose of some activity and the rationality of the means that are employed). Specifically, firms that have profit-maximizing competitors will have to base their actions on the best possible forecasts of the future, and rational means-end analysis can then be applied also to formulate hypotheses about these forecasts. By contrast, economic analysis does not appear to be very useful for explaining the activities of the ancient Oracle at Delphi, unless both the aim of its predictive work and the extent of competition in this trade can be known!

Another reason why Sahlins has been quoted at length is because of his observation that production and consumption have not lost their symbolic significance in a capitalist society. Wants and preferences, however, are assumed to be given exogenously in economic analysis, and if the term "rational" is applied -- by non-economists -- to the preferences of individuals or groups, then its meaning is quite different. Economic rationality is concerned solely with the optimal selection of (costly) means to achieve a given, positively valued, aim. Hypothesis testing should show the "coverage" of this rationality assumption, but many people are not satisfied with such a pragmatic approach. The remainder of this section will therefore be devoted to three common objections to the economist's assumption of rational behaviour.

First, it is feared that the stress on rationality makes people egoistic. In an influential book, Titmuss (1971) showed that the introduction of payment for blood has the effect of drying up the supply of voluntary, unpaid blood. More generally, it has been argued:

"Cooperation can develop into an extended relation of
mutual concern and respect. But such a relation cannot
be recommended on conceptions of rational self-interest
alone, for each person involved may well at any time
maximize individual gain by taking advantage of the
other and turning the relation into a competitive one
on grounds of rationality."
(Held, 1977, p. 743).

The obvious answer to these and similar remarks is that
the assumption of rationality has an "as if" character and is
not concerned with the way in which people think (Knight, 1951,
Simon, 1978a, b).

A second line of argument against the rationality
postulate points out:

"Once one goes beyond the rationality of individuals to
rationality in groups, new difficulties arise."
(Vickrey, 1977, p. 698).

We encounter these difficulties since we shall need to
describe the behaviour of a bureaucracy at two points. In the
next chapter we shall formulate a hypothesis about the money
supply behaviour of the Central Bank, and in chapter 5 we shall
need to discuss the behaviour of the Dutch Central Planning
Bureau, a government agency that publishes price forecasts. When
the economist tries to analyse such political entities he will
-- by definition -- continue to assume that the officers of these
institutions act rationally and attempt to maximize their chance
of survival and success in the bureaucracy. Brunner (1972) argues
that the pursuit of these objectives will not create the amount
of "cognitive rationality" needed both for optimal policy-making,
and for insight in the bureaucracy's actions.

The work of Brunner and others helps to explain many
aspects of government and Central Bank behaviour and shows at
the same time that one would be naive to expect that rational
bureaucrats automatically do what is best for society as a whole.
On the contrary, when we analyze groups or organizations it is
often impossible to derive the utility-probability combination

that is being maximized by the group from assumptions about the preferences of the group's members, particularly if they play a game that is predominantly non-cooperative (Harsanyi, 1976, chapter 6). Also, one cannot use the same observations to determine both what the group's utility function is and whether it is maximized in a rational way. Consequently, when discussing Central Bank behaviour, we shall exclude only *obviously* suicidal paths for the money supply in those economies in which economic and political "markets" still work. Each of a number of simple hypotheses about the money supply -- constant, fixed growth, random walk, etc. -- is considered in chapter 2. The attempt to derive a *single* money supply hypothesis from considerations about the optimal path of money would work better in a context where money is not produced by a government monopoly but by contract with a private firm.

When the official Dutch price forecasts are discussed in chapter 4, we shall find that they are far from optimal and we shall try to account for this by assuming that the Central Planning Bureau has other aims than just producing the best possible forecasts. In both cases we have to do with a *large bureaucracy* instead of the single actor of economic analysis and, moreover, with a *monopoly situation*, without competition to eliminate behaviour that is consistently sub-optimal. It is true that in such situations predictive power will be lost if we refuse to view the bureaucracy otherwise than as a single decision-making unit that maximizes a well-defined and simple utility function (see Allison, 1971, for a fascinating example of applying first rational actor analysis and then other paradigms to different aspects of a historical episode).

Finally, there are those who object to the assumption of rationality, and specifically rationality in the formation of expectations, because it is too demanding on economic subjects. In fact, however, only one thing is asked, namely that people spot systematic opportunities for profit and try to exploit these. Darwinian selection then makes it seem as if the representative firm (not: the typical firm) behaves rationally

(Alchian, 1950). The system induces rationality and it is not necessary for economic analysis to make assumptions about the way in which individuals reach their decisions (cf. Simon, 1978a, b).

The argument against the thesis that rational expectations are too difficult can also be made by considering what will happen when the cost of mistaken predictions increases, so that people want to improve their efforts to forecast as accurately as possible. Which aim will they set themselves, as they review their current forecasting practices? Assume, for example, that the rate of inflation increases and people make greater efforts to anticipate the future course of prices. Does it make sense to assume that they will now more and more trust predictive formulas such as the adaptive expectations scheme with its predictable errors? It is more attractive to assume that expectations are intendedly rational (Gordon and Hynes, 1970, p. 388); every other assumption has an unstable character.

Of these three objections to assuming rationality, only the second point -- rationality in groups and organizations -- indicates important limitations to the rational actor model of economic analysis. But, as long as individual behaviour in a market context is discussed, economists must work with the assumption that economic agents are rational, so that they can use the tools of their trade. We shall find that as far as inflationary expectations by individuals and firms are concerned, the evidence nowhere contradicts the assumption that such fore-casts are formed rationally. A neo-Keynesian approach to inflation may ostensibly have a similar explanatory force, but as long as it is based on ad-hoc assumptions about economic power and on irrational expectations, it should be rejected in favour of a theory which assumes rational behaviour. The rational actor paradigm should come first, *and there is no need to return to those questions that can be answered satisfactorily with the assumption that people behave rationally.*

1.3. RATIONAL EXPECTATIONS

In this section we shall discuss two consequences of the
assumption that expectations are formed rationally. The first
concerns the way in which expectations are modelled, and is
being accepted by a growing minority of economists. A second
aspect of rational expectations -- namely its implications for
the term structure of expectations -- has been mentioned
occasionally in the literature, but has not yet, to our
knowledge, been strictly applied in empirical work.

What the rationality assumption means for the specification of economic models may be illustrated with an example.
Suppose we have an economic model in which the expected rate of
growth of output depends on many factors, such as world trade,
agricultural production, government policies, etc. Now let the
expected rate of growth of output be included in one of the
equations of the model, for example the equation for imports,
and let it be proxied by the lagged growth of output. But, if
expected output growth $E(\hat{y})$ is proxied by a distributed lag on
$\hat{y}$ in one equation of the model (with $E(\hat{y}) = \hat{y}_{-1}$ as the simplest
case), whereas one of the aims of the model as a whole is
to show how $\hat{y}$ depends on various economic factors, then the
model is self-contradictory. Also, systematic opportunities for
profit are left open, and these are unlikely to exist in a
competitive import sector for much the same reason that the stock
market is efficient. Importers who use the regularities that are
expressed in the complete model to forecast $\hat{y}$ will drive those
who forecast according to $E(\hat{y}) = \hat{y}_{-1}$ out of business. Presumably
the lagged rate of growth of output has been included in the
imports equation because it happens to improve the statistical
fit of that equation and the assertion that it represents an
expectation may be unfounded.

The proper way to model an expectational variable is to
make the expectation a function of all those economic factors
that should be relevant, according to the postulated economic
model. This approach is followed, for example, in recent work

by Korteweg (1978a, b), and has also been used in this study.
We begin by estimating models for exogenous variables that are
used in the analysis. On the basis of these results, we subsequently model the expectations of the endogenous variables.
In Korteweg's work, the expectations of the endogenous variables
are functions of exogenous variables. For example:

$$(1.1) \qquad \hat{p}^e = \alpha \hat{M}^e + \beta \hat{p}^{*e} \qquad\qquad , \qquad \alpha, \beta > 0$$

Here, $\hat{p}^e$ is the expected rate of inflation in a small open
economy, $\hat{M}^e$ stands for the expected rate of domestic money
growth, and $\hat{p}^{*e}$ is the expected rate of inflation in the world.

In the present study, a generalization of the format used
in equation (1.1) is developed (see chapter 2), and expectations
are also determined by behavioural equations. For example, we
shall use:

$$(1.2) \qquad \hat{p}^e = \hat{M}^e - (1 - \delta_1)\hat{y}^e \qquad\qquad , \qquad \delta_1 \gtrless 0$$

with $\hat{p}^e, \hat{M}^e$ as above, and $\hat{y}^e$ the expected rate of growth of
domestic output. This equation will be derived from the demand
for money function under certain simplifying assumptions. Only
when series for the expected values of some endogenous variables
have been generated, can we estimate the behavioural equations
in which expectations about output growth or other endogenous
variables are required.

Until now, we have discussed the case of a given equation
in an econometric model which included a term that might represent an expectation. The rationality assumption also has its
consequences for the theoretical specification of the behavioural
equations. Take, for example, the case of the demand for money
function:

$$M = p + \alpha y + \beta r_1 + \gamma r_2 \qquad (\alpha > 0 \; ; \; \beta, \gamma < 0)$$

with M,p,y as before and r_1, r_2 rates of return on alternative assets. In a context of comparative statics, this relation can be put on a choice-theoretic basis (aggregation problems remain, but these are another matter). People decide at the margin whether to hold money, stores of goods, or financial assets.

Whether the equation still describes the behaviour of rational maximizers in a dynamic context entirely depends on the assumptions made about the stochastic behaviour of p, y, r_1 and r_2. Assume, for example, that money, prices, and income have been stable for some time, but that in two years time an electoral contest will be held between the current government and an opposition party which favours an expansionary economic policy that will result in sharp increases in the money stock (cf. Brock, 1974, p. 751). Those people who expect that such a policy will affect prices rather than output, and are afraid that the opposition has a chance of winning the forthcoming election, will start buying goods now. The rate of interest will increase, the demand for money will fall, and prices will have to go up. The old demand for money function no longer describes optimal behaviour, because not just the current price level, but the complete expected future course of prices as well are relevant for determining the quantity of money demanded.

It will be clear from this example that in a dynamic model, before we can trust its demand for money function, we need to know whether economic agents are capable of predicting the future of any of the exogenous and endogenous variables that influence money holdings. For if they can, they will certainly base their portfolio behaviour also on these expectations. In other words, the behavioural equations of an economic model can only be specified, conditional on the stochastic behaviour of all the exogenous and endogenous variables in the model.

If economic subjects are capable of looking far into the future, these behavioural equations will have to contain a whole term structure of expectations, not only for the next year, but also for a number of subsequent years. It will then be hard to derive the proper functional forms from economic

theory (see Brock, 1972, 1974, for an example). The obvious
mathematical tool, the calculus of variations, is only
applicable in a limited number of cases, and not, for example,
for the determination of the links between expected money growth
and inflation (see chapter 2).

In this study we have made a simplifying assumption about
the term structure of expectations, so that we do not require
more than just the expectation about the next period in the
behavioural equations:

$$_t E\hat{z}_{t+1} = {}_t E\hat{z}_{t+2} = {}_t E\hat{z}_{t+3} = \ldots$$

with $_t E\hat{z}_{t+k}$ the expectation of $\hat{z}$ for period t+k, held during
period t. This simple term structure of expectations is
imposed on a number of endogenous variables. It will imply that
theorizing about the equations does not become infinitely more
complicated in a dynamic context than in a static one, because
behaviour in the dynamic case is no longer dependent upon a whole
string of differently dated anticipations. People's expectations
about the future are compressed into a single, representative
number, and we can still derive their behaviour from the
assumption that they are rational optimizers.

1.4. CALCULATION OF EXPECTATIONS

Rationality implies that economic subjects extend the information set I on which the expectations about a variable $\hat{z}$ are
based, until the cost of collecting and processing extra relevant
information is equal at the margin to the benefits to be
obtained from further accuracy in predicting $\hat{z}$. Whether the
information set consists of past values of $\hat{z}$ only, or whether it
also includes other variables, the forecast errors have to be
serially uncorrelated. Correlation in the residuals means that
inspection of previous errors can contribute to improve the
current predictions, and it is to be assumed that this error-

learning process is costless and will therefore always be under-
taken without delay.

The time series methodology of Box and Jenkins provides
the statistical techniques for calculating series for z^e, the
expected rate of growth of z, and for $(\hat{z} - \hat{z}^e)$, that satisfy
this requirement, both in the univariate and the multivariate
case. Therefore, Box-Jenkins techniques have been used everywhere for the calculation of expectations.

For each Box-Jenkins model, approximate standard errors
of the coefficients are presented, and a value of $\bar{R}^2$, adjusted
for degrees of freedom is also given, although the non-
linearity of most models implies that many of the usual properties that $\bar{R}^2$ possesses in the multivariate linear model do
not apply (see Nelson, 1976, for a justification of using $\bar{R}^2$
for time-series models).

Care has been taken to remove all outliers from the
series before the models were estimated, with an outlier
defined as an observation more than 2.5 standard deviations
away from the mean. In series of sufficient length, one would
replace an outlier $\hat{y}_t$ in period t = T by the weighted mean of
two forecasts for $\hat{y}_T$, one ordinary forecast based on the values
of $\hat{y}$ that occurred for t < T , and one backward forecast, based
on subsequent observations with t > T . The number of observations does not allow this, so that any outliers have been replaced by predictions from one model only. Details are given in
Appendix 2.

The short length of the time series also means that the
standard Box-Pierce test of the appropriateness of the chosen
model (see Ljung and Box, 1978, for a modification to this test)
will have limited power. Often it will not be possible to discriminate, for example, between an AR(1) and a MA(1) model. In
such cases, we have preferred moving-average models to auto-
regressive models for two reasons.

In the first place, the popularity of the autoregressive
models has been more a matter of statistical convenience than
anything else, whereas the moving-average model has a natural

interpretation as random walk plus noise. Consider, for example, the following useful model:

$$\hat{x}_t = \hat{y}_t + u_t$$

$$\hat{y}_t = \hat{y}_{t-1} + v_t$$

Here, u_t and v_t are independent white noise series. $\hat{y}_t$ can be considered as the unobservable underlying growth rate of some economic variable, and $\hat{x}_t$ as the observed value of this growth rate. u_t then has an interpretation as a measurement error or as a temporary disturbance that does not permanently affect $\hat{y}$. The optimal predictor of $\hat{y}$ (and of $\hat{x}$) is the first-order moving-average model (Nerlove, 1967). Muth (1960) uses this model with y_t as permanent income and x_t as measured income. Mussa (1976b, 1978) chooses it to describe the money supply. Here we shall also use it for money supplied and many other series.

   The second argument for preferring moving-average models is that they result in a simpler term structure of expectations. This holds particularly for the first-order moving-average model, which was found adequate for many series (see section 2.2.).

   One remaining problem is to decide whether to use univariate models for the exogenous variables or whether to specify multi-variate "economic" prediction formulas. The forecast errors can usually be reduced by adding explanatory variables, but the difficulty is that we do not know at which point economic agents stop extending the information set (McCallum, 1976).

   An important consideration is that univariate models for $\hat{E}(x)$ can lead to inconsistency in equations where $\hat{E}(x)$ is one of the explanatory variables, as explained by Nelson (1975). Let $\hat{x}^*$ be the optimal univariate predictor of $\hat{x}$ and $\hat{x}^{**}$ the pre-dictor based on a wider information set which includes the other variables z_i, z_j. Both $\hat{x}^*$ and $\hat{x}^{**}$ are unbiased (Shiller, 1973), but $\hat{x}^{**}$ will be more accurate, of course. Suppose we estimate the behavioural equation:

(1.3) $$y = \alpha E(\hat{x}) + \beta_1 z_1 + \ldots \beta_N z_N + u_t$$

with z a vector of explanatory variables. If now $\hat{x}^*$ is used for $E(\hat{x})$, although $\hat{x}^{**}$ is the proper proxy, then least squares will be inconsistent if z_i or z_j also appears in equation (1.3), because the error term u_t is then correlated with one of the explanatory variables. When $\hat{x}^{**}$ is used instead, such problems do not arise.

A second reason for preferring multivariate models for the calculation of expectations is that a simple multivariate model can often more easily be based on economic theory than a complicated univariate one. Sometimes, the simplest univariate models for a (seasonally adjusted) variable $\hat{x}$ are inadequate, as shown by the residual autocorrelation function. Economic agents apparently do not limit the information set to the values of $\hat{x}$ over the past one or two periods plus the previous one or two errors. In such cases, it seems more likely that they will consider the current or immediate past values of other economically relevant variables than that they will include observations from the more distant past of $\hat{x}$ in their information sets.

These are two strong arguments in favour of using multivariate formulas for the generation of expectations. In chapters 3 and 4 some multivariate models will indeed be developed, but other exogenous expectations, notably those that relate to government expenditure, will still be proxied by univariate, extrapolative models. Further discussion of the issues will be found in the two empirical chapters.

All the expectations are calculated on the basis of an information set that consists solely of actually observed data from the past. Evidence from surveys of expectations or intentions, for example, will be briefly discussed in section 4.6. but not used in the regressions of chapters 3 and 4. The fact that all expectational variables in our empirical models are calculated objectively causes an ambiguity in the interpretation of these models (Sargent, 1976a, b). Assume, for example, that the expected growth rate of some z is hypo-

thesized to influence a variable x , and that this expected
growth rate is given by the actual growth rate during the
previous period. In that case, there would be no way of
distinguishing between the hypothesis that expectations about z
are important for the determination of x , and the alternative
hypothesis that the actual growth rate of z during the previous
period is what influences x . But, if the stochastic nature of
the process that generated z underwent a change, then it would
become possible to discriminate between the two competing
hypotheses, for the observational equivalence between $_{t-1}E\ \hat{z}_t$
and the actual lagged value $\hat{z}_{t-1}$ would hold for part of the
period only. Neftci and Sargent (1978) present an example, but
our time series are too short for such tests.

   In principle, an alternative explanation in terms of
lagged effects is possible for all cases in which we shall speak
in terms of expectations. However, in those cases where the
influence of an unanticipated change in some variable z is
postulated, such distributed lags may show a pattern of lag
coefficients that would be difficult to explain in any other way
than that the distributed lag must stand for the unexpected
change in some variable. Barro (1977) gives an example of this.
Similarly, the equations in chapters 3 and 4 will contain many
terms that stand for unexpected changes in some variable,
$(\hat{x} - \hat{x}^e)_t$; substituting the appropriate distributed lag for
$\hat{x}^e_t$ would often result in a series of lag coefficients on $\hat{x}_t$
that defies an alternative explanation.

1.5. THE REST OF THE BOOK

The mathematical notation used in this study follows the usual
conventions. M , for instance, is used to denote the nominal
money stock, whereas lower-case y represents gross national
product in constant prices. The letter e is used everywhere to
indicate an expectation. x^e relates to the same period as does x,
and has therefore already been formed before the current period

starts. A full list of all the notations in this and subsequent
chapters is contained in Appendix 1, but in order to facilitate
reading, the meaning of each symbol has been repeated at more or
less regular intervals throughout the text. A caret (^) has been
used everywhere to indicate rates of growth. The models contain
identities of the type "rate of growth of variable x in current
prices = real rate of growth of x plus rate of growth of the
price of x", which is one sufficient reason for preferring first
differences of logarithms to percentage growth rates. A second
reason is that average rates of growth cannot be meaningfully
computed when percentage changes are used. Consider, for
example, a variable which takes the following values in four
consecutive years:

$$100 \ , \ 120 \ , \ 80 \ , \ 100$$

The average rate of growth is 0 when measured in the form
$100 \times \Delta \log(\text{variable})$, but 3.9% when percentages are used. Everywhere in chapters 4 - 6, $\Delta \log(\text{variable})$ has been multiplied by
100, so that the resulting numbers are directly comparable to
percentage rates of growth. In chapter 3, this was not always
possible, because sometimes the level of a series is used. There,
it has been indicated if necessary whether the calculations refer
to $\Delta \log$ or to $100 \times \Delta \log$.

The main time series used are either presented in the text
or given in Appendix 1, apart from the data for the U.S., which
are easily accessible in Barro (1978). Equations and tables are
numbered sequentially in each chapter, so that equation (4.2) is
the second referenced equation in chapter 4. All references to
the literature are made by the name of the author(s) and the
year of publication. The length of the bibliography at the end
of the book may serve as an illustration that this study is an
application of the only inflation theory that is as old as
inflation itself.

The content of the remaining chapters is as follows. The
next chapter is concerned with the theoretical model that
connects money, prices and output. Two empirical applications are
subsequently presented in chapters 3 and 4. First, we study the

relation between money growth, output growth, and inflation in
the U.S. in chapter 3, so that a comparison may be made with
the recent work by Barro (1977, 1978), who also uses the
quantity theory, but -- just to mention the main difference --
uses levels of logarithms for money, output, and prices, as
against the logarithmic first-difference form used here.
In chapter 4, the theoretical model is applied to the Netherlands
for the period 1954-1976. The same conclusions are obtained, but
the equations are rather more complicated than in the case of
the U.S. After that, the present approach is compared to the
work by Korteweg (1978b), who has followed a different approach
to the modelling of foreign influences on Dutch inflation.
We also make a comparison with the price predictions of the
Dutch Central Planning Bureau, an agency of the Ministry of
Economic Affairs. Both the acutal forecasts and the underlying
models are considered. Chapter 5 has the aim of meeting the
obvious criticism that the approach chosen here results in the
estimation of reduced-form equations and is therefore inferior
to a more structural analysis. A short, final chapter attempts
to offer some remarks about the relevance of our research and
its possible weaknesses.

Chapter 2

THE QUANTITY THEORY AND THE PRICE EQUATION

2.1. INTRODUCTION

In this chapter we shall develop the theoretical model that will
be tested in chapters 3 and 4 against data for the U.S. and the
Netherlands. The model is very small as only two markets are
described, the market for money and the market for aggregate
output of goods and services. In order to introduce the model,
a simplified version of it will be discussed in the present
section. In the subsequent sections of this chapter, we shall
put forward the actual form of each equation as it will be
estimated later.

In essence, the structure of the model is as follows:

$$(2.1) \qquad \hat{M}_t = \hat{M}_{t-1} + a_{1,t}; \quad \hat{M}^e_t = \hat{M}_{t-1} \qquad \text{-- supply for money}$$

$$(2.2) \qquad \hat{M}_t = \hat{P}_t + \hat{Y}_t - \varepsilon \Delta i_t + a_{2,t} \qquad \text{-- demand for money}$$

$$(2.3) \qquad \hat{y}^e_t = c \qquad \text{-- expected growth of output}$$

$$(2.4) \qquad (\hat{y} - \hat{y}^e)_t = - \beta_1 \Delta r_t - \beta_2 (\hat{p} - \hat{p}^e)_t + \beta_3 (\hat{g} - \hat{g}^e)_t + a_{4,t} \quad \text{--}$$
$$\text{-- actual demand for output}$$

$$(2.5) \qquad (\hat{y} - \hat{y}^e)_t = \alpha_1 (\hat{p} - \hat{p}^e)_t + a_{5,t} \qquad \text{-- short-run supply curve}$$

$$(2.6) \qquad r_t = i_t - \hat{p}^e_{t+1} \qquad \text{-- Fisher relationship}$$
$$\text{between real and nominal interest rate}$$

Here, M represents the stock of money, p the price index of
output, y, i a nominal rate of interest, r the real rate of
interest and g the rate of real government expenditure on goods
and services. A caret (^) stands for a relative rate of growth.
$a_{1,t}$, $a_{2,t}$, $a_{4,t}$ and $a_{5,t}$ are serially uncorrelated error terms.
c is a constant, and $\varepsilon, \beta_1, \beta_2, \beta_3, \alpha_1$ are positive coefficients.
$\hat{M}_t^e$, $\hat{y}_t^e$, $\hat{p}_t^e$, $\hat{g}_t^e$ are the rational expectations of $\hat{M}_t$, $\hat{y}_t$, $\hat{p}_t$ and
g_t respectively, as held before the beginning of period t.
Similarly, $\hat{p}_{t+1}^e$ is the rational expectation of $\hat{p}_{t+1}$ as held
during period t. It was argued in the previous chapter that it
is inconsistent to assume that the demand and supply schedules
in an economic model are consistent with optimizing behaviour,
but that the same economic agents who are fully rational when
they decide at the margin about supply and demand, become
systematically irrational when they have to form expectations.
Therefore, all expectations are held to be rational, i.e. based
on the solution of the complete model. As a further consequence
of rational expectations, we assume that expected supply equals
expected demand in both the money and the output market.

In the remainder of this section we shall first discuss
the six equations (2.1) - (2.6). After that, eqs. (2.1) - (2.6),
together with two further equations that are obtained through
applying the expectations operator to eqs. (2.1) and (2.2),
will be solved for the eight endogenous variables $\hat{M}$, $\hat{M}^e$, $\hat{y}$, $\hat{y}^e$,
$\hat{p}$, $\hat{p}^e$, Δr, Δi.

THE EQUATIONS

Equation (2.1) represents a formula for the supply of money.
It says that the monetary authorities plan a growth rate of
money that is equal to the actual rate of growth during the
previous period. In each period, however, an error is made,
equal to $a_{1,t}$. With this stochastic model for money growth, the
expected growth rate for the next period is also expected to be
maintained in all subsequent periods:

$$_t E \, \hat{M}_{t+1} = \, _t E \, \hat{M}_{t+2} = \, \ldots .$$

Whether this last assumption is a realistic one to make has, of course, to be tested. We shall see that it agrees with the evidence obtained from annual time series for the U.S. and the Netherlands that cover the post-war period.

The second equation of the model is a standard demand for money function, written in terms of the relative rates of growth of M, p and y. We assume that shocks $a_{2,t}$ have a temporary effect on the growth rate of money demand and therefore a permanent effect on the level of the demand for money. It would seem more likely that changes in the technology with which money is produced and utilized are permanent rather than transitory, so that the stochastic term is best attached to a money demand function that is formulated in terms of growth rates.

Substitution of eq. (2.6) in (2.2) gives:

$$\hat{M}_t = \hat{p}_t + \hat{y}_t - \varepsilon(\Delta\hat{r}_t + \hat{p}_{t+1}^e - \hat{p}_t^e) + a_{2,t},$$

where $\hat{p}_{t+1}^e = {}_t E\hat{p}_{t+1}$ and $\hat{p}_t^e = {}_{t-1}E\hat{p}_t$. Taking expectations at time t-1 and applying the chain principle of forecasting, which allows us to replace ${}_{t-1}E_t(E\hat{p}_{t+1})$ with ${}_{t-1}E\hat{p}_{t+1}$, we get:

(2.7) $$\hat{M}_t^e = \hat{p}_t^e + \hat{y}_t^e - \varepsilon {}_{t-1}E(\Delta\hat{r}_t) - \varepsilon({}_{t-1}E\hat{p}_{t+1} - {}_{t-1}E\hat{p}_t).$$

At the end of this section, it will be shown that the complete model has one solution with the following two properties: First, economic agents are unable to forecast future changes in real interest rates:

(2.8) $${}_{t-1}E(\Delta r_{t+j}) = 0, \text{ for all } j > 0.$$

Second, the change in the rate of inflation that will take place between period t and period t+1 cannot be predicted before the start of period t, since it depends only on unforeseen events that may take place during periods t and t+1:

$${}_{t-1}E\hat{p}_{t+1} = {}_{t-1}E\hat{p}_t; \text{ or more generally:}$$

(2.9) $_{t-1}E\hat{p}_{t+j} = {}_{t-1}E\hat{p}_t$, for all $j > 0$.

It is important that the model has a solution which satisfies (2.8) and (2.9). To see this, consider what would happen in the opposite situation, i.e. if future changes in the real rate of interest, or changes in the rate of inflation beyond the next period could be predicted successfully. Such predictions presumably would be based on predictions of future fluctuations in important exogenous variables. In that case, all the behavioural equations of the model ought to take this into account, and the demand for money function, for example, would have to be extended with a whole string of differently dated future expectations of interest rates and inflation rates:

$$M_t = p_t + y_t - \varepsilon_1(r_t + \hat{p}^e_{t+1}) - \varepsilon_2 \, {}_tE(r_{t+1} + \hat{p}_{t+2}) +$$

$$- \varepsilon_3 \, {}_tE(r_{t+2} + \hat{p}_{t+3}) - \ldots.$$

Fortunately, our empirical work will not reject the hypothesis that the exogenous variables behave according to simple time-series models, so that future changes in their growth rates cannot be predicted. It then follows that there is no need to include differently dated expectations in the behavioural equations of our theoretical model; in particular, it suffices to specify the current nominal interest rate and the currently expected rate of price change in the demand for money function.

The more general model that will be developed in the following sections of this chapter has a somewhat richer specification than the model of eqs. (2.1) - (2.6), but both models are constructed in such a way that they have a solution consistent with a constant term structure of expectations for $\hat{p}$:

$$_tE\hat{p}_{t+1} = {}_tE\hat{p}_{t+2} = \ldots.$$

Also both the real and the nominal rates of interest will satisfy the martingale property:

$$r_t = {}_t^{}Er_{t+1} = {}_t^{}Er_{t+2} = \dots \qquad i_t = {}_t^{}Ei_{t+1} = {}_t^{}Ei_{t+2} = \dots$$

Consequently, it is sufficient to include the current nominal rate of interest only in the demand for money function. With the two conditions (2.8) and (2.9), equation (2.7) simplifies to

$$\hat{M}_t^e = \hat{p}_t^e + \hat{y}_t^e.$$

This equation for the expected growth in the demand for money will serve to determine the expected rate of inflation in the model:

$$\hat{p}_t^e = \hat{M}_t^e - \hat{y}_t^e,$$

with the expected growth rates of money and output determined by eqs. (2.1) and (2.3).

Equation (2.3) is concerned with the expected rate of growth of output. In this simplified version of the model, it is assumed that the optimal prediction of $\hat{y}$ is given by the naive model

$$\hat{y}_t^e = c \qquad , \text{ with } c \text{ a constant.}$$

With $\hat{y}^e$ constant, all changes in the expected rate of inflation are caused by the fluctuations in $\hat{M}^e$. In section 2.7. we shall put forward a more realistic equation for $\hat{y}^e$, but it will remain true in the empirical applications that variation in expected money growth is more important for the determination of $\hat{p}^e$ than changes in $\hat{y}^e$. This explains why equations of the form

$$\hat{p}_t^e = d + \hat{M}_t^e \qquad , \text{ with } d \text{ a constant,}$$

familiar from many studies of inflation (Meltzer, 1977a, Stein, 1978) are quite successful in explaining the course of expected inflation.

Equation (2.4) deals with the differences between the actual and expected rate of change in the demand for output, y. Because $\hat{y}^e$ is an optimal predictor of $\hat{y}$, only new, unexpected developments can cause differences between actual and expected growth in demand. Three such "impulse" variables explain $(\hat{y}-\hat{y}^e)$: first, (unexpected) changes in the real rate of interest; second, unexpected changes in the price level; third, unexpected changes in the rate of real government expenditure (see Korteweg, 1978a for the original development of the "impulse" approach to the determination of the current unforeseen change in demand).

Because suppliers of output are unable to forecast the actual level of demand, they have to move along their short-term supply curve and can only produce the actually demanded y at a price which differs from p^e. This is shown in equation (2.5), which explains the difference between the expected rate of inflation and the actual rate of price change. Equation (2.5) is a short-term supply curve, which connects the difference $(\hat{p} - \hat{p}^e)$ to $(\hat{y} - \hat{y}^e)$ (see Lucas, 1972a, b, Meltzer, 1977a, b, Korteweg and Meltzer, 1978). The equation can be written both with $(\hat{p} - \hat{p}^e)$ and with $(\hat{y} - \hat{y}^e)$ as the dependent variable (Parkin, 1977a).

The final equation of the model, eq. (2.6) defines the real rate of interest as equal to the nominal rate minus the inflation premium.

REMAINDER OF THIS CHAPTER

The simple model (2.1) - (2.6) is constructed in such a way that the deviations $(\hat{p} - \hat{p}^e)$ and $(\hat{y} - \hat{y}^e)$ are purely temporary and have no effects on the formation of expectations. Later on, we shall relax this assumption with respect to the expected growth of output, so that the impulses that cause a deviation between expected and actual output growth in period t can also have an effect on the expected growth of output in subsequent periods. As regards the formation of inflationary expectations, we shall maintain throughout the assumption that $\hat{p}^e$ will be based on expectations about the systematic cause of rising prices, namely

expected growth of money relative to output, and not on the
history of actual rates of price change. Empirical tests of this
hypothesis in section 2.6. will show that the demand for money
function is sufficiently stable to be useful for the formation of
inflationary expectations, whereas in contrast, the actual rate
of price change in a given year apparently depends on such a great
number of unique and one-time events that a distributed lag of
past rates of price change is an inferior predictor of future
inflation. In the words of Meltzer (1977a), we shall maintain
a distinction between the rate of inflation (a longer-term
concept), and the rate of price change (associated with short-
term events).

Everywhere in the model, we need the distinction between
the expected part and the unanticipated part of the change in
each variable. It is assumed that all the expectations are
formed in a rational manner. The next two sections of this
chapter are devoted to the different ways in which these rational
expectations are to be proxied, first for the univariate case in
section 2.2., then for the case that more variables are included
in the information set in section 2.3.

When that has been done, we return to the different
equations of the model and introduce the actual form that will
be tested later on. In section 2.4. the dynamics of the money
supply are discussed. In this section we shall work on the basis
of the assumption that the monetary authorities are indeed able
to plan the growth of money supply. In section 2.5. we then
confront the supply and the demand for money.

In section 2.6. evidence is presented against the obvious
alternative hypothesis that the stock of money is demand-
determined, so that the causality goes from the expected rate of
inflation to the expected rate of growth of money demanded to
the actual growth rate of the money stock.

Section 2.7. deals with the determination of output. We
shall relax the restriction $\hat{y}^e = c$, and allow for a changing
"mean" of $\hat{y}$ and for permanent effects of the impulses on the
growth rate of y. Section 2.8. on the determination of $(\hat{p}-\hat{p}^e)$ can

then be short, because the role of the impulses have already been discussed in the context of the output equation.

SOLUTION OF THE SIMPLIFIED MODEL

After this brief survey of the equations, we conclude the section with a solution of the simplified model of equations (2.1) – (2.6). Equations (2.2) – (2.6) can be reduced to the following three equations:

$$(2.10) \qquad \hat{p}_t + (\hat{y} - \hat{y}^e)_t - \varepsilon \Delta \hat{r}_t = -c + \hat{M}_t + \varepsilon \Delta \hat{p}^e_{t+1} - a_{2,t}$$

$$(2.11) \qquad \beta_2 \hat{p}_t + (\hat{y} - \hat{y}^e)_t + \beta_1 \Delta \hat{r}_t = \beta_2 \hat{p}^e_t + \beta_3 (\hat{g} - \hat{g}^e)_t + a_{4,t}$$

$$(2.12) \qquad -\alpha_1 \hat{p}_t + (\hat{y} - \hat{y}^e)_t = -\alpha_1 \hat{p}^e_t + a_{5,t};$$

with
$$\Delta \hat{p}^e_{t+1} = {}_t E \hat{p}_{t+1} - {}_{t-1} E \hat{p}_t.$$

Eliminating $(\hat{y} - \hat{y}^e)_t$ and $\Delta \hat{r}_t$ from the equation (2.10) we get this expression for $\hat{p}_t$:

$$(2.13) \qquad \hat{p}_t = \frac{1}{A} \Big[-\beta_1 c + (\alpha_1 \beta_1 + \varepsilon \alpha_1 + \varepsilon \beta_2) \hat{p}^e_t + \beta_1 \varepsilon \Delta \hat{p}^e_{t+1} +$$
$$+ \beta_1 \hat{M}_t + \varepsilon \beta_3 (\hat{g} - \hat{g}^e)_t - \beta_1 a_{2,t} + \varepsilon a_{4,t} - (\varepsilon + \beta_1) a_{5,t} \Big]$$

with
$$A = \beta_1 (1 + \alpha_1) + \varepsilon (\alpha_1 + \beta_2).$$

Applying the expectations operator $_{t-1}E$ to equation (2.13), gives:

$$(2.14) \qquad \hat{p}^e_t = -c + \hat{M}^e_t + \varepsilon \, _{t-1}E (\Delta \hat{p}^e_{t+1}).$$

Equation (2.14) describes the expected growth in the demand for money. As regards the supply side of the money market, economic agents expect stable growth for the whole future (see equation (2.1.)):

$$(2.15) \qquad _{t-1}E \, \hat{M}_t = {}_{t-1}E \, \hat{M}_{t+1} = \ldots .$$

The two equations (2.14) and (2.15) have infinitely many
solutions for $\hat{p}_t^e$, $\hat{p}_{t+1}^e$, ... given $\hat{M}_t$, all but one of which
lead to hyperinflation or hyperdeflation for every value of $\hat{M}_t$.
The price level explodes, although the money supply is expected
to grow at a fixed rate. There is one stable solution, namely:

(2.16) $\hat{p}_t^e = -c + \hat{M}_t^e$.

  We assume that economic agents deduce from the constant term
structure of expectations with respect to the rate of money
growth (equation 2.15), that there is no need to fear for a
self-propelling hyperinflation of -deflation. On the contrary,
as long as they expect stable monetary growth, they should
expect correspondingly stable rates of inflation as well.
Because of this assumption, we select the single stable dynamic
solution of equations (2.14) - (2.15):

(2.16) $\hat{p}_t^e = -c + \hat{M}_t^e$.

To obtain this solution we must assume:

$$_{t-1}E(\Delta\hat{p}_{t+1}^e) = 0.$$

In words: since agents are unable to forecast changes in the
rate of money growth beyond the next period, they are also
unable to forecast changes in the rate of inflation after the
next period (cf. Black, 1974).

  Shifting equation (2.16) one period forward in time:

(2.17) $\hat{p}_{t+1}^e = -c + \hat{M}_{t+1}^e$.

Subtracting (2.16) from (2.17) and substituting from (2.1):

$$\Delta\hat{p}_{t+1}^e = \hat{p}_{t+1}^e - \hat{p}_t^e = (\hat{M} - \hat{M}^e)_t = a_{1,t}.$$

Substituting this expression for $\Delta \hat{p}^e_{t+1}$ in equation (2.13) and using the identity (2.16), we get the reduced form solution for $\hat{p}_t$:

$$\hat{p}_t = \hat{p}^e_t + \frac{1}{A} \Big[\beta_1 (1 + \varepsilon)(\hat{M} - \hat{M}^e)_t + \varepsilon \beta_3 (\hat{g} - \hat{g}^e)_t +$$

$$- \beta_1 a_{2,t} + \varepsilon a_{4,t} - (\varepsilon + \beta_1) a_{5,t} \Big],$$

with $A = \beta_1 (1 + \alpha_1) + \varepsilon (\alpha_1 + \beta_2)$.

The solution for $(\hat{y} - \hat{y}^e)$ becomes:

$$(\hat{y} - \hat{y}^e)_t = \frac{\alpha_1}{A} \Big[\beta_1 (1 + \varepsilon)(\hat{M} - \hat{M}^e)_t + \varepsilon \beta_3 (\hat{g} - \hat{g}^e)_t +$$

$$- \beta_1 a_{2,t} + \varepsilon a_{4,t} + \frac{1}{\alpha_1} (\beta_1 + \varepsilon \beta_2) a_{5,t} \Big]$$

It follows from our assumptions regarding the signs of the co-efficients that A is positive; therefore a positive shock $(\hat{M} - \hat{M}^e)$ or $(\hat{g} - \hat{g}^e)$ has a positive short-run effect on both prices and output.

Finally, the final form equation for Δr_t is:

$$\Delta r_t = \frac{1}{A} \Big[- (1 + \varepsilon)(\alpha_1 + \beta_2)(\hat{M} - \hat{M}^e)_t + \beta_3 (1 + \alpha_1)(\hat{g} - \hat{g}^e)_t +$$

$$+ (\alpha_1 + \beta_2) a_{2,t} + (1 + \alpha_1) a_{4,t} - (1 - \beta_2) a_{5,t} \Big].$$

A positive monetary impulse will lower the real interest rate, whereas a positive g-impulse -- holding the money stock con-stant -- will lead to a higher real rate. Shifts in the demand for money and in the demand and supply for goods also have an effect on the real rate of interest: an impulse or a stochastic shock will lead to a single change Δr_t in the current period. Changes in the real rate of interest in the next period will depend on the values of the impulses and the error terms in period t+1, so that they cannot be predicted: the solution of the model for Δr_t satisfies the requirement (2.8) that changes in the real rate of interest must always be unpredictable.

2.2. THE ARIMA (0,1,1) MODEL

In this section and the next, time series $\hat{x}$ will be considered that possess the property:

(2.18) $\qquad {}_t E\hat{x}_{t+1} = {}_t E\hat{x}_{t+j}$ for all $j > 1$

where $\hat{x}$ is the growth rate of some economic variable.

First we discuss the univariate model, when no information is used for the predictions apart from that contained in the past of $\hat{x}$. After that, the multivariate case is described, where the information set also contains the present and past values of other variables. Readers who are familiar with this material may wish to proceed directly to section 4 of the chapter.

In order to satisfy equation (2.18), changes in the growth rate of x must be unpredictable for all future periods after the next period:

$$ {}_t E(\Delta\hat{x}_{t+j}) = 0 \qquad \text{for all} \quad j > 1 $$

It follows that if we write $\Delta\hat{x}$ as a function of present and past shocks:

$$ \Delta\hat{x}_t = a_t + \theta_1 a_{t-1} + \theta_2 a_{t-2} + \theta_3 a_{t-3} + \dots $$

with the a's serially uncorrelated random errors, the coefficients θ_2, θ_3, ... must be zero, so that we are left with

$$ \Delta\hat{x}_t = a_t + \theta_1 a_{t-1}, \text{ or, with } \theta = -\theta_1: $$

(2.19) $\qquad \Delta\hat{x}_t = (1 - \theta B) a_t$

where B is the back-shift operator, defined by $B(..)_t = (..)_{t-1}$.

(see Appendix 2 for the notation that has been used with respect to Box-Jenkins models).

Equation (2.19) is known as the integrated first-order moving average model, as it may be written in the form:

$$(2.20) \qquad (1 - B)\hat{x}_t = (1-\theta B)a_t.$$

It follows that:

$$(2.21) \qquad \hat{x}_t = \frac{1 - \theta B}{1 - B} a_t = (1 - \theta B)\{a_t + a_{t-1} + a_{t-2} + ...\}$$

$$= a_t + (1 - \theta)\{a_{t-1} + a_{t-2} + ...\}$$

Each shock a_t leads to an increase in the "level" of $\hat{x}$ with $(1 - \theta)$ as the factor of proportionality. Taking expectations on both sides of equation (2.21) gives:

$$(2.22) \qquad \hat{x}_t^e = {}_{t-1}E\hat{x}_t = (1 - \theta)\{a_{t-1} + a_{t-2} + ...\}$$

$$= (1 - \theta)(\hat{x}_{t-1} - \hat{x}_{t-1}^e) + (1 - \theta)\{a_{t-2} + a_{t-3} + ...\}$$

We get:

$$(2.23) \qquad \hat{x}_t^e - \hat{x}_{t-1}^e = (1 - \theta)(\hat{x} - \hat{x}^e)_{t-1} = (1 - \theta)a_{t-1}$$

which is the familiar adaptive expectations formula.

It is also possible to express $\hat{x}^e$ as a function of previous values of $\hat{x}$ only.

$$(1 - B)\hat{x}_t = (1 - \theta B)a_t$$

implies:

$$\frac{(1 - B)}{1 - \theta B}\hat{x}_t = a_t;$$

thus:

$$\frac{1 - \theta B - (1 - \theta)B}{1 - \theta B} \hat{x}_t = a_t.$$

It follows that:

$$\left\{1 - \frac{(1 - \theta)B}{1 - \theta B}\right\} \hat{x}_t = a_t;$$

therefore:

$$\hat{x}_t = (1 - \theta)(1 + \theta B + \theta^2 B^2 + \theta^3 B^3 + \ldots)\hat{x}_{t-1} + a_t;$$

so that:

(2.24) $\qquad \hat{x}_t^e = (1 - \theta)\hat{x}_{t-1} + \theta(1 - \theta)\hat{x}_{t-2} + \theta^2(1 - \theta)\hat{x}_{t-3} + \ldots$

Both equations (2.23) and (2.24) show that, the greater θ, the more slowly does the "level" of $\hat{x}$ change over time. In the limiting case, when $\theta = 1$, the model changes into

$$(1 - B)\hat{x}_t = (1 - B)a_t,$$

so that

$$\hat{x}_t = c + a_t \qquad \text{with } c \text{ a constant.}$$

The level of $\hat{x}$ is now a constant, or, in other words, each observed deviation of $\hat{x}$ from its level is purely temporary.

ECONOMIC ARGUMENTS FOR THE (0,1,1) MODEL

Even when the estimated value of θ is close to one, the ARIMA (0,1,1) model may still be attractive as against the alternative

$$\hat{x}_t = c + a_t \qquad \text{with } c \text{ a constant}$$

because it allows for a slowly changing "mean" of the series $\hat{x}$. Take, for example, the time series for real gnp in the U.S. With annual values for 1949-1973, this series can be modelled either as:

$$(2.25) \qquad (1 - B)\hat{y}_t = (1 - .74\ B)a_t$$
$$(.14)$$

or as:

$$(2.26) \qquad \hat{y} = 3.52 + a_t$$

with $\hat{y}$ equal to 100 x Δln (gnp) and a_t white noise.

If one wishes to test the hypothesis that gnp growth in 1974 was exceptionally low, then in the first case (eq. (2.25)) one would calculate:

$$\hat{y}^e_{1974} = .26\ \hat{y}_{1973} + .26 \text{ x } (.74)\hat{y}_{1972} +$$

$$+ (.26) \text{ x } (.74)^2\hat{y}_{1971} + \ldots$$

and investigate the difference between actual growth in 1974 and this expected value. In the second case (eq. 2.26)) one would take the mean value over the period 1949-1973 as the ex-pectations for 1974 and test whether $\hat{y}_{1974}$ is significantly different from this arithmethic average.

If one accepts that the structure of the economy changes slowly over time, then in testing this hypothesis one would want to attach more importance to growth rates in the years just before 1974 than to data from a more distant past. The expectation calculated with the ARIMA (0,1,1) model does just that, whereas the model $\hat{y}$ = c gives the same weight to all previous observations (see Box and Tiao, 1965). Closely related to this argument is the fact that with a moving average model for $\Delta\hat{y}$, the amount of uncertainty in predictions of future output growth quickly increases with the length of the forecast horizon.

On the other hand: accurate predictions for the long-term can be made when it is assumed instead that $\hat{y}$ is stationary. The

latter assumption is made by Barro (1978) in his paper that will be
discussed in chapter 3, and, for example, by the O.E.C.D.'s
McCracken Report (1977, p. 323) where ways are discussed to
"restore the system to the target track when sufficient evidence
of deviation from it has accumulated". Our assumption that annual
series for important macroeconomic variables such as output
growth, $\hat{y}$, and money growth, $\hat{M}$, are non-stationary, is at variance
with much econometric practice, but is in agreement with the implicit assumption of all those people who distinguish between short-
term and long-term contracts just because of the *"greater uncer-*
tainty .... with more distant points of future time" (Gray, 1978,
p. 7).

These are two economic arguments for differencing a series
$\hat{x}$ that are relevant even when $\hat{x}$ appears to be stationary. As
shown by Gonedes and Roberts (1977), there is even a good case to
be made on Bayesian grounds for differencing when the series $\hat{x}$
is actually stationary, but short (in the order of 20-50 observations) and highly autocorrelated.

Consequently, we shall fit models to $\Delta\hat{x}$ in all cases in
which there can be doubt about the stationarity of $\hat{x}$. In particular, the ARIMA (0,1,1) model will be found to be appropriate for
many exogenous variables $\hat{x}$, where we do not want to model explicitly the shocks a_t that influence $\hat{x}$. In chapters 3 and 4 either
this or some other univariate model will be fitted for every exogenous variable $\hat{x}$ that is used in the analysis, so that we can
work with time series for $\hat{x}^e$ and $(\hat{x} - \hat{x}^e)$ in each model equation
in which $\hat{x}$ appears. Because all our empirical work will be based
on yearly data for the post-war period, the data series are short
by the standards of time series analysis. The problems of estimating θ in the ARIMA (0,1,1) model for such short series has been
investigated by Nelson (1974) who performed a Monte-Carlo study
for series with 30 observations. He found that θ can still be
determined quite accurately, but that the estimated variance of
θ will be biased upwards. Details about the Box-Jenkins models
employed are in Appendix 2 at the back of the book.

Before we turn to the multivariate case in the next section,

we mention two other properties of the ARIMA (0,1,1) process.
First, this time series model is obtained when we combine a pure
random walk for $\hat{x}$:

$$\Delta \hat{x}_t = a_t$$

with the assumption that a white noise error, for example a measurement error, influences $\hat{x}_t$. The contaminated series is now
ARIMA (0,1,1). An application to the money supply process is given
by Mussa (1976b, p. 244, example 2). Second, the sum of two or
more ARIMA (0,1,1) processes is again an ARIMA (0,1,1) process
(see Box and Jenkins, 1970, p. 121). It follows that in equation
(2.11), specifying this process for two out of three variables $\hat{p}$,
$\hat{M}$ and $\hat{y}$ implies that the remaining variable has the same properties,
in particular that the expected value for the next period holds
for all later periods as well.

2.3. VARIABLES WITH THE SIMPLEST
TERM STRUCTURE OF EXPECTATIONS

The discussion of the multivariate case can be limited to that
of one exogenous variable, extensions to more input variables
being straightforward. Let $\hat{x}$ be the endogenous variable and $\hat{b}$
the exogenous input. If we consider $(\hat{b} - \hat{b}^e)$ as a second "noise"
in equation (2.19), then it is clear that we can write:

(2.27) $\Delta \hat{x}_t = (\mu_1 + \mu_2 B)(\hat{b} - \hat{b}^e)_t + (1 - \theta B)a_t$

so that:

(2.28) $(\hat{x} - \hat{x}^e)_t = \mu_1(\hat{b} - \hat{b}^e)_t + a_t$

Equation (2.27) expresses the general form of a fixed-coefficient
model for $\hat{x}$ that satisfies our requirements about the term
structure of expectations. Multiply both sides of (2.27) with the
lag operator B, subtract, and take expectations in order to get:

$$(2.29) \qquad \hat{x}^e_t - \hat{x}^e_{t-1} = (\mu_1 + \mu_2)(\hat{b} - \hat{b}^e)_{t-1} + (1 - \theta)a_{t-1}$$

Equation (2.29) is the multivariate analogue to the adaptive expectations formula (2.23). In the univariate case, the change in $\hat{x}^e$ depended solely on the unanticipated shock that took place during the previous period. Now, the change in $\hat{x}^e$ is a linear function of $(\hat{b} - \hat{b}^e)_{t-1}$, last period's unanticipated change in the exogenous variable, and a_{t-1}, last period's error term, so that the rational expectation $\hat{x}^e$ can no longer be written as a distributed lag on past $\hat{x}$ alone. If, for example, $\hat{x}$ represents the actual growth rate of income, then with a univariate model for $\hat{x}^e$, there would be no way to distinguish between permanent income and a distributed lag on actual income; with a multivariate model, one could discriminate between permanent and (lagged) actual income (Hall, 1978, p. S77).

Equation (2.28) connects the unexpected changes in $\hat{x}$ and $\hat{b}$. Only if the moving-average parameter θ is equal to 1, does it become possible to derive a relation between the expected rates of growth $\hat{x}^e$ and $\hat{b}^e$. The precise form depends on the stochastic model for $\hat{b}$. Suppose, for example, that $\hat{b}$ itself can be represented by the first-order moving average process:

$$\Delta \hat{b}_t = (1 - \theta_1 B)(\hat{b} - \hat{b}^e)_t$$

We then can change equation (2.29) into:

$$(2.30) \qquad \hat{x}^e_t - \hat{x}^e_{t-1} = \frac{(\mu_1 + \mu_2)}{1 - \theta_1}(\hat{b}^e_t - \hat{b}^e_{t-1})$$

so that:

$$(2.31) \qquad \hat{x}^e_t = c + d\hat{b}^e_t$$

with c a constant of integration and $d = \dfrac{(\mu_1 + \mu_2)}{1 - \theta_1}$.

If, on the other hand, $\theta \neq 1$, then the relation between $\hat{x}$ and $\hat{b}$ cannot be specified in terms of

$$\hat{x}^e_t = f(\hat{b}^e_t, \ldots.)$$

One has to take the differences of the growth rates $\hat{x}$ and $\hat{b}$, and work with $\Delta\hat{x}$, $\Delta\hat{b}$ as in equation (2.27).

We have presented economic arguments for preferring $\Delta\hat{x}$ to $\hat{x}$ in the univariate case, whenever there could be doubt about the stationarity of $\hat{x}$. These arguments also apply in the multivariate context. A further economic reason for differencing is that one eliminates the large constant terms which often appear in regressions for the growth rates of output, world trade, investment, and similar variables. Such large constant terms may be impossible to explain theoretically, and should therefore be avoided (Brunner and Meltzer, 1963, p. 342).

Statistical arguments for differencing series that may or may not be stationary are given by Plosser and Schwert (1977, 1978). They show that the danger of "overdifferencing" is not as important as the risk of spurious regression when non-stationary series are correlated. When the researcher is certain that the series which he wants to connect are non-stationary, then he should certainly difference them, because otherwise the usual significance tests on the estimated coefficients and the F-test on $\bar{R}^2$ cannot be applied (Granger and Newbold, 1977, p. 203). Because of all this, the time series that we shall try to explain by multivariate economic models are often differenced one more time than is usual in much econometric practice.

2.4. DYNAMICS OF THE MONEY SUPPLY

"We have gone one derivative beyond Hume"
Friedman (1975, p. 177).
The supply and demand schedules for money, as is the case with many other goods, are not independent of one another. The monetary authorities have to take into account the public's demand for money function when they plan their policies. Conversely, the actual form of the demand for money function depends on

what the public thinks the monetary authorities will do.

In this section we shall not be too specific about the demand for money function, and concentrate on the supply side of the money market. In the next section, our preferred model for the supply of money will be combined with an explicit demand for money function. The reason for choosing this particular order for the discussion is that the demand for money is market-determined, whereas the supply depends on a single political entity, the monetary authority. Therefore, the demand function can and must be firmly grounded in economic theory, and a discussion of the supply function will, of necessity, be more speculative.

A general price-theoretic demand for money function must contain many more terms than the simple demand for money equation (2.2). Our equation contained the current change in the rate of interest only, whereas expectations about the complete future course of interest rates should be included:

$$(2.32) \qquad M_t = p_t + y_t - \varepsilon_1 i_t - \varepsilon_2 (_t E i_{t+1}) - \varepsilon_3 (_t E i_{t+2}) - \cdots ,$$

with M, p and y the natural logarithms of money, prices and income, i_t a vector of rates of return on substitutes for money and ε_1, ε_2, ... corresponding vectors of coefficients (Cf. Motley, 1967).

This function contains an infinite number of future variables, and is too general to be of any practical use. A specific assumption about the supply of money, however, can help to simplify the demand function in a correct manner. This approach is taken by Sargent (1976b, 1977a) and also in this study. A difference with Sargent's procedure is that he begins with an arbitrary demand for money function and then chooses the money supply rule that fits this demand for money function best. In the present section we shall try to give economic arguments for our choice of money supply rule, and then formulate a corresponding demand for money function.

We may distinguish the following four basic types of

money supply rules according to whether M has to be differenced
0,1,2 or 3 times to achieve stationarity:

Money supply		Price expectations
(2.33)	$M_t = M_{t-1} + a_t$ or $\Delta M_t = a_t$	expectations are neutral: no inflation or deflation
(2.34)	$\hat{M}_t = c + a_t$ c a constant	a constant, stable rate of inflation
(2.35)	$\hat{M}_t = \hat{M}_{t-1} + a_t$ or $\Delta \hat{M}_t = a_t$	new information (a_t) changes inflationary expectations; each expected rate of inflation is assumed to hold for all future periods
(2.36)	$\Delta (\hat{\Delta M})_t = a_t$	unstable expectations, possible leading to hyperinflation

Notation:

M_t :   logarithm of the money stock in period t

$\hat{M}$:   logarithmic growth rate of M between period $_{t-1}$ and period t

a_t :   uncorrelated shock term in period t

Δ :   difference operator: $\Delta x_t = x_t - x_{t-1}$.

In each case the simplest possible model in its class has been
selected. The actual time series models for money may of course
be more complicated, which would imply a number of additional
future terms in the demand for money function, but that would
make no essential difference to the rules for the formation of
inflationary expectations. The consequences for the behaviour of
future prices are given for each model on the assumption that
variations in income and velocity can be neglected and that
a standard demand for money function connects money and prices.
Throughout we assume that expectations are formed rationally.

The first rule for price expectations is the one used by
Patinkin (1965). All changes in the level of prices are unforeseen. Patinkin uses a demand for real balances function in which

the expected rate of price change is always zero. Such a demand
function puts restrictions upon the thought-experiments that we
are allowed to perform with the money supply. Obviously, it
would not make sense to combine his demand for money function
with the hypothesis that the money supply grows at a certain
constant rate. Neither would it be correct to assume that the
growth rate of money follows some type of random walk. The only
possible model for the supply of money which is compatible with
Patinkin's demand for real balances is one in which the money
stock is constant almost all of the time and in which changes
in the stock are discrete and always completely unforeseen.
We then have a consistent combination of a money supply process
and a demand for money function which satisfies the requirement
that expectations are rational, albeit be it in a trivial way,
since the possibility that economic agents have advance knowledge of future movements in the money stock has been excluded.

The next two models correspond better to the post-war
experience. They can be combined into the more general
formulation:

$$(2.37) \qquad \Delta \hat{M}_t = (1 - \theta B) a_t \qquad \text{with } 0 \le \theta \le 1$$

As discussed in section 2.2., the model (2.37) lies in between
the two models (2.34) and (2.35). If the parameter θ equals 1,
we have the case of a constant rate of monetary growth, whereas
if θ equals 0, equation (2.37) becomes the pure random walk
model, $\Delta \hat{M}_t = a_t$ (equation 2.35) (Cf. Mussa, 1976a).

In the next section we shall work with equation (2.37) as
a description of the supply side, and confront this model with
the appropriate relation for the expected growth of the demand
for money. In section 2.6. we shall discuss whether θ is likely
to be equal to 1, so that there is a "normal" rate of money
growth and thus a "normal" rate of inflation, or whether the
"level" of money growth and thus the trend rate of inflation
change with time.

The final model for the supply of money equation (2.36)

implies

$$_t\hat{EM}_{t+k} > {}_t\hat{EM}_{t+k-1} \qquad \text{for all } k > 1$$

when a positive shock a_t has taken place. The rate of monetary expansion is assumed to increase further and further. Such a process is neither politically nor economically stable (Jacobs, 1977a, b). It may have dramatic consequences, either a process of de-monetization when a hyper-inflation runs its full course, or the overthrowing of the government. When in the model (2.35) a number of positive shocks occur in a row, then the money stock data may suggest that equation (2.36) is now operative. However, the transition to a state of hyper-inflation is very hard to predict ex ante. Many economists must have realized this recently when the rate of inflation in the United Kingdom decreased after there had been much talk about inflationary expectations moving into a "higher gear".

Of the four basic models (2.33) - (2.36), the first and the last have to be rejected for either being completely at variance with the facts (equation (2.33)) or for being unstable (equation (2.36)). The remaining two models have been subsumed in the more general model

$$(2.37) \qquad \Delta\hat{M}_t = (1 - \theta B) a_t$$

which will be combined with a demand for money function in the next section.

2.5. THE DEMAND FOR MONEY

Having made an assumption about the supply of money, we can now return to the demand for money function. To begin, we assume that y_t is constant and that the only relevant substitution takes place between money and goods. In that case eq. (2.32) can be written as follows (omitting the constant term):

$$(2.38) \qquad M_t = p_t - \varepsilon_1 ({}_t\hat{Ep}_{t+1}) - \varepsilon_2 ({}_t\hat{Ep}_{t+2}) - \varepsilon_3 ({}_t\hat{Ep}_{t+3}) - \cdots$$

Eq. (2.38) can be combined with eq. (2.37) for the supply of money into a two-equation model for the determination of the rate of money growth, the rate of inflation and the expected rate of inflation. Our discussion of the dynamic relations between these three variables, based on the work by Brock (1972, 1974), will lead to a simple one-to-one relationship between expected money growth and expected inflation:

$$\hat{M}_t^e = \hat{p}_t^e$$

After that, we relax the assumption that income is constant and make an assumption about the income velocity of money, but in such a way that the link between expected money growth and expected inflation remains intact. Next, we allow for substitution between money and other assets, so that one ore more interest rates enter the demand for money function. Finally, we look at the stochastic term in the money demand function.

BROCK'S MODEL

Let us start by considering the demand for money function on the assumptions that real wealth, y, is constant and that the only significant substitution is between money and goods. These restrictive assumptions are familiar from studies of hyper-inflation: extremely rapid changes in the price level disrupt the supply of assets that bear a fixed rate of interest, and the flight from money into goods can explain most of the changes in real balances during the hyperinflation (Cagan, 1956, Frenkel, 1977, but see also Abel et al., 1979, for evidence about substitution between domestic and foreign money during the German hyperinflation).

Substitution between money and goods occurs because of changes in inflationary expectations. With money, M, and the price index, p, the only variables in the model, these ex-pectations must be based on an information set that consists of

present and past values of M or p or both. In this section we
shall assume that rational inflationary expectations depend on
univariate projections of future growth in the money stock M;
in the next section we shall discuss tests of the hypothesis that
past rates of price change are included in the information set.

The dynamics of money and prices under the assumptions that
expectations are rational and based on projections of future
money growth have been treated by Brock (1972, 1974). The
mathematics is quite involved, because the link from money to
prices cannot be derived by aggregating individual actions.
Relevant here is the important distinction made by Patinkin
(1965) between theorizing on the basis of *individual* experiments,
for example in arguing from an increase in interest rates to
a fall in the demand for money, and theorizing on the basis of
market experiments, for example establishing the link between
an increase in money and changes in prices and interest rates.
The latter type of experiment is much more difficult to
formalize correctly.

Brock studies the movements in p on the assumption that
agents have perfect foresight about the following path of the
money supply:

$$\hat{M}_t = c(1 \leq t \leq \tau_1), \qquad \hat{M}_t = d(\tau_1 < t < \infty)$$

c and d are constants; we can set c equal to zero and assume
that d is positive with no loss of generality. In that case,
the stock of money and the price level have been constant for
a long time, but at period $t = 1$ it becomes known that the rate
of monetary growth will increase to d at some specific time
$t = \tau_1$. Brock does not combine this supply path with an
arbitrary demand for money function, but assumes utility
maximizing wealth holders and then derives the unique path for
the price level that satisfies the following three conditions.

First, there is equilibrium in the money market: in each
period the price level, p, adjusts so that agents willingly
hold the stock of real balances, M/p. Second, expectations are

rational, which means under perfect foresight that there is
complete correspondence between actual and expected prices.
Third, there is long-term stability; after the adjustment period
from t = 1 to t = τ_1, the economy is on a stable path with both
M and p growing at the same constant rate d.

The link between money and prices in our model can be
regarded as a simplified stochastic version of Brock's model in
which perfect foresight is replaced by rational expectations.
The essential simplification consists of the assumption that
the interval from t = 1 to t = τ_1 can be condensed into a single
period. In Brock's model, agents receive information during
period t=1 about a change in $\hat{M}$ that may be scheduled for a period
far into the future. By contrast, in our model for the growth of
the money supply, eq. (2.37), a signal a_t which agents receive
during period t=1 implies a change in the rate of money growth
that will be effective from period t=2 onwards.

With this simplification, we are able to retain the main
result of Brock's work: every foreseeable future change in the
growth rate of money has its effects on current desired real
balances. For the choice of the first-order moving average
process for $\Delta \hat{M}$ means that there is only one foreseeable change
in $\hat{M}$, namely that between the current and the next periods. As
regards subsequent periods, agents expect:

$$ _t E\ \hat{M}_{t+1} = {}_t E\ \hat{M}_{t+2} = {}_t E\ \hat{M}_{t+3} = \ \dots $$

If rational agents hold these expectations about future money
growth, they will also expect:

$$ _t E\ \hat{P}_{t+1} = {}_t E\ \hat{P}_{t+2} = \ \dots = {}_t E\ \hat{M}_{t+1} = {}_t E\ \hat{M}_{t+2} = \ \dots $$

It follows that eq. (2.38) simplifies to:

(2.39) $ M_t = p_t - \varepsilon ({}_t E \hat{p}_{t+1}) $

Taking first differences we get:

(2.40) $\hat{M}_t = \hat{p}_t - \varepsilon(_t E\hat{p}_{t+1} - _{t-1} E\hat{p}_t)$

Applying the expectations operator at time t-1 to eq. (2.40) gives:

(2.41) $_{t-1} E\hat{M}_t = _{t-1} E\hat{p}_t - \varepsilon(_{t-1} E\hat{p}_{t+1} - _{t-1} E\hat{p}_t)$,

where we have used the chain principle of forecasting in equating

$$_{t-1} E(_t E\hat{p}_{t+1}) \text{ to } _{t-1} E\hat{p}_{t+1}.$$

Because of the constant term structure of expectations for $\hat{p}$, eq. (2.41) reduces to

$$\hat{M}_t^e = \hat{p}_t^e;$$

a one-to-one relation between expected money growth and expected inflation. With $\hat{M}_t^e$ determined by eq. (2.37), we now have a formula for the expected rate of inflation that corresponds to rational expectations and is not based adaptively on actual past rates of price change, but on the expected growth of the money supply.

  It is worth noting that the equation for $\hat{p}$ has not been obtained by combining a given demand for money function with a convenient assumption about the supply of money and then imposing rational expectations. Instead, we have followed Brock and assumed only that rational holders of money have a certain type of knowledge about the future growth in the money supply, and written down the corresponding equation that correctly describes the stock of real balances in each period.

  If a different assumption had been made about the supply of money, then another demand for money function would have described the amount of real balances that is desired during each period. Let $\hat{M}$ be described, for example, by an auto-regressive, process, instead of by eq. (2.37):

$$\hat{M}_t = c + \alpha \hat{M}_{t-1} + a_t \quad , \text{ with c a constant, } 0 < \alpha < 1,$$
$$\text{and } a_t \text{ uncorrelated white noise.}$$

Now, the growth rate of M returns to $c(1 - \alpha)^{-1}$ after each shock, but if α is close to one, the return-to-normality takes a long time. It would be purely arbitrary to combine this rule for the supply of money with the demand for money function

$$M_t = p_t - \varepsilon(_t\hat{Ep}_{t+1}),$$

since the complete expected future course of the price level has an influence on currently desired real balances. An auto-regressive process for $\hat{M}$ does not permit us to compress the term structure of inflationary expectations into the single term

$$_{t-1}\hat{Ep}_{t+1}.$$

Admittedly, there would be one simple solution, namely to assume

$$_{t-1}\hat{Ep}_{t+k} = c(1-\alpha)^{-1}$$

for all k, so that the expected rate of inflation is constant and does not depend on variations in the rate of money growth at all (Sweeney, 1978). However, this extreme assumption is contrary to the evidence about positive serial correlation in the time series for the actual rate of inflation: the only realistic solution is to repeat Brock's analysis in order to derive the demand for money function that is appropriate if an autoregressive process describes the growth of the money supply.

EXTENSIONS

Having established the link between expected money growth and expected inflation, we can turn to other aspects of the demand for money. First, how can the relation

$$\hat{M}_t^e = \hat{p}_t^e$$

be modified to take account of expected changes in income and velocity? Second, which assumptions about interest rates are

compatible with the present approach to the demand for money?
Third, what difference does it make that the signal of a future
change in monetary growth is not just an announcement by the
monetary authorities, as in Brock's model, but an actual unanticipated increase in the stock of money? Finally, what do we
assume about the error term in the demand for money relation?

The determination of income, y, will be dealt with in
section 2.7. At present, we postulate:

$$_t E \; \hat{y}_{t+1} = \; _t E \; \hat{y}_{t+2} = \; \ldots$$

so that the constant term structure of expectations for $\hat{M}$ can
be combined with the constant term structure of expectations
for $\hat{y}$ to give a constant term structure of expectations for
$\hat{M} - \hat{y}$. Under these assumptions, Brock's results can be retained,
and we get the following relation between $\hat{p}^e$, $\hat{M}^e$ and $\hat{y}^e$:

$$\hat{p}_t^e = \hat{M}_t^e - \hat{y}_t^e.$$

In words: the expected rate of inflation is equal to the expected growth of money per unit of output, and the expected
rates of growth for the next period apply also to all subsequent periods. If we further assume that the difference between
desired and actual real balances in each period is proportional
to the difference between expected and actual income, we get:

$$(2.42) \qquad \hat{M}_t = \hat{p}_t + \hat{y}_t^e + \delta_2 (\hat{y} - \hat{y}^e)_t - \epsilon (\hat{p}_{t+1}^e - \hat{p}_t^e)$$

In eq. (2.42), the expected rate of growth of income has
a coefficient of unity. This restriction was imposed for ease of
exposition, but will be lifted now for two reasons. First,
because the income elasticity of the demand for money by
individual asset-holders at any given moment may not necessarily
be equal to unity. A second reason why the coefficient of $\hat{y}_t^e$ in
a time series analysis of the demand for real balances may not
be equal to one is that the way money is used changes over time.

New substitutes for money are offered, the state of technology
in the money industry is not constant, and people's payment
habits change over time. It is generally difficult to model this
type of change in the demand for money function, and we shall
follow the convention of making it a function of time, t, and
income (see Melitz and Correa, 1970, Wallich, 1971, Graves,
1978). When we accept these two reasons for lifting the
restrictions on the coefficients of y_t^e, the demand for money
function takes the following form:

$$\hat{M}_t = -d + \hat{p}_t + (1-\delta_1)\hat{y}_t^e + \delta_2(\hat{y}-\hat{y}^e)_t - \varepsilon(\hat{p}_{t+1}^e - \hat{p}_t^e)$$

Having made assumptions about money, prices, expected prices
and income, we proceed to the three remaining issues concerning
the demand for money: the role of interest rates, the effect on
the demand for money of an unanticipated increase in the money
supply, and the stochastic element in the demand for money.

The theoretical model contains a single, representative
rate of interest

$$i_t = r_t + {}_tE\,\hat{p}_{t+1}$$

We have already made the assumption that economic agents cannot
foresee future changes in the inflation premium; it remains to
make an assumption about future changes in the real rate of
interest. Let us postulate that the complete model has a solution that makes the current change in the real rate of
interest, Δr_t, a function of the current unforeseen changes in
the exogenous variables and of the current stochastic shocks
$a_{1,t}$, $a_{2,t}$, etc.

As the determinants of Δr_t cannot be predicted in advance,
the current rate of interest is the optimal predictor of the
future:

$$r_t = {}_tEr_{t+1} = {}_tEr_{t+2} = \ldots$$

Consequently, we also have:

$$i_t = {}_tE^ii_{t+1} = {}_tE^ii_{t+2} = \cdots$$

In other words, both the nominal and the real rate of interest satisfy the martingale property. With this assumption about the predictability of future interest rates, we can write the demand for money function as:

$$(2.43) \qquad \hat{M}_t = -d + \hat{p}_t + (1-\delta_1)\hat{y}^e_t + \delta_2(\hat{y}-\hat{y}^e)_t - \varepsilon\Delta r_t -$$

$$- \varepsilon(\hat{p}^e_{t+1} - \hat{p}^e_t) \ .$$

If r_t is unpredictable, then there is no need to include expectations about changes in interest rates in the demand for money function. The assumption that the rate of interest is a martingale is a natural one to make for long-term rates of interest in an economy with efficient capital markets (see Sargent, 1979, and the references he cites). If it does not hold for certain short-term interest rates then there will be predictable future changes in velocity that undermine the validity of equation (2.39) (see chapter 4). In this theoretical chapter, we shall assume that the demand for money depends on one endogenous rate of interest, i_t, and construct our model in such a way that future changes in i_t are unpredictable (see, for example, Hamburger, 1977a, b, about the importance of long-term interest rates in the demand for money).

The next issue to be considered with respect to the actual demand for money, concerns the signal which the monetary authorities emit during each period, and that causes agents to revise their estimates of future money growth. In our model this signal consists of an actual (unanticipated) change in the level of the money stock. We know that monetary shocks affect inflationary anticipations which in turn leads to a change in the current demand for real balances. But the sudden increase in M must also by itself have an influence on current levels of prices

and income. The final-form equations for $\hat{p}-\hat{p}^e$ and $\hat{y}-\hat{y}^e$ in
sections 2.7. and 2.8. will incorporate these short-run effects
in such a way that our assumptions about the term structure of
expectations are not violated.

One final element of the demand for money function has been
neglected until now: an assumption about the kind of stochastic
disturbances that affect the demand for money. We can allow only
for purely temporary, random shocks in the growth rate of the demand for money. Any other assumption would upset our requirements
with respect to the term structure of expectations for $\hat{M}$, $\hat{y}$ and $\hat{p}$.
Serially uncorrelated shocks in the growth rate of the demand for
money correspond to permanent shifts in the level of the demand
for money real balances. When eq. (2.43) is extended with a serially uncorrelated error term, we get the equation that describes the
growth in the demand for money in the model:

$$(2.44) \qquad \hat{M}_t = -d + \hat{p}_t + (1-\delta_1)\hat{y}_t^e + \delta_2(\hat{y}-\hat{y}^e)_t - \varepsilon\Delta i_t + a_{2,t}.$$

And, in terms of expectations:

$$(2.45) \qquad \hat{M}_t^e = -d + \hat{p}_t^e + (1-\delta_1)\hat{y}_t^e.$$

2.6. THE BEHAVIOUR OF THE MONETARY AUTHORITIES

In this section we will concentrate on the expected rate of
growth of money as the main determinant of expected inflation.
$\hat{y}^e$, the expected rate of growth of income, tends to fluctuate
much less than $\hat{M}^e$ and will be assumed to be constant for the
remainder of this section, so that equation (2.45) simplifies to

$$(2.46) \qquad \hat{p}_t^e = d_1 + \hat{M}_t^e$$

with d_1 a constant, which will be neglected for the time
being.

IS THE MONEY SUPPLY DETERMINED ON THE DEMAND SIDE?

The behaviour of the monetary authorities is described in our model by equation

$$(2.37) \qquad \Delta \hat{M}_t = (1-\theta B) a_t.$$

In each period the authorities miss their expected target by a_t, which not only implies a positive or negative monetary impulse for that year, but also leads to a revision of the money growth targets for all following years by $(1-\theta) a_t$ (see section 2.2. for the mathematics). Economic agents form their expectations about future money growth on the basis of equation (2.37), and because this future rate of money growth is expected to hold for all future periods and we have assumed that there are no changes in the expected growth rate of income, they will use equation (2.46) and also expect:

$$(2.47) \qquad {}_t\hat{Ep}_{t+1} = {}_t\hat{Ep}_{t+2} = {}_t\hat{EM}_{t+1} = {}_t\hat{EM}_{t+2} = \ldots.$$

In this bivariate model for money growth and inflation, expected money growth drives inflation. It will now be juxtaposed to that of Sargent (1977a), who lets expected inflation determine the growth in the money stock (Cf. Sargent and Wallace, 1973a, b).

In his study of the dynamics of hyperinflation under rational expectations Sargent, too, abstracts from all economic variables except money and prices. He assumes the following bivariate stochastic process for money growth and inflation.

$$(2.48) \qquad \Delta \hat{M}_t = \{(1+\mu_1) - (\lambda + \mu_1) B\} a_{2,t} + (1-B) a_{1,t},$$

$$(2.49) \qquad \Delta \hat{p}_t = (1-\lambda B) a_{2,t},$$

with $a_{1,t}$, $a_{2,t}$ uncorrelated white noise processes.

The particular coefficient restrictions are the consequence of Sargent's decision to construct a model in which, first, adaptively formed expectations of $\hat{p}$ are rational, and, second,

(2.50) $_t EM_{t+1} = _t EM_{t+2} = \cdots = _t Ep_{t+1} = _t Ep_{t+2} \cdots$

This means that each observed discrepancy between the expected
and the actual rate of inflation must have the same effect on
the next period's expected rate of inflation:

$$\hat{p}^e_{t+1} = \hat{p}^e_t + (1 - \lambda)(\hat{p}_t - \hat{p}^e_t)$$

Equation (2.50) can then be used to derive the expected rate of
money growth: the growth in the money supply is now demand-
determined. It follows that there are only two ways in which an
independent noise a_{1t} in the money supply process can affect the
rate of price change. Either

$$\hat{\Delta p}_t = (1 - \lambda B) a_{2,t} + (1 - \lambda B) a_{1,t}$$

$$\hat{\Delta M}_t = \left[(1 + \mu_1) - (\lambda + \mu_1) B\right] a_{2,t} + (1 - \lambda B) a_{1,t}$$

or

(2.49) $\hat{\Delta p}_t = (1 - \lambda B) a_{2,t} + 0.a_{1,t}$

(2.48) $\hat{\Delta M}_t = \left[(1 + \mu_1) - (\lambda + \mu_1) B\right] a_{2,t} + (1 - 1.B) a_{1,t}$

The first case is trivial, as the $a_{1,t}$'s are indistinguish-
able from the $a_{2,t}$'s. Therefore, Sargent uses the second specification, so that, in the terminology of Meltzer (1977a), *the rate of
inflation* has become a deterministic function of *the rate of
price change*. Each disturbance $a_{2,t}$, even those that are caused
by changes in relative prices, has an effect on $\hat{p}^e_t$ and thus on
the rate of inflation in all future periods. Nominal disturbances,
$a_{1,t}$, have no influence at all on the expected rate of inflation.
Sargent's model satisfies equation (2.50), which is equivalent to
our equation (2.47), although the underlying economic mechanism
is the opposite of what we have assumed. Now, the noise in the
price equation drives the system, whereas in our model it was

the noise a_t in the money growth equation that caused changes in the expectations about future growth in money and prices.

Whether Sargent's model is relevant for the study of hyper-inflation can be doubted. Jacobs (1977a) has a diagram which shows that the $\hat{M}$-series cannot be assumed to be stationary with a zero mean for the German hyperinflation: economic agents should have been able to infer that the probability of further increases in the rate of money growth was higher than the probability of decreases in $\hat{M}$, at least in the final stage of hyperinflation. Statistical tests by Evans (1978) and Friedman (1978) also show that Sargent's model is not compatible with the hyperinflation data.

However, Sargents model is useful as it expresses in the simplest possible form the popular hypothesis that the supply of money is completely demand-determined. Each change in the demand for money -- expressed here by a change $\hat{p}$ -- is accommodated by the monetary authorities, either because they do not want to disturb the economy, or because they lack the power to be independent. If by chance the supply of money diverges from what is required by the change in demand (a non-zero value for the noise term $a_{1,t}$), then such a deviation in the growth path of the money stock is purely temporary and does not at all affect the price level. The contrast with equations (2.37) and (2.46) becomes even more clear when we write Sargent's model in the form

$$(2.49) \qquad \Delta \hat{p}_t = (1 - \lambda B) a_{2,t}$$

$$(2.51) \qquad \hat{M}_t^e = \hat{p}_t^e$$

Price expectations are now determined by the past history of prices, and the expected rate of inflation determines the expected rate of money growth. It follows that watching the money supply does not help in predicting inflation. If the money stock always increases by just as much as it should to accommodate the expected rise in the demand for money

$(a_{1,t} = 0$ in eq. (2.48)), then past rates of growth of M are
as useful in predicting the rate of inflation as are past
inflation rates. If the monetary authorities make errors
(significant non-zero values for $a_{1,t}$ in Sargent's model), then
money growth rates are not informative about future inflation.
At no time can inflationary expectations be made more accurate
by paying attention to money growth rates:

$$\hat{M}_t^{S^e} \leftarrow \hat{M}_t^{D^e} \leftarrow \hat{p}_t^e \rightarrow \hat{p}_t$$

$$\uparrow$$

$$\hat{p}_{t-1, t-2, \ldots}$$

M^S --   money supply

M^D --   money demand

p --   price level

$p_{t-1,t-2}$ --   the set of past price level data.

Once lagged inflation rates are taken into account, lagged
money growth rates do not help predict current inflation
(Sargent, 1977a, p. 65). This is a testable proposition, derived
from the hypothesis that the behaviour of the monetary
authorities is completely demand-determined.

By contrast, in our model (equations (2.37) and (2.46))
past money growth rates are useful for predicting current
inflation:

$$\hat{M}_t^{S^e} \rightarrow \hat{p}_t^e \rightarrow \hat{M}_t^{D^e}$$

$$\uparrow$$

$$M_{t-1,t-2, \ldots}$$

$M_{t-1,t-2}$ --   the set of past money stock data.

Inflationary expectations are now based on the path of
another variable, the money stock, and not on past rates of
price change. This has the advantage that not every one-time
discrepancy between $\hat{p}^e$ and $\hat{p}$ has an infinite influence on

future rates of inflation, as in Sargent's model.

In order to test the two alternative hypotheses, we have
regressed actual rates of price change in the U.S. and the
Netherlands on two measures of expected inflation rates, one
built on past rates of money growth and one on past rates of
price change. The models for expected money growth are based on
equation (2.37) (see chapters 3 and 4). The univariate models
for $\hat{p}$ can be found in Appendix 2. The simple correlations between
$\hat{p}$, the actual rate of price change, and $\hat{p}^e(\hat{p}_{-1,-2},\ldots)$, the
univariate predictor of $\hat{p}$, are .69 for the U.S. and .72 for
the Netherlands. This indicates that past rates of price change
do contain information about the future course of inflation.

However, the regressions in table 2.1. indicate not only
that money growth rates are useful for predicting inflation,
which is sufficient to reject Sargent's model, but also that
past rates of price change are superfluous, given past rates of
money growth. Because of heteroskedasticity in equation (2.52)
for the U.S., that equation has also been estimated for the
shorter period 1953-1973. The rate of inflation never fluctuated
as much during these years as during the period of the Korean
war. Still, the coefficient on $\hat{M}^e_t$ remains positive and significant, and information that is contained in past rates of price
change is not required, even though the year-to-year variability
in $\hat{p}_t$ was less than in 1949-1953. When the omitted-variables
bias in these equations is reduced by adding some variables that
explain part of $(\hat{p} - \hat{p}^e)$ (see chapters 3 and 4), the results
remain the same: the coefficient on $\hat{M}^e$ is close to one and
significant, whereas $\hat{p}^e(\hat{p}_{-1,-2},\ldots)$ has a coefficient which is
not significantly different from zero. Equations (2.52) - (2.54)
strongly reject Sargent's model in which the money supply is
simply demand-determined. The proponents of this view will have
to offer a multivariate model for inflationary expectations that
does not include past rates of money growth in its information
set, but manages to dominate $\hat{M}^e$ in an empirical price equation.
Additional tests for the Netherlands show that extending the
information set by past rates of wage change is not sufficient:

Table 2.1. EXPECTED INFLATION AND MONEY GROWTH

(2.52) U.S.: $\hat{p}_t = .003 + .70 \; \hat{M}^e_t + .34 \; \hat{p}^e_t(\hat{p}_{t-1,t-2},\dots)$

$\qquad\qquad\qquad (.007) \quad (.31) \qquad\quad (.33)$

$\qquad \bar{R}^2 = .53; \quad \sigma_a = 1.6; \quad D.W. = 1.6; \quad \text{years:} \quad 1949\text{-}1976$

(2.53) U.S.: $\hat{p}_t = - .009 + .64 \; \hat{M}^e_t + .46 \; \hat{p}^e_t(\hat{p}_{t-1,t-2},\dots)$

$\qquad\qquad\qquad (.006) \quad (.18) \qquad\quad (.31)$

$\qquad \bar{R}^2 = .74; \quad \sigma_a = 0.7; \quad D.W. = 1.4; \quad \text{years:} \quad 1953\text{-}1973$

(2.54) Netherlands:

$\qquad\qquad \hat{p}_t = - 1.05 + .77 \; \hat{M}^e_{t-.5} + .10 \; \hat{p}^e(\hat{p}_{t-1,t-2},\dots)$

$\qquad\qquad\qquad\;\; (1.27) \quad (.28) \qquad\qquad (.34)$

$\qquad \bar{R}^2 = .61; \quad \sigma_a = 1.4; \quad D.W. = 1.7; \quad \text{years:} \quad 1954\text{-}1976$

Meaning of symbols:

p_t -- gnp deflator (U.S.); gdp deflator (Netherlands)

$\hat{M}^e_t$ -- expected rate of money growth

$\hat{M}^e_{t-.5} = .5(\hat{M}^e_t + \hat{M}^e_{t-1})$ -- expected rate of money growth, lagged 0.5 years (see Argy, 1978, for an economic justification for a short lag)

$\hat{p}^e_t(\hat{p}_{t-1,t-2},\dots)$ -- optimal univariate predictor of inflation (in contrast with the multivariate predictions, given by equation (2.45)).

$\bar{R}^2$ -- coefficient of determination, corrected for degrees of freedom

σ_a -- residual standard error

D.W.   -- Durbin-Watson coefficient

See chapters 3 and 4 for more details and a justification of the choice of initial years for the regressions.

when $\hat{w}^e(\hat{w}_{-1}, _{-2}, \ldots)$ is added to equation (2.54), its coefficient does not differ significantly from zero either. Until a more powerful model of non-monetary inflationary expectations is offered, we can continue to regard the money supply as the driving force behind inflation.

AIMS OF THE MONETARY AUTHORITIES

The important question now remains: is it possible to give a more economic interpretation of the statistical equation (2.37)? Mussa (1976b, p. 247) has this to say about the same stochastic model:

> ".... (T)he process generating disturbances in the money supply was an arbitrary prescribed stochastic process, a stochastic black box. In fact, there is likely to be a good deal of economic structure which lies behind the nature of disturbances to the money supply, including the structure of the banking system, the aggressiveness of "stabilization" policy, and the extent to which the government ment resorts to the printing press as a means of financing its deficits."

Now that the tests have shown that the money supply is not wholly demand-determined, we should try to formulate hypotheses about what does determine the course of money, so that the statistical equation (2.37) is given economic content.

Let us first consider a closed economy. The monetary base may grow because the government finds it convenient to extract revenue from a tax on real balances. One natural hypothesis (Gordon, 1975) would be that whenever the authorities have to find additional income, they try to spread the burden over different forms of taxation and raise part of it by recourse to the inflation tax. Barro (1977) offers this rationale as one of two arguments for including the lagged rate of unemployment in his money growth equation: when the U.S. economy is in recession, revenue from other taxes decreases, so that real balances are taxed more heavily.

Barro's second reason for having the lagged unemployment rate in the money growth equation is that it may express

a political reaction function: when unemployment is high, the
authorities are under pressure to provide a monetary stimulus to
the economy. A difficulty with a systematic reaction function
-- noted by Barro in his paper -- is that rational agents will
anticipate the government's behaviour, which in this case
implies that the monetary stimulus will lead only to a higher
anticipated rate of money growth and not to less unemployment.
Similar problems cast doubt on the value of some other theoretical
attempts to model a political reaction function for money growth
(Sjaastad, 1976, Laidler, 1976). These authors assume that the
government engineers cyclical patterns in the growth rate of
money either to maximize revenue from the inflation tax
(Sjaastad) or to make it easy to issue new government debt and
then reduce its real value (Laidler), but they have to assume
persisting opacity on the part of the public, as stressed by
Johnson (1977a) in his diagrammatic exposition of Sjaastad's
hypothesis. When Barro's assumption about high unemployment
leading automatically to faster money growth was used by Parkin
in 1975, it led to the following prediction, based on the high
rates of unemployment in the U.K. at the time of the forecast:

> "The result is going to be a 1976 of rapid real growth
> and falling unemployment and a 1977 with inflation rates
> into the 20's and 30's rather than the mere 'teens'."
> (p. 202).

The fate of this prediction illustrates that it is hazardous
to predict money growth on the basis of political reaction
functions that assume irrational behaviour by the public.
People cannot be fooled all the time, it seems; reaction
functions should assume rationality.

Let us now consider the case of an open economy under
fixed or quasi-fixed exchange rates. The U.S. and the Netherlands must be discussed separately. The U.S. was the main
supplier of international reserves during the period under
review, so that its monetary policy was not faced with the type
of constraint that applies to a small open economy such as the
Netherlands. The exchange-rate regime explains why the U.S.

authorities could easily validate any upward pressure on prices
in the U.S. with additional money (Meltzer, 1977b). Movements in
the aggregate price level did not tend to be reversed quickly,
as under the gold standard, but were usually indicative of
further changes in the same direction during subsequent years.
This is the reason why "we have gone one derivative beyond
Hume" (Friedman, 1975, p. 177), and must now think in terms of
the rate of money growth and the rate of inflation, and not in
terms of the level of the money stock or the level of prices
(Klein, 1976, 1978, Meltzer, 1977a).

Our statistical tests have already shown that the U.S.
authorities do not just keep the growth rate of the money stock
equal to last year's rate of price increase. Actual money growth
rates can be significantly increased or lowered so that
monetary policy influences the real sector in the short run and
the rate of inflation in the longer run. As indicated earlier,
however, we have not been able to specify the economic
determinants of these changes in the rate of money growth.
The Netherlands maintained a fixed rate of exchange with the
U.S. dollar for most of our estimation period. At least in the
longer run, the Dutch rate of money growth must have been
determined by international factors. Much theoretical and
descriptive work has been done on these linkages, for example
Fausten (1975) for the U.K., and Corden (1976), who gives a
six-way theoretical classification of reasons for increases in
the money supply in open economies. But, when the Dutch rate of
money growth was regressed on past values of $\hat{M}^*$ and $\hat{p}^*$, with
$\hat{M}^*$, $\hat{p}^*$ the rates of money growth and inflation in the world
(see chapter 4), no satisfactory relationships could be found
for the fixed-rate period 1954-1972.

Genberg (1978) has argued that the explanatory variables
$\hat{M}^*$ and $\hat{p}^*$ should be replaced by their determinants, which would
imply regressing changes in Dutch money growth on monetary and
other impulses in important foreign countries. Some preliminary
experiments are reported in chapter 4. The only significant
finding was a close connection between unanticipated money

growth in the Netherlands and unanticipated monetary impulses in
West Germany. For the interpretation of this result, however,
a more structural model would be required, in the absence of
which it is of no use for predicting Dutch money growth.

Once again, there is only one firm conclusion that can be
drawn from this discussion: because of the exchange rate regime,
the hypothesis that there exists a "normal" rate of money growth
or a "normal" rate of inflation (Frenkel, 1975, Mussa 1975,
Barro, 1977) must be rejected. Money growth and inflation are
more or less noisy random walks, which explains the empirical
success of models such as:

$$\hat{M}^e_t = (\hat{M}_{t-1} + \hat{M}_{t-2} + \hat{M}_{t-3})/3 \quad \text{Meltzer (1977a), Stein (1978);}$$

$$\hat{M}^e_t = \hat{M}_{t-1} \qquad \qquad \text{Korteweg (1978a, b);}$$

$$\hat{M}^e_t = \hat{M}^e_{t-1} + (1 - \theta)a_{t-1} \qquad \text{equation (2.25).}$$

That much is clear, but the modelling of the economic determinants
of changes in the rate of money growth is still very much an
unfinished business, because of the problems in specifying reaction functions that are compatible with the assumption of
rational expectations.

2.7. THE DETERMINATION OF REAL INCOME

The simplified model of section 2.1. contained the following pair
of equations for the demand and supply of output:

$$(2.4) \quad (\hat{y}-\hat{y}^e)_t = -\beta_1 \Delta r_t - \beta_2 (\hat{p}-\hat{p}^e)_t + \beta_3 (\hat{g}-\hat{g}^e)_t + a_{4,t}, \quad \text{demand}$$

$$(2.5) \quad (\hat{y}-\hat{y}^e)_t = \alpha_1 (\hat{p}-\hat{p}^e)_t + a_{5,t}, \qquad \qquad \text{supply.}$$

It is assumed throughout that the market for output clears, so
that the single symbol y can represent both sides of the market.

According to equation (2.4) the demand for output depends on the (unanticipated) change in the real rate of interest, unanticipated changes in prices, unanticipated growth in government expenditure, $(\hat{g}-\hat{g}^e)$, and on an error term $a_{4,t}$. If we replace the variable $(\hat{g}-\hat{g}^e)_t$ by the more general expression:

$$(\hat{z}-\hat{z}^e)_t$$

where Z is a vector of exogenous variables that influence demand, then the demand for output equation becomes:

$$(2.55) \qquad (\hat{y}-\hat{y}^e)_t = -\beta_1 \Delta r_t - \beta_2 (\hat{p}-\hat{p}^e)_t + \beta_3 (\hat{Z}-\hat{Z}^e)_t + a_{4,t}$$

with β_1 and β_2 positive constants, β_3 a constant vector of co-efficients, and $a_{4,t}$ an uncorrelated error term. This type of aggregate demand schedule has been common in recent theoretical work (Barro and Fischer, 1976), and was used in empirical work by Korteweg (1978a, b); McCallum (1978, p. 421) shows that it can also be derived from a Keynesian model. The demand curve is not a matter of contention between monetarist and non-monetarist economists, but there is disagreement about the modelling of the other side of the market for output, the schedule for aggregate supply.

THE SHORT-RUN SUPPLY CURVE

Two main strands can be distinguished in the literature (see the survey by Barro and Fischer, 1976, and the entertaining article by Gordon, 1976a). The first explanation, the so-called Lucas-Sargent proposition, stresses informational problems in a complex economy. For the sake of analytical tractability, the complexity is usually not modelled by assuming that many different goods are produced and consumed, but by postulating that a single homogeneous good is traded in a large number of spatially segregated markets (the islands hypothesis).

After rational expectations for the current period have been formed, agents do not have a chance to monitor markets

other than the single market in which they trade before actual
"closing" prices and volumes in their own market are determined.
Each market is cleared, but the equilibrium values for price
and volume in the market have to be based on somewhat out-of-
date figures for prices and quantities in all the other markets.
Traders find it impossible or at least not worth the cost to
collect information about every market all the time, so that they
have to make their decisions without full knowledge of what is
happening in the aggregate.

Assume now that a firm experiences an unanticipated
increase in the demand for its product. Whether this shift in
demand is caused by a change in preferences that benefits this
firm at the expense of its competitors, or whether the cause is
a nominal shift in aggregate demand that affects each firm in
the same way makes a difference as to the optimal response of
the firm. Real shifts should induce permanent changes in the
composition of output; nominal shifts do not change the
equilibrium values of any real measures, but should lead to
a proportional increase of all absolute prices. However, the
firm cannot discern immediately between the two types of demand
shifts, and must make its decisions for the current period on
the basis of limited knowledge. Its rational response will
consist of an average of the decisions appropriate to the two
extremes that it cannot distinguish: the firm will raise prices
and expand output, which is to say that it moves along a short-
run supply curve with a positive slope (Gordon and Hynes, 1970,
Lucas, 1977). The slope of this curve increases with the
expected variance of unannounced shifts in nominal aggregate
demand, ceteris paribus. Loosely speaking, if a country tries
to revive its economy by repeatedly inflating nominal demand,
then each successive monetary stimulus will generate more
inflation and less real growth.

An alternative foundation for a short-run supply curve
that has a positive slope rests on temporary rigidities in the
markets for productive factors. Assume, for example, that at
the beginning of each period labour has been contracted at

a wage that will be maintained until contracting for the next period takes place. If the bargaining parties are rational, then the agreed wage rate will be based on an estimate of the state of the economy during the period of the contract. However, unforeseen changes in nominal aggregate demand may occur, and their effect will be temporarily to decrease real wages. As a consequence, there will be a short-term rise in output, even if the increase in demand is perceived correctly as a nominal shock. This so-called contract theory would be incomplete without a rational explanation for the existence of contracts that do not allow for constant renegotiation of wages, hours of work, etc. Recently, much progress has been made in this area (see, for example, Grossman, 1978, Mortensen, 1978), so that the assumption of fixed contracts is losing the arbitrariness for which it used to be criticized.

Both the Lucas-Sargent proposition and the contract theory explain why output and prices change because of an unforeseen shift in the aggregate demand curve. We find the actual changes by solving the four equations (2.5), (2.37), (2.44) and (2.55). The solutions differ from those obtained in section (2.1) (see eq. (2.16)) in some minor aspects, but $(\hat{y}-\hat{y}^e)_t$ and $(\hat{p}-\hat{p}^e)_t$ remain linear combinations of the current unexpected changes in the exogenous variables and the current error terms:

$$(2.56) \qquad (\hat{p}-\hat{p}^e)_t = \frac{1}{A} \left[\beta_1 (1+\varepsilon(1-\theta)) \ (\hat{M}-\hat{M}^e)_t + \varepsilon\beta_3 (\hat{Z}-\hat{Z}^e)_t + \right.$$

$$\left. - \beta_1 a_{2,t} + \varepsilon a_{4,t} - (\beta_1 \delta_2 + \varepsilon) a_{5,t} \right];$$

$$(2.57) \qquad (\hat{y}-\hat{y}^e)_t = \frac{1}{A} \left[\alpha_1 \beta_1 (1+\varepsilon(1-\theta)) \ (\hat{M}-\hat{M}^e)_t + \alpha_1 \varepsilon\beta_3 (\hat{Z}-\hat{Z}^e)_t + \right.$$

$$\left. - \alpha_1 \beta_1 a_{2,t} + \alpha_1 \varepsilon a_{4,t} + (\beta_1 + \varepsilon\beta_2) a_{5,t} \right],$$

with $A = \beta_1 (1+\alpha_1 \delta_2) + \varepsilon(\alpha_1 + \beta_2)$.

The reduced form for $(\hat{y}-\hat{y}^e)$ will be discussed in the remainder

of this section; the equation for $(\hat{p}-\hat{p}^e)$ is on the agenda for
section 2.8. together with the restrictions that hold across
equations (2.56) and (2.57) with respect to the coefficients of
$(\hat{M}-\hat{M}^e)$ and $(\hat{Z}-\hat{Z}^e)$.

THE DYNAMICS OF THE OUTPUT MARKET

Before proceeding to a survey of the impulses that influence
$(\hat{y}-\hat{y}^e)$, we consider the form of equation (2.57). To begin, note
that all the dependent or independent variables in the final
form equations for $(\hat{y}-\hat{y}^e)$ and $(\hat{p}-\hat{p}^e)$ are of the form:

$$(\hat{x}-\hat{x}^e)$$

where x represents M or the elements of the vector Z. Furthermore, it has been assumed that the error terms $a_{2,t}$, $a_{4,t}$, and
$a_{5,t}$ are serially uncorrelated. Consequently, this model for the
determination of unexpected short-run changes in output and
prices can be combined with a variety of assumptions about the
expected growth rates of y. However, one constraint on the
formation of expectations about output growth follows from our
derivation of the demand for money in section 2.5.: the term
structure of expectations for $\hat{y}$ must collapse into the single
number $\hat{y}^e_t$.

The way to transform equation (2.57) into a (multivariate)
model that satisfies a constant term structure of expectations
was discussed in section 2.3. First, rewrite equation (2.57):

$$(2.58) \qquad (\hat{y} - \hat{y}^e)_t = \kappa_1 (\hat{M} - \hat{M}^e)_t + \kappa_2 (\hat{Z} - \hat{Z}^e)_t + w_t$$

with κ_1 a positive constant, κ_2 a constant vector of coefficients
and w_t a serially uncorrelated error term.

The general form of the equation for $\Delta\hat{y}$ now becomes:

$$(2.59) \qquad \Delta\hat{y}_t = (\kappa_1 + \lambda_1 B)(\hat{M} - \hat{M}^e)_t + (\kappa_2 + \lambda_2 B)(\hat{Z} - \hat{Z}^e)_t +$$

$$+ (1 - \theta_o B)w_t$$

with λ_1 an additional constant, λ_2 a fixed vector of coefficients, and θ_o a moving average parameter in the noise model. Note, that eq. (2.58) can be derived from eq. (2.59), but not vice-versa; eq. (2.59) is just one of the expressions that contain the relation (2.58) for unexpected growth in demand, namely the final form equation for $\Delta \hat{y}$ that leads to a constant term structure of expectations for $\hat{y}^e$:

$$(2.60) \qquad \hat{y}^e_t - \hat{y}^e_{t-1} = (\kappa_1 + \lambda_1)(\hat{M} - \hat{M}^e)_{t-1} + (\kappa_2 + \lambda_2)(\hat{Z} - \hat{Z}^e)_{t-1} +$$

$$+ (1 - \theta_o) w_{t-1}$$

Equation (2.60) will from now on replace equation (2.3) that postulated a constant expected growth rate for y. Instead, an impulse in period t may cause a permanent change in the "level" of $\hat{y}$, for $\hat{y}$ is no longer assumed to be a stationary series. The impulse will have this effect if the relevant κ and λ do not add to zero in equation (2.60).

The assumption of a constant term structure of expectations for $\hat{y}$ was introduced in order to simplify the demand for money function. However, it can also be defended in its own right. For, consider the hypothetical opposite situation in which economic agents are capable of predicting future fluctuations in the rate of economic growth. In that case, each firm will try to reduce unit costs by making its own rate of production a smooth function of time, accumulating stocks during periods of slack and selling from stock when aggregate demand is above average (Alchian, 1959). Such off-setting intertemporal behaviour makes it unlikely that complete trade cycles can be anticipated; market forces would go a long way towards eliminating the cycles before they could have materialized. Instead, we assume that a positive impulse in period t leads only to higher expected growth in that period and -- possibly -- to a small increase in the expected rate of growth for periods t+1, t+2 etc. If this impulse is followed by another positive impulse in year t+1, then the rate of growth of y will continue to be high: a prolonged economic

boom. Only after a negative shock has occurred does the economy
enter the second half of the cycle with lower-than-average
economic growth. This phase in turn will last until the next
positive impulse affects the economy and a new cycle begins.
According to this hypothesis, complete cycles do not have a
fixed period and are therefore not foreseeable. The observed
cyclical movements in $\hat{y}$ are caused by random sequences of positive and negative shocks that hit the economy.

Equations (2.59) and (2.60) have been developed from the
reduced form equation (2.58) and not directly from dynamic
structural demand and supply equations, since we want to impose
rational expectations together with the restriction that in
period t agents cannot foresee changes in $\hat{y}$ beyond period t+1 --
the hypothesis of a constant term structure of expectations. If
instead the reduced form equations, or, more precisely, the final
form equations of a model are derived from structural equations
that include distributed lags on the jointly dependent variables,
then these final forms will contain error terms with complicated
serial correlation patterns (cf. Pierce and Mason, 1978). As
a consequence, a series of future changes in the growth rate of
income can be predicted with the help of such a final form
equation, which is something we have wanted to eliminate, both
to keep the derivation of the expected growth in the demand for
money manageable, and because of Alchian's argument that rational
firms would tend to exploit and thereby nullify any foreseeable
fluctuations in economic activity. The alternative assumption,
namely that the errors in the final form equations have simple
properties (for example, the first-order moving average model as
in equation (2.59)), has the advantage that one retains a correspondingly simple term structure of expectations for the endogenous variables. For this reason, equation (2.59) is a dynamic
generalization of the reduced form equation (2.58), and not the
solution of a pair of dynamic supply and demand equations.

Concern about the formation of expectations also explains
why the expected rate of growth of output has not been derived
from the theory of the production function. Suppose that we wish

to use a production function, not to analyze the causes of
long-term economic growth, nor to calculate some hypothetical
volume of output that might be produced in the next period if all
productive factors were fully employed, but to derive an expectation of the actual growth of output in the next period. One
necessary input for the calculation of $_t\hat{E}y_{t+1}$ will be a forecast
of the utilization rate of capital in the next period. However,
this leads to two difficulties. First, which theory is available
to derive such a forecast? Second, is the use of a capital stock
variable that is adjusted for the rate of utilization of capital
not contrary to the theoretical assumptions that underlie the
production function? According to Sargent and Sims (1977, p. 46):

> "no micro-theory leading to an aggregate production
> function with utilization-adjusted capital has been put
> forward."

These are two formidable difficulties, in view of which the use
of a production function for the generation of short-term forecasts of output has been rejected.

THE IMPULSES

Having discussed the formal structure of the reduced-form
equation for output, we proceed with some remarks about the impulses that influence y. One impulse that is already explicit in
equation (2.59) is the unanticipated growth in the money supply,
$(\hat{M} - \hat{M}^e)$. As explained above, such a monetary impulse will have
a short-term influence on current output, but it may also have
consequences for the longer-term. If the moving average parameter in the equation (2.37) for money growth is not equal to
one, then a positive monetary impulse will lead to an upward
revision of inflationary expectations and that can have an influence on $\hat{y}$ for three reasons: first, because of the non-
neutralities in every real economy (tax rates that are not
adjusted for inflation, changes in the effective rate of
interest if interest changes are tax-deductible, the impossibility of paying interest on currency, etc.). Some of these non-
neutralities will tend to increase $\hat{y}^e$, others will lead to less

economic growth. Second, because the probability of an attempt
by the government to break inflationary expectations through
controls or through sudden monetary restraint will be a positive
function of the actual rate of inflation, and any increase in
the likelihood of such actions will have depressing effects on
output and spending plans. Finally, and this argument holds for
every impulse in the equation for output, if a positive shock
leads to an increase in employment, then it will increase the
stock of human capital and thus the potential for future economic
growth, because workers who were outside the labour force will
acquire useful experience.

All the other impulses in equation (2.59) were subsumed
in the vector $(\hat{Z}-\hat{Z}^e)$. In the empirical work of chapters 3 and 4
we shall exploit, for example, the positive association between
unanticipated changes in government expenditure, $(\hat{g}-\hat{g}^e)$, and
$(\hat{y}-\hat{y}^e)$. Unforeseen increases in $\hat{g}$ apparently do not lead to
immediate opposite reactions in private output; in other words,
there is no complete real crowding-out in the very short-term.
Some recent theoretical literature explains this by assuming that
agents do not fully discount the future burden of the increase
in government debt that pays for the additional government expenditure. Alternatively, there may be informational problems
similar to those discussed in connection with the Lucas-Sargent
proposition. Our model is unfit to analyze the issue, if only
because it does not contain an equation for the government
budget. In the time series models an unforeseen impulse $(\hat{g}-\hat{g}^e)_t$
simply has an influence on the future expectations $_t E\hat{g}_{t+1}$ etc.
In principle, the impulse can affect $_t E\hat{y}_{t+1}$ as well. Such longer-
term effects will depend on many factors, including the way in
which any deficits are financed, the efficiency of the public and
private sectors of the economy and the degree to which government
expenditure results in additions to the nation's productive stock
of human or physical capital. Further impulses may be significant
in open economies. We shall find an important influence of
$(\hat{m}_w - \hat{m}_w^e)$, unexpected changes in world trade, on the Dutch
economy. Changes in tariffs also come to mind (Wanniski, 1978,

chapter 7). Korteweg further includes $(\hat{p}^* - \hat{p}^{*e})$, the unexpected change in world prices as a determinant of $\Delta\hat{y}$ in his theoretical model (see also Laidler, 1977). He measures $\hat{p}^*$ as the rate of price inflation in the developed economies that are Holland's competitors in international markets, so that $(\hat{p}^* - \hat{p}^{*e})$ has a short-term positive influence on demand.

A final impulse that will be included in some of our equations, is the unexpected change in agricultural production. This impulse is different from, for example, an M or g impulse, as it does not imply the competitive bidding for productive factors that causes the economy to move along a positively sloped short-run supply curve, and prices to increase together with output. With a positive agricultural impulse, both the short-run supply curve and the demand curve shift in the same direction; output increases but the sign of the impulse in the reduced form for prices cannot be easily predicted.

Most of the impulses in this list originate in the government sector of the economy. An exception is the agricultural impulse, which will be mainly caused by the weather, although changes in government policy are also important determinants of agricultural production. Changes in world trade and world prices must be assumed to depend mainly on monetary and fiscal policies and on tariff decisions in the different trading nations. It follows that empirical success of such an output equation provides evidence against the hypothesis that output fluctuations are mainly caused by unstable, erratic behaviour in the private sector of the economy. As was already pointed out in chapter 1, economists should begin by assuming rational behaviour on the part of market participants. If rational actor analysis is capable of accounting for the evidence, then there is no need to develop other, non-economic hypotheses. Therefore, one impulse that is often mentioned as a major cause of price and output fluctuations, has been omitted from our list on methodological grounds: the unexpected change in wages $(\hat{w} - \hat{w}^e)$. Observed large changes in wages may have economic causes: for example, a change in the expected rate

of inflation, a large increase in government demand for labour,
or a sudden increase in foreign demand for domestic output. In
such situations, it is preferable to specify these economic
determinants of the change in wage rates, instead of $(\hat{w} - \hat{w}^e)$.
The empirical research in chapters 3 and 4 will show that those
large changes in wage rates that occurred in the U.S. and in the
Netherlands must have had predominantly economic causes, because
the patterns over time of prices and output can be explained
without a variable for $(\hat{w} - \hat{w}^e)$. This fits in which the argument
of Lucas (1977) that wage changes cannot be the major determinant
of the trade cycle, because there is no systematic correspondence
between changes in real wages and changes in output.

In concluding this section, it should be stressed once
again that the impulses do not pretend adequately to describe
the determination of the *trend* growth of output, but only serve
in a simple reduced-form equation for $\Delta\hat{y}$, needed for tests of
the usefulness of the equation of exchange in predicting
inflation. Moreover, it is quite possible that in empirical work
many impulses will not be significant, if only because the
restrictions on the term structure of expectations imply that
we should use annual data, which means that few degrees of
freedom are available in regressions for $\Delta\hat{y}$.

2.8. THE ACTUAL RATE OF PRICE CHANGE

A final-form equation for $(\hat{y} - \hat{y}^e)_t$ was obtained in the previous
section:

$$(2.58) \qquad (\hat{y} - \hat{y}^e)_t = \kappa_1 (\hat{M} - \hat{M}^e)_t + \kappa_2 (\hat{Z} - \hat{Z}^e)_t + w_t$$

After that we wrote down a dynamic generalization of this final-
form equation for output:

$$(2.59) \qquad \Delta\hat{y}_t = (\kappa_1 + \lambda_1 B)(\hat{M} - \hat{M}^e)_t + (\kappa_2 + \lambda_2 B)(\hat{Z} - \hat{Z}^e)_t + (1 - \theta_0 B)w_t$$

Equation (2.59) does not only express the effects of the impulses on the current rate of growth of output, it also provides a way of calculating expectations of the future growth of output that are rational and based on all the available information:

$$(2.60) \qquad \hat{y}_t^e - \hat{y}_{t-1}^e = (\kappa_1 + \lambda_1)(\hat{M} - \hat{M}^e)_{t-1} + (\kappa_2 + \lambda_2)(\hat{Z} - \hat{Z}^e)_{t-1} +$$
$$+ (1 - \theta_0) w_{t-1}$$

Proceeding to the determination of the rate of price change, we find that the situation is different, for we have assumed already that inflationary expectations are based on equation (2.45):

$$\hat{p}_t^e = d + \hat{M}_t^e - (1 - \delta_1)\hat{y}_t^e$$

Therefore, in contrast with the output equation, this time we cannot allow for effects of the impulses on $\hat{p}^e$ or introduce serial correlation in the error terms of the equation for $(\hat{p} - \hat{p}^e)$. The reduced form equation (2.56) satisfies both these restrictions, for it relates the differences $(\hat{p} - \hat{p}^e)_t$ to the values of the impulse variables in period t plus a serially uncorrelated error term. In the notation that was also used for equation (2.58).

$$(2.61) \qquad (\hat{p} - \hat{p}^e)_t = \mu_1(\hat{M} - \hat{M}^e)_t + \mu_2(\hat{Z} - \hat{Z}^e)_t + v_t$$

with μ_1 a positive constant, μ_2 a vector of constant coefficients, and v_t a serially uncorrelated error term.

No connection exists in our model between the equation for $(\hat{p} - \hat{p}^e)$ and the equation for expected inflation which is based on the equation of exchange. Some other models which do assume a feedback between $(\hat{p} - \hat{p}^e)$ and $\hat{p}^e$, neglect the distinction between one-time and permanent influences on the rate of price change that has been stressed in this chapter. We have seen in section 2.6. above that prediction formulae which do use past rates of price change for the determination of $\hat{p}^e$ produce inferior

forecasts (see also Gordon, 1978). Models with that property,
for example

(2.62) $\hat{p}_t = f(p_t^* - p_{t-1})$ (Barten et al., 1976)

with p^* a desired price level,

or

(2.63) $\Delta\hat{p}_t^e = \alpha(\hat{p}_{t-1} - \hat{p}_{t-1}^e)$ (Aghevli and Khan, 1977)

not only suffer from a confusion between one-time and permanent
influences on the rate of price change, but can be criticized more
generally for not being derived from economic theory. It is
significant that Ando, in specifying expected inflation as
dependent on past rates of price change had to conclude:

> ".... the response of the expected rate of change of prices
> to the actual rate of change of prices is a very much un-
> settled empirical question, and the estimates of this
> process incorporated in the MPS model are probably among
> the least reliable of all estimates in it."
> (1974, p. 566).

In the empirical chapters 3 and 4 the theoretical
distinction between the determinants of $\hat{p}^e$ on the one hand and
those of $(\hat{p} - \hat{p}^e)$ on the other will be maintained. $\hat{p}^e$ will be
calculated from equation (2.45) and equation (2.61) will be our
relation for the difference between the expected and the actual
rate of price change. The impulse variables that explain $(\hat{p}-\hat{p}^e)$
have already been discussed in the previous section, so that we
proceed to the deferred issue of the coefficient restrictions
that hold across the two reduced-form equations for output and
prices.

Inspection of the equations (2.56) and (2.57) shows that
the short-term output elasticities of the different impulses are
in the same proportions to each other as the short-term price
elasticities: if the coefficient of impulse 1 in the output
equation is, say, double the coefficient of impulse 2, then the

coefficient of 1 must also be twice the coefficient of impulse 2 in the price equation. This condition applies only to impulses that shift the demand curve. It should not hold for all those impulses that lead to unforeseen shifts in both the supply and demand curves for output.

The proportionality of the coefficients in the price and output equations rests on one assumption that we have made which may be too restrictive. We have assumed that agents are totally unable to discover during the current period why $\hat{y}_t$ differs from $\hat{y}_t^e$, and $\hat{p}_t$ from $\hat{p}_t^e$. Only at the end of the period do they learn about the values of all the impulses during period t, so that they can form fully rational expectations about future values of the impulses and of $\hat{M}$, $\hat{p}$, and $\hat{y}$. If, however, we assume that they obtain some information about the current impulses in the course of period t, then their reactions will differ according to whether an impulse is seen as completely temporary or as partly, possibly wholly permanent. An impulse with continuing positive effects on $\hat{y}$ will lead more readily to changes in asset prices and to plans for future expansion than a purely temporary impulse. It still remains true, however, that the same set of impulses should be present in the two reduced forms.

Finally, a remark has to be made about the error term in the price equation. It seems likely that the errors will not be normally distributed, for large positive discrepancies between $\hat{p}$ and $\hat{p}^e$ are more likely to occur than large negative differences. Relevant here is a study by Aigner et al. (1977), who worked with a composite error term that consisted of a normally distributed error plus a second stochastic term that took positive values only. They showed that such "half-normal" error terms make a difference to the estimate of the constant terms in the regressions, but do not affect the other regression coefficients.

THE EQUATIONS THAT WILL BE ESTIMATED

Now that all the changes to the original simple model of equation (2.1) - (2.5) have been discussed, we can conclude this chapter by presenting the four equations that have been derived from the theoretical model and will be estimated in chapters 3 and 4.

$$(2.37) \qquad \Delta \hat{M}_t = (1 - \theta B) a_{1,t}$$

$$(2.45) \qquad \hat{p}_t^e = d + \hat{M}_t^e - (1 - \delta_1) \hat{y}_t^e$$

$$(2.59) \qquad \Delta \hat{y}_t = (\kappa_1 + \lambda_1 B)(\hat{M} - \hat{M}^e)_t + (\kappa_2 + \lambda_2 B)(\hat{Z} - \hat{Z}^e)_t + (1 - \theta_0 B) w_t$$

$$(2.61) \qquad (\hat{p} - \hat{p}^e)_t = \mu_1 (\hat{M} - \hat{M}^e)_t + \mu_2 (\hat{Z} - \hat{Z}^e)_t + v_t.$$

Here, $\hat{M}$ is the rate of money growth and $\hat{p}$, $\hat{y}$ are the rates of growth of prices and output. Z is an index of exogenous impulse variables that influence y and p. θ, θ_0 are coefficients in the moving-average models for $a_{1,t}$ and w_t. All other Greek letters indicate constant coefficients. d is a fixed constant. $a_{1,t}$, w_t, and v_t are serially uncorrelated error terms. All expectations $\hat{M}^e$, $\hat{p}^e$, $\hat{y}^e$, and $\hat{Z}^e$ are rational and relate to the current period. Finally, the model is such that

$$\hat{x}_t^e = {}_{t-1}E\hat{x}_t = {}_{t-1}E\hat{x}_{t+1} = {}_{t-1}E\hat{x}_{t+2} = \ldots$$

for $x = M$, p, and y: a constant term structure of expectations. Equations (2.37), (2.45), and (2.59) will be estimated and then equation (2.61) will be estimated with $\hat{p}^e$ replaced by its determinants in the two empirical chapters that follow. By contrast, the actual demand for real balances, eq. (2.44) is not going to be estimated, since our model implies correlation between the error term in that equation and some of the explanatory variables.

Chapter 3

APPLYING THE QUANTITY THEORY:
THE CASE OF THE U.S.

3.1. INTRODUCTION

The theoretical model of the previous chapter has a number of
implications that will be investigated empirically in this
chapter and the next. Some examples of testable propositions
are:

-- the estimated coefficient of expected money growth, $\hat{M}^e$,
   in the price equation should be 1;

-- expected growth rates of money and real income for next
   year should also be representative of the expected growth
   rates for all subsequent years;

-- there should not be long lags in the effects of unanticipated impulses on $(\hat{p}-\hat{p}^e)$, the difference between the actual
   and expected rates of price change, and $(\hat{y}-\hat{y}^e)$, the discrepancy between the actual and expected growth of output,
   because the theory assumes that such shocks have a surprise
   effect, which becomes implausible when there are lags of
   several years between the impulse and its effects.

Apart from testing a number of implications of our theoretical
model, there is the equally interesting question whether the
model does a good job in tracking the past course of inflation
and whether it might be useful for predictions. While tests such
as those mentioned above can be performed against the null-
hypothesis, an overall investigation of the usefulness of the
model should be carried out through comparisons with other
models of inflation. To find that the $\bar{R}^2$ of our two reduced-
form price and output equations is significantly different from

zero, is of no particular interest, as there may be one or more
alternative models that result in even higher correlation
coefficients. Consequently, when our theoretical model is
implemented empirically with annual data for two countries,
the U.S. and the Netherlands, a comparison will be made in both
cases with a model from the literature that covers the same
country and the same period.

In the case of the U.S. our model will be juxtaposed to
that of Barro (1977, 1978). Barro also uses the equation of
exchange for the determination of prices, and he separates
money growth into an anticipated and unanticipated component.
In both aspects, his model and the present one are similar. But
two main differences remain: first, Barro works with the equation
of exchange in the form:

$$\log p = \log M - \log y + \log V,$$

where V stands for the income velocity of money. By contrast,
our theory uses

$$\hat{p}^e = \hat{M}^e - \hat{y}^e + \hat{V}^e.$$

Barro's use of the actual levels of p, M, y, and V implies that
a more worked-out theory of velocity is needed than in our
model, where

$$\hat{v}^e = c + \delta_1 \hat{y}^e$$

will be seen to be an acceptable simplification.

The second major point of difference between the two
models is the estimated duration of the period during which
the economy adjusts to its new equilibrium path after an
unanticipated monetary impulse. In Barro's model, it takes four
years for the rate of output to return to its equilibrium path
after a monetary shock, and the price level requires no less
than six years to adjust fully to an unanticipated change in

the level of the money stock. In our alternative model, the
period of adjustment takes only one year for both output and
prices. In the remainder of the present chapter we discuss these
and other differences between the two models.

A second comparison will be made with a model by Korteweg
(1978b) for the Dutch economy. Here, the resemblance between
the two structures is even greater than in the case of the U.S.
Korteweg also works with rational expectations and distinguishes
between anticipated and unanticipated changes of all his
variables. What is different, however, is the modelling of
foreign influences on inflationary expectations. Korteweg
calculates $\hat{p}^e$ as a weighted average of two series: expected
domestic money growth, $\hat{M}^e$, determined simply from its own past,
and expected world inflation, $\hat{p}^{*e}$. In our alternative model,
expected world inflation is not used for the formation of
inflationary expectations in Holland, but the expectations about
money growth are formed in a more complicated way, and utilize
information from financial markets. The two Dutch models are
discussed in chapter 4 below.

In order to make a meaningful comparison between the
explanatory power of each pair of models, they should be built
on more or less the same data bases. In the U.S. case, a subset
of Barro's collection of time series was used, and the need for
additional data did not arise. For the Netherlands, only two
further time series were used in addition to a subset of
Korteweg's data. With such minor differences, the explanatory
power of the two models for the U.S. and those for the Netherlands can be compared. We shall see that there is not much
difference, which provides some support for the present model,
because it satisfies a greater number of theoretically desirable
constraints than the models of Barro and Korteweg.

The model for the Netherlands is rather richer in detail
than the model for the U.S. Also, the stochastic structure of
some of the time series used is more complicated for the Dutch
economy. For these reasons, the comparison between the somewhat simpler U.S. models will be taken up first. In the next

section of this chapter, we shall discuss the division of actual
U.S. money growth into expected and unexpected parts. Section 3.3.
then deals with the determination of output, and section 3.4. is
concerned with the price equation. Each time Barro's equation
will be introduced first, and then compared to an alternative
that uses the same data, but corresponds to the theoretical model
of chapter 2. In section 3.5. the differences between the two
complete models are highlighted through comparing the outcomes
of Barro's simulation exercise with the results of the same
simulation when performed with the alternative model. The chapter
ends with a short summary.

3.2. MODELS FOR MONEY GROWTH

Equation (3.1) in table 3.1 presents the money growth equation
in Barro (1978). The rate of growth of M1 is regressed on its
own past and on two other explanatory variables, FEDV and UN,
defined as:

$$FEDV = \frac{.8}{1 - .8B} \hat{FED},$$

with   FED   the real expenditure of federal government.

$$UN = \log(u/1 - u),$$

with   u   the annual average unemployment rate.

The equation shows that when federal expenditure increases, money
balances are taxed more heavily, and also that a high level of
unemployment makes an expansionary monetary policy more likely.
The regression covers the years 1941-1976 with a reduced weight
for the war-time years. It implies belief in a return-to-
normalcy theory of money creation, because the coefficients on
the lagged money growth terms do not sum to unity.

     The residuals of equation (3.1) are Barro's measure of

unanticipated money growth. Expected money growth is given by:

$$\hat{M}_t^e = .082 + .41\ \hat{M}_{t-1} + .21\ \hat{M}_{t-2} + .072\ FEDV_t + .026\ UN_{t-1}$$

The variable FEDV thus appears in *current* form in an equation for *anticipated* money growth. Barro has this defence:

> "The rationale is that the principal movements in FEDV, which are dominated by changes in wartime activity, would be perceived sufficiently rapidly to influence $\hat{M}$ without a lag. For example, in 1946 the value of $\hat{M}$ is much lower than in 1945 because of the contemporaneous downward movement in FEDV."
>
> (1977, p. 106, footnote 9).

In other words: re-write FEDV as:

$$FEDV_t = 0.8\ \hat{FED}_t + 0.8\ FEDV_{t-1}$$

and assume that the first term on the R.H.S. is either negligible or perceived in time to influence anticipations of money growth.

Estimation of equation (3.1) over different periods shows that the coefficient of FEDV changes according to whether movements in the variable FEDV are large or small. Barro finds a value of .072 for the years 1941-1976 (with a smaller weight for the observations of the war years). The coefficient has increased to .102 when the equation is re-estimated over the shorter period 1953-1976, but then almost doubles again when the initial year is advanced further. Equation (3.3) in the table shows a (just significant) coefficient of .180 for FEDV when the regression begins in 1955. The jump in the coefficient coincides with a large decrease in the variability of FEDV: the variable is hardly significant for periods that exclude the aftermath of the Second World War and the Korean conflict. Barro's variable and the interpretation he gives it are suited only to the abnormal years in the first part of the estimation period. For these special years, the current change in federal

Table 3.1.   Equations for money growth

(3.1) $\hat{M}_t = .082 + .41\ \hat{M}_{t-1} + .21\ \hat{M}_{t-2} + .072\ FEDV_t + .026\ UN_{t-1}$
        (.027) (.14)   (.12)   (.016)   (.009)

$\bar{R}^2 = .77,\ \sigma_a = .015,\ D.W. = 1.9$, years: 1941–1976, with
                                              reduced weight for
                                              1941–1945

(3.2) $\hat{M}_t = .073 + .44\ \hat{M}_{t-1} + .26\ \hat{M}_{t-2} + .102\ FEDV_t + .026\ UN_{t-1}$
        (.034) (.20)   (.20)   (.074)   (.012)

$\bar{R}^2 = .49,\ \sigma_a = .015,\ D.W.\ 1.7$, years: 1953–1976

(3.3) $\hat{M}_t = .038 + .41\ \hat{M}_{t-1} + .22\ \hat{M}_{t-2} + .180\ FEDV_t + .017\ UN_{t-1}$
        (.039) (.20)   (.20)   (.085)   (.013)

$\bar{R}^2 = .54,\ \sigma_a = .014,\ D.W. = 2.0$, years: 1955–1976

(3.4) $\Delta\hat{M}_t = (1 - .59\ B)a_t$
                (.16)

$\bar{R}^2 = .15,\ \sigma_a = .016,$ years: 1949–1976

(3.5) $\Delta\hat{M}_t = (1 - .71\ B)a_t$
                (.17)

$\bar{R}^2 = .30,\ \sigma_a = .014,$ years: 1955–1976

(3.6) $\Delta\hat{M} = .000 + .038\ \Delta UN_{-1}$
          (.003) (.013)

$\bar{R}^2 = .28,\ \sigma_a = .014,\ D.W. = 2.3$, years: 1955–1976

expenditure may be an acceptable indicator of expectations which
agents could possess before the beginning of the year. But, in
more normal times, expectations should preferably be based on
information that is actually available, not on ex-post data.

The fact that $\hat{M}_{t-1}$, the once lagged growth rate of money,
is the only variable that has a stable and significant coefficient
when equation (3.1) - (3.3) are compared, suggests that a univariate model for money growth may be appropriate. With a view
to achieving a simple term structure of expectations, the ideal
model would be the first-order moving average model for $\Delta \hat{M}$:

$$\Delta \hat{M}_t = (1 - \theta B) a_t$$

Such a univariate model has been estimated for the years
1949-1976, on the assumption that the war years with their very
high money growth rates, and the immediate post-war period when
the rate of money growth was swiftly and *systematically* reduced
to "normal" levels, are not representative of later periods.
Equations (3.4) and (3.5) indicate that the residual errors are
similar in size to those of Barro's multivariate models
(equation (3.1) has a S.E.E. of .016 for 1949-1976). Re-
estimation of the moving-average model for the shorter period
1955-1976, which eliminates the influence of the Korean war on
money growth, hardly changes the value and the significance of
the parameter. Therefore, equation (3.4) will be our model for
U.S. money growth.

Equation (3.6) shows that it is also possible to regress
$\hat{M}$ on ΔUN_{-1}. In fact, the significance of ΔUN_{-1} in this equation
is higher than that of the *level* UN_{-1} in Barro's equation over
the same period. However, the explanatory power of equations (3.5)
and (3.6) is the same, so that the simpler univariate model has
been preferred. In the next two sections, the residuals of
equation (3.1) will be included in Barro's relations for output
and prices, whereas the alternative relations will utilize the
residuals of equation (3.4) as a measure of unanticipated money
growth in the U.S.

3.3. THE DETERMINATION OF OUTPUT

A model for output which shows the influence of unanticipated
money growth is both interesting for its own sake, and necessary
if one wishes to use the equation of exchange for the determination of prices. Equation (3.7) in table 3.2. is Barro's preferred relation for the level of gross national product, y;
it will be substituted in his price equation:

$$\log p = \log M - \log y + \log V.$$

DMR represents unanticipated money growth as measured by the
residuals of his equation (3.1). The other two variables in the
equation are MIL, which is defined as:

$$MIL \equiv \text{military personel} \div \text{male population aged 15-44,}$$

and a linear time trend t.

Barro's equation may be compared to the alternative
equation (3.8). The form of this equation, with $\hat{\Delta y}$ as the
dependent variable that is explained by current and once-lagged
values of unanticipated impulses plus a first-order moving
average term, corresponds to the theoretical model in chapter 2
and satisfies the requirement,

$$_t\hat{E}y_{t+1} = {}_t\hat{E}y_{t+2} = \ldots .$$

$(\hat{M} - \hat{M}^e)$ are the differences between expected and actual money
growth, as measured by the residuals of equation (3.4) and g is
the real expenditure on goods and services by the federal
government. This variable was tried (in level form, of course) by
Barro, and retained in his price equation, but had to be
rejected on empirical grounds in his output equation. In our
alternative model, $(\hat{g} - \hat{g}^e)$ appears in both the output and
price equations. To use the unanticipated changes in g requires
a model for $\hat{g}^e$, the expected growth rate of real government

expenditure, to be developed below. Eq. (3.8) contains one
further variable, D, designed to account for the effects of the
recent oil crisis on economic output. Finally, the equation has
a first-order moving average model for the residual errors. In
what follows, we first discuss the determination of $\hat{g}^e$, and
after that we present a defence of the dummy variable. The final
part of the section consists of a comparison between the two
output equations (3.7) and (3.8).

CHANGES IN REAL GOVERNMENT EXPENDITURE

The data for g are shown in table 3.4. below. They indicate that
this series has to be divided into three separate segments. First,
the years 1945, 1946 and 1947 when government expenditures were
reduced to peace-time levels. Second, the period 1948-1955 with
fairly large swings in $\hat{g}$, largely because of the Korean war.
Third, the remaining years in the sample period, with a much
reduced variation in $\hat{g}$. A time series model can be estimated for
the latter period, 1955-1976, and results in the model:

$$\Delta\hat{g}_t = (1 - .45\ B)a_t \qquad \bar{R}^2 = .17$$
$$(.20)$$

Residuals of this equation are indeed significant in an output
equation estimated over the same short period. However, this
model is not appropriate for the determination of $\hat{g}^e$ and $(\hat{g}-\hat{g}^e)$
in earlier years, for which no univariate model is really
satisfactory. The course of $\hat{g}$ was determined by large changes in
military expenditure in those years and one solution, therefore,
would be to make subjective ad-hoc assumptions about whether
economic agents could foresee that military activities were to
be increased or reduced, and to construct a series for $\hat{g}^e$
accordingly. Subjective assumptions about the degree to which
agents are capable of predicting changes in government expenditure
will indeed be made for two special years in the case of the
Netherlands, but there we can simply use the same hypothesis as
Korteweg. But Barro opted for an objective, statistical formula

Table 3.2.   Output equations

(3.7) $\log y_t$ = 2.95 + 1.04 DMR_t + 1.21 DMR_{t-1} + .44 DMR_{t-2} +
     (.004) (.21)   (.22)   (.21)

      + .26 DMR_{t-3} + .55 MIL_t + .0354 t
      (.16)   (.09)   (.0004)

    $\bar{R}^2$ = .998, σ_a = .016, D.W. = 1.8 , years: 1946-1976

(3.8) $\hat{\Delta y}_t$ = $(1.04 - 1.06\ B)\,(\hat{M} - \hat{M}^e)_t$ +
     (.25)   (.23)

      + $(.028\ -\ .068\ B)\,(\hat{g} - \hat{g}^e)_t + \Delta D_t + (1\ -\ .84\ B)\,a_t$
      (.030)   (.019)   (.11)

    $\bar{R}^2$ = .71, σ_a = .019,   years: 1949-1976

(3.8a) $\hat{y}_t^e$ = $\hat{y}_{t-1} - 1.06\ (\hat{M} - \hat{M}^e)_{t-1} - .068\ (\hat{g} - \hat{g}^e)_{t-1}$ +

      + $\Delta D_t - .84\ a_{t-1}$

Notes:

D is a dummy variable that is equal to - .025 in 1974 and 1975,
and 0 otherwise, in order to model the influence of the oil
crisis on income expectations (see text).

DMR_t is the residual in period t of Barro's equation for anticipated money growth.

$(\hat{M} - \hat{M}^e)_t$ is the residual in period t of the alternative univariate model for anticipated money growth.

in the case of FEDV instead, and to avoid the charge of
arbitrariness we shall do the same for $\hat{g}$.

The simple model

$$\hat{g}^e_t = \hat{g}_{t-1}$$

has been used for the determination of $\hat{g}^e$ from 1948 to 1976. This
model is not very different from the first-order moving average
model for 1955-1976, and agrees with the autocorrelation function
of $\hat{g}$ for the complete period. With the help of this model for $\hat{g}^e$,
we can now estimate the output equation beginning in 1949. To start
our model for $\Delta\hat{y}$ in 1948, which would correspond best to the
initial year 1946 in Barro's equation for the level of y is clearly
inappropriate, as the coefficient on $(\hat{g} - \hat{g}^e)_{-1}$ would be completely
dominated by the value of $(\hat{g} - \hat{g}^e)_{-1}$ in 1948.

THE EXPECTED GROWTH OF OUTPUT

In the theoretical equation for $\hat{y}^e$, that variable is a function
of *lagged* impulses and *lagged* error terms. With our data in the
form of yearly averages of quarterly or monthly data, this seems
unrealistic in the case of the recent "oil crisis". The pattern
over time of the shift in the relative price of imported energy
(see Rasche and Tatom, 1977a, b) meant that the higher price
would appear mainly in the yearly average index for 1974, so that
expected output would not be affected until 1975. Instead, we
have preferred to assume here that an episode which began in the
autumn of 1973 could still influence expectations for 1974,
although this invalidates for two years our maintained hypothesis
of a constant term structure of expectations. We make the
assumption that U.S. citizens perceived the rise in the price of
imported energy during late 1973 and most of 1974 as a permanent,
or, at least, long-run change in the relative price of
imported energy in terms of the domestic price level. OPEC was
supposed to be able to indicate the *relative* price of energy
for a substantial period of time, if need be through indexation
with the U.S. domestic price level.

According to Rasche and Tatom, the increase in this relative price must have meant a once-and-for-all fall of about 5% in the economic capacity of the U.S. private economy. The 5% figure is a rough estimate, but gets support from independent calculations by P.K. Clark for the C.E.A. (see Rasche and Tatom, 1977b, for a discussion of Clark's results). Clark found a once-and-for-all shift of 4.2% in the potential output of the private sector. Econometric work by Griffin and Gregory (1976) also supports the estimates by Rasche and Tatom, but Perloff and Wachter (1979) obtain a somewhat smaller estimate. Gordon (1979) and De Leeuw (1977) provide critical surveys of this literature.

If we accept, as a working hypothesis, that economic capacity suffered a once-and-for-all 5% loss during 1974, how did the fall in economic capacity influence anticipated output? We have assumed that the effect in continuous time can be modelled by a so-called ramp function that changes by - .05 in the course of 1974. The corresponding discrete version was used to adjust the values of $\hat{y}^e$, so that $\hat{y}^e_{1974}$ and $\hat{y}^e_{1975}$ are .025 lower than they would have been otherwise. Equation (3.8) has therefore been estimated with a dummy variable. The size of the dummy has not been determined after experimentation but was taken from the above-mentioned studies, which should minimize the degree of arbitrariness inherent in the use of a dummy variable.

COMPARING THE TWO OUTPUT EQUATIONS

Having discussed the alternative output equation, we turn to a comparison with Barro's model. As regards the empirical fit to the data, there is not much to choose between the two equations. The residual errors of equation (3.8) are slightly higher than those of Barro's equation, which has a S.E.E. of .017 when re-estimated for 1949-1976. A striking difference between the two equations, however, is the specification of the way in which an unforeseen monetary impulse affects the rate of output. Barro's equation for $\log y_t$ contains the current plus three lagged terms of his measure of the unanticipated monetary impulse; our equation for $\Delta \hat{y}$ has the current and once-lagged values of the monetary impulse, and, if we divide both sides of eq. (3.8) by the (almost) common factor $(1-B)$, we get an equation for $\hat{y}$ in which the growth rate of output is affected by the current value of the monetary impulse only.

In other words, if economic agents make their output decisions in terms of the *level* of y, then their current decisions still depend on the unexpected impulses of the past three years. Concomitantly, a monetary impulse that has just taken place leads to *foreseeable* changes in the level of output for three more years. By contrast, we assume that agents formulate their decision problem differently and decide whether output this period will be higher, lower, or unchanged in relation to last year's, i.e. decide in terms of the rate of change of output. Thus, the influence of the current unexpected impulse is limited to the agents' current decisions; their decisions on the long-term growth rate of output are always based on a constant term structure of expectations.

The question which of these two formulations has to be preferred will be discussed below, after we have compared the two alternative price equations. But it is worth pointing out at this stage that the difference in the lag cannot be attributed to the fact that two different series for unanticipated money growth have been used. When the residuals from our equation (3.4) are inserted in Barro's equation (3.7), the coefficients for $(\hat{M}-\hat{M}^e)$ are .82 (.28) for current $(\hat{M}-\hat{M}^e)$ and .83 (.26), .42 (.26) and .35 (.27) for the three lagged values. Conversely, when DMR_t, DMR_{t-1}, and DMR_{t-2} are taken as measures of unanticipated money growth in our equation (3.8), we get:

$$\Delta \hat{y}_t = (.80 - .93B - .032B^2) \, DMR_t + \ldots$$
$$\quad\quad (.34) \quad (.48) \quad (.36)$$

which shows that even DRM_{t-2} is no longer significant, just as $(\hat{M}-\hat{M}^e)_{t-2}$ is insignificant (coefficient .29 with standard error of .26) when added to equation (3.8).

THE EXPECTED GROWTH OF OUTPUT

Equation (3.8) can be used to derive a time series for $\hat{y}^e$, the expected growth rate of g.n.p. We add $\hat{y}_{t-1}$ on both sides of equation (3.8) and substitute zero for all unknown values of the impulses and the error terms. The result is equation (3.8a), which shows that the expected growth rate is based on the previous growth rate, but with corrections for the temporary influences that acted on $\hat{y}_{-1}$. If the previous growth rate was higher than expected because of a positive monetary impulse, then the equation (3.8a) shows that $\hat{y}^e$ falls back to almost exactly its "underlying" value, because the coefficients 1.04 and - 1.06 are practically equal in size. Temporary movements in $(\hat{g} - \hat{g}^e)$ are also reversed after one period, but the low t-values of the coefficients on $(\hat{g} - \hat{g}^e)_t$ and $(\hat{g} - \hat{g}^e)_{t-1}$ make it impossible to make any firm statements about the permanent effect of a g-impulse on $\hat{y}$; the hypothesis that the permanent effect is zero is not rejected. However, the coefficient of - .84 on a_{t-1} shows that the remaining influences on $\hat{y}$, not modelled here, cause the "level" of $\hat{y}^e$ to change slowly over time.In the following section we shall use this non-stationary series for $\hat{y}^e$ in an empirical price equation.

3.4. THE PRICE EQUATION

In our theoretical model, the time series for $\hat{M}^e$ and $\hat{y}^e$ were combined with a simple assumption regarding the expected rate of change of velocity, to get an expression for the expected rate of price change:

(2.45) $\hat{p}_t^e = d + \hat{M}_t^e - (1 - \delta_1)\hat{y}_t^e$

The actual rate of price change, $\hat{p}$, was subsequently explained by letting various impulses determine the yearly differences between $\hat{p}$ and $\hat{p}^e$.

Barro proceeds in a different way. He uses the equation

of exchange for the actual levels of M, V, p, and y. His theoretical price equation is:

$$\log p = \log M - \log y' + \log V$$

y' is based on equation (3.7) for the level of real output, but
with a correction for the fact that government holdings of
money are not including in the money stock data. y' is defined as

$$\log y' \equiv \log y - \gamma g/y$$

with γ approximately .5 (cf. Gordon, 1950, Selden, 1975). By
contrast, we shall use the uncorrected growth rate of y, and
include $(\hat{g} - \hat{g}^e)$ as an impulse variable. Barro's model for
velocity, V, is:

$$V = b_2 r + b_3 t$$

with r the AAA corporate bond rate and t a linear time trend.
The choice of a long-term interest rate is in agreement with
recent work by Hamburger (1977a, b) on the demand for money
function, whereas the time trend represents gradual changes
in velocity that are not modelled explicitly.

Equation (3.9) in table 3.3. shows the results of an
empirical implementation of Barro's price equation. All the
variables have the correct signs, and the only aspect in which
the equation differs from what the theory predicts is that
the lagged coefficients of unanticipated money growth are not
exactly the opposite of what was found in equation (3.7) for
output. However, Barro points out that if money holdings adjust
with a lag to changes in the transitory component of income,
the longer average lag in the price equation can be accounted for.

An alternative price equation is shown as equation (3.10)
in the table. It is cast in terms of the rate of change of prices,
$\hat{p}$, not the level of prices, and should therefore start one year
later than Barro's equation. Equation (3.10) is a regression in

which both $\hat{M}^e$ and $\hat{y}^e$ have unconstrained coefficients. The co-efficients on $\hat{M}^e$ and $\hat{y}^e$ are not significantly different from 1 and -1 respectively. There is no reason to reject the simple model

$$\hat{p}^e = c + 1.\hat{M}^e - 1.\hat{y}^e$$

for the expected rate of inflation. (Parenthetically, replacing $\hat{M}^e$ and $\hat{y}^e$ by $.5(\hat{M}^e + \hat{M}^e_{-1})$ and $.5(\hat{y}^e + \hat{y}^e_{-1})$ respectively gives an equivalent alternative series for $\hat{p}^e$ (cf. equation (4.10).) Substituting for $\hat{p}^e$ and adding the impulse $(\hat{g} - \hat{g}^e)$ from the output equation gives our price equation (3.11). For the complete estimation period, a term $(\hat{M} - \hat{M}^e)$ may be added to the equation, as equation (3.12) shows. In that case, the same impulses would appear in both the output and the price equations. However, when the estimation period is shortened, the term in $(\hat{M} - \hat{M}^e)$ becomes yet more insignificant and even assumes the wrong sign, so that it has not been included in our preferred equation. Because $\hat{y}^e$ exhibits little variation before 1974, the estimated coefficient becomes highly correlated with the estimated coefficient of the constant term in the regression. Inclusion of the variable in the regressions for inflation that do not go beyond 1973, has to be justified therefore by theoretical arguments, for empirically nothing much is lost when the price equation is changed into:

$$\hat{p}^e = c' + f(\hat{M}^e)$$

Karnosky (1976), for example, studied the link between money and prices with quarterly data for merely these two variables. The rate of inflation is explained by a constant term and a number of lagged money growth terms with the sum of the weights equal to one. In a simulation of Karnosky's equation with the actual post-sample rates of money growth, his regression indicated the temporary effect of the wage-price freeze of 1971 and pre-dicted again the correct value for the price level in the final quarter of 1973. After that, the model produces a price level that

Table 3.3.   Price Equations

(3.9) $\log p_t$ = $-$ 4.60 + 1.0 $\log M_t$ $-$ .74 DMR_t $-$ 1.48 DMR_{t-1} +
                     (.26)   ($-$)   (.17)   (.20)

             $-$ 1.78 DMR_{t-2} $-$ 1.34 DMR_{t-3} $-$ .69 DMR_{t-4} +
                (.24)   (.22)   (.17)

             $-$ .32 DMR_{t-5} + .59 $(g/y)_t$ + 3.8 r_t $-$ .0106 t
                (.14)   (.14)   (.9)   (.0018)

        $\bar{R}^2$ = .99, σ_a = .012, D.W. = 1.7 , years: 1948-1976

(3.10) $\hat{p}_t$ = .041 + .76 $\hat{M}_t^e$ $-$ .92 $\hat{y}_t^e$ + .081 $(\hat{g} - \hat{g}^e)_t$
                     (.014) (.14)   (.27)   (.015)

        $\bar{R}^2$ = .79, σ_a = .011, D.W. = 1.8 , years: 1949-1976

(3.11) $\hat{p}_t$ = 1 $\hat{p}_t^e$ + .085 $(\hat{g} - \hat{g}^e)_t$
                     ($-$)   (.014)

        $\bar{R}^2$ = .77, σ_a = .011, D.W. = 1.6 , years: 1949-1976

(3.12) $\hat{p}_t$ = 1 $\hat{p}_t^e$ + .082 $(\hat{g} - \hat{g}^e)_t$ + .18 $(\hat{M} - \hat{M}^e)_t$
                     ($-$)   (.014)   (.13)

        $\bar{R}^2$ = .78, σ_a = .011, D.W. = 1.5 , years: 1949-1976

Notes:
- D.W.-coefficients in equations (3.11) and (3.12) relate to the
  same equation with an (insignificant) constant term added.
- $\hat{p}_t^e$ in equation (3.11) and (3.12) is calculated as:

        $\hat{p}_t^e$ = .036 + $(\hat{M}^e - \hat{y}^e)_t$

Table 3.4.

U.S. data

	(1)	(2)	(3)	(4)	(5)	(6)
1945	232.7	–	–	–	–	–
1946	58.4	–	.6	–	–	–
1947	36.1	186.4	.1	–	–	–
1948	42.4	64.2	.2	–	– .1	–
1949	48.9	– 1.8	– 1.2	– 1.3	– 1.6	– 1.4
1950	47.0	– 18.2	.7	2.6	.3	3.5
1951	81.3	58.8	– .6	– 2.0	1.6	1.5
1952	107.0	– 27.3	– 1.5	.0	.1	– .5
1953	114.6	– 20.6	1.4	2.5	– .6	– .8
1954	95.2	– 25.4	– .7	– 3.3	.9	1.2
1955	86.9	9.4	1.5	.6	– .4	.2
1956	85.9	8.0	1.2	– 1.2	.0	.8
1957	89.8	5.6	1.1	– .9	.3	1.4
1958	92.8	– 1.2	– 2.5	– 3.9	.5	.6
1959	91.8	– 4.4	– 1.9	.1	– 1.0	1.0
1960	90.8	.0	– .6	1.1	1.2	– .6
1961	95.6	6.3	– .4	– 2.4	– .3	– .7
1962	103.1	2.4	.2	1.7	– 1.1	– .3
1963	102.2	– 8.4	.5	– .5	– .6	.2
1964	100.6	– .7	– .3	– .3	.0	– .4
1965	100.5	1.5	.9	.6	1.5	– .7
1966	112.5	11.4	2.4	.6	1.5	– .9
1967	125.3	– .5	1.7	– .9	.2	– .9
1968	128.3	– 8.4	– .1	– 2.0	– 1.5	1.1
1969	121.8	– 7.6	– 3.2	– 1.8	– 1.6	.4
1970	110.7	– 4.4	.4	– 2.0	– 1.2	.0
1971	103.9	3.2	– .5	– 2.4	1.3	– .2
1972	102.1	4.6	.4	1.1	.3	– 2.4
1973	96.6	– 3.8	2.8	1.2	.0	– .7
1974	95.3	4.2	– 1.0	– 1.4	– .3	.0
1975	95.7	1.8	– 2.9	– .6	.9	– .3
1976	96.7	.6	1.1	3.3	– .2	– .9

NOTES TO TABLE 3.4.

(1)   g, federal expenditure on goods and services in billions
         of 1972 dollars
         Source: Economic Report of the President, 1977, p. 189
(2) $\Delta \hat{g}$ with g defined as in (1)
(3)   Residuals of Barro's output equation
(4)   Residuals of equation (3.8) for $\Delta \hat{y}$
(5)   Residuals of Barro's price equation
(6)   Residuals of equation (3.11) for $\hat{p}$

All entries in columns (2) - (6) have been multiplied by 100.
so that the numbers can be interpreted as percentages.

increases parallel to the actual p but runs about 4.5% lower.
Karnosky's interpretation of this result as a 4.5% drop in
productive capacity during 1974 has since been underpinned by
Rasche and Tatom and has also been used in this chapter.

COMPARING THE TWO PRICE EQUATIONS

Proceeding to a comparison between the two price equations, we
note that, as in the case of the money and output equations,
there is not much difference in explanatory power between
Barro's equations and the proposed alternative, with this time
a slight superiority for our equation (3.11). Although equally
successful in empirical terms, the two equations differ in three
respects. First, Barro assumes that agents decide in terms of
the level of prices, whereas we hypothesize that they have to
decide whether prices will be higher or lower compared with
prices in the previous period. Second, Barro finds that
unanticipated monetary impulses act on the price level;
by contrast, we let the expected rate of growth of money
determine the expected rate of inflation and conclude that
unforeseen monetary impulses do not have a significant effect
on the rate of price change (see eq. 3.12). Finally, Barro's
equation shows a very long period of adjustment after a
monetary shock, while in our model expected money growth
affects the rate of inflation immediately and there are no
lagged effects.

As in the case of the output equations, the discrepancies
cannot be attributed to the alternative modelling of the money
growth process. When Barro's equation (3.9) is re-estimated with
our $(\hat{M}-\hat{M}^e)$ instead of his DMR, the coefficient values are:
- 1.07 (.24) for current $(\hat{M}-\hat{M}^e)$, and - 1.06 (.26), - .94 (.24),
- .98 (.25), - .72 (.22), and - .49 (.22) for $(\hat{M}-\hat{M}^e)_{t-1}$ ......,
$(\hat{M}-\hat{M}^e)_{t-5}$.

Once again, if agents formulate their pricing decisions in
terms of the level of prices, as in Barro's equation, then they
have to take into account the unanticipated monetary impulses
of the previous five years. Also, each monetary impulse causes

foreseeable changes in prices for the subsequent five years.
If, however, agents decide in each period whether prices will be
higher, lower or the same as compared with last period's prices,
i.e. think in terms of the rate of change of prices, then the
unexpected impulses from only the previous year have an influence
on their current decisions. Agents can never foresee changes in
the rate of inflation after the next period, since such changes
depend on impulses that have not yet taken place. This follows
from the fact that in our model, current changes in the rate of
inflation are caused by revisions in the expected rate of growth
of money which depend on last year's value of the unanticipated
monetary impulse.

The finding of a long period of adjustment in Barro's model
as against a quick adjustment to a new equilibrium path in our
alternative model corresponds to what we saw in the case of the
two output equations. In the next section of the chapter, we
consider both the price and the output effects of a monetary
impulse in the two models, and try to determine whether there are
theoretical grounds for preferring one of the two scenarios to
the other.

3.5. A SIMULATION WITH THE TWO MODELS

Barro ends his 1978 paper with a simulation in which the effects
of a monetary impulse on output and prices are shown. In tables
3.5. and 3.6. his main results have been copied and compared
to the outcome of a similar experiment with our rational
expectations model. Barro assumes that an unanticipated monetary
impulse, DMR, temporarily changes the actual rate of money growth
(line 1). He uses his equation for money growth to calculate the
effects of the impulse on the actual growth rate of the money
stock:

$$(3.1) \qquad \hat{M}_t = .082 + .41\ \hat{M}_{t-1} + .21\ \hat{M}_{t-2} + .072\ FEDV_t +$$
$$+ .026\ UN_{t-1} + DMR_t$$

The size of the impulse -- assumed to be 1 per cent of the
money stock -- determines the value of $\hat{M}$ in year 1. The figures
for subsequent years depend not only on the lagged growth rates
$\hat{M}_{t-1}$ and $\hat{M}_{t-2}$, but also on the effects of the monetary impulse
on unemployment, UN. For this, Barro has made use of a relation
between unanticipated money growth and unemployment (see Barro,
1977, for the details). According to this equation, the monetary
impulse leads to a temporary drop in unemployment, which slightly
lowers future rates of money growth.

In our model, a single monetary impulse would permanently
change the growth rate of money; therefore we have made the
assumption that an unforeseen impulse $(\hat{M}-\hat{M}^e)$ in year 1 is
followed by an equal but opposite impulse in year 2 (line 2 of
the tables 3.5. and 3.6.). The size of the impulses differs in
the two tables: in table 3.5. we are concerned with the short-
run effects of monetary impulses on output; therefore the initial
impulses in year 1 are equal in magnitude. For the purpose of
comparing the effects on output, what matters is that the shocks
are of the same size; the long-term implications of these shocks
for the levels of money and prices are different, but that is not
relevant here. By contrast, in table 3.6. we are interested in
the effects on prices. In this table, the experiment with Barro's
model is as in table 3.5.; it leads to a one percent increase in
the money stock. The size of the impulses in our model has been
chosen in such a way that the money stock increases also by one
percent, so that the effects on prices can be directly compared.

As regards the effects on the rate of growth of real gnp,
we note that the basic pattern is identical (lines 5 and 6 in
table 3.5.), with a strong positive effect of the monetary
impulse on $\hat{y}$ in the current period and no permanent effect on
the growth rate of output. The difference is that in Barro's
model output growth is only gradually reduced to its original
level, whereas in our model the negative impulse in year 2
immediately reduces $\hat{y}$ to zero. Corresponding to this difference,
the actual level of output remains above the original level for
some years in Barro's experiment (line 7), whereas it falls back

Table 3.5.　　EFFECTS OF UNANTICIPATED MONEY GROWTH ON OUTPUT

Y E A R	(1)	(2)	(3)	(4)	(5)	(6)	(7)	(8)	(9)	(10)
I Changes in money										
1. Barro's DMR	1.00	0	0	0	0	0	0	0	0	0
2. Alternative $(M-\hat{M}^e)$ (eq. 3.4)	1.00	-1.00	0	0	0	0	0	0	0	0
3. Barro's $\hat{M}$	1.00	.24	.01	-.09	-.04	-.03	-.02	-.02	-.01	-.01
4. Alternative $\hat{M}$ (eq. 3.4)	1.00	-.59	0	0	0	0	0	0	0	0
II Effects on output										
5. Barro's $\hat{y}$	1.0	.2	-.5	-.4	-.3	0	0	0	0	0
6. Alternative $\hat{y}$ (eq. 3.8)	1.0	-1.1	0	0	0	0	0	0	0	0
7. Barro's log y	1.0	1.2	.7	.3	0	0	0	0	0	0
8. Alternative log y (eq. 3.8)	1.0	-.0	-.0	-.0	-.0	-.0	-.0	-.0	-.0	-.0

Note:

All entries have been multiplied by 100.

quickly in our model (line 8). There is no disagreement about
the longer-term effects, only about the speed with which the
effects of an impulse are dissipated.

This also holds for the price equation (table 3.6.).
In Barro's model there are still perceptible changes in the rate
of inflation half a dozen years after the original shock. By
contrast, in the alternative model everything occurs in year 2.
Again, the long-term results are the same, but the period of
adjustment is much longer in Barro's model.

To highlight the different implications of the two models,
let us consider the state of the economy at the end of year 2.
There will be no unexpected events after period 2; therefore
agents should be capable of using either Barro's or the
alternative model to form forecasts for years 3 and beyond.
According to our model, rational agents will assume that the
money stock, the rate of output and the price level will all
remain unchanged. On the other hand, if agents believe that
Barro's model correctly depicts the economy, they will foresee
a rate of output that will be above its equilibrium level for
another two years, and they will forecast that the price level
will remain far below its long-run level for one more year,
after which it will start to rise for some years.

The complicated term structure of expectations which
agents are assumed to hold in Barro's model is implausible for
the reasons that have been given in chapter 2. Rational agents
will not merely hold such a complicated term structure of
expectations at the end of period 2; they will plan their actions
for period 3 and beyond in such a way that they can exploit
individually the possibilities for profit that are implied by
it (see the discussion of Sweeney, 1978, and Alchian, 1959 in
chapter 2). However, in that case, the aggregate effect of their
individual actions will be to nullify the term structure of price
expectations as it is shown in the tables. For example, agents
will try to shift some purchases of durable goods forward in time,
because the price level in period 3 is lower than that in period
4, 5, etc. But such actions will tend to have a positive effect

Table 3.6.

EFFECTS OF UNANTICIPATED MONEY GROWTH ON PRICES

Y E A R	(1)	(2)	(3)	(4)	(5)	(6)	(7)	(8)	(9)	(10)
I Changes in money										
1. Barro's DMR	1.00	0	0	0	0	0	0	0	0	0
2. Alternative $(M-\hat{M}^e)$ (eq. 3.4)	2.44	-2.44	0	0	0	0	0	0	0	0
3. Barro's log M	1.00	1.24	1.25	1.16	1.12	1.09	1.06	1.05	1.04	1.03
4. Alternative log M (eq. 3.4)	2.44	1.00	1.00	1.00	1.00	1.00	1.00	1.00	1.00	1.00
II Effects on prices										
5. Barro's $\hat{p}$	.2	-.4	.0	.3	.5	.2	.1	.1	.1	.0
6. Alternative $\hat{p}$ (eq. 3.11)	.0	1.0	0	0	0	0	0	0	0	0
7. Barro's log p	.2	-.2	-.2	.1	.5	.7	.8	.9	1.0	1.0
8. Alternative log p (eq. 3.11)	0	1.0	1.0	1.0	1.0	1.0	1.0	1.0	1.0	1.0

Note:

All entries have been multiplied by 100.

on prices in year 3 and negative effects on prices in subsequent years. Not only the private sector, but also the
authorities may try to exploit the complicated term structure
of expectations in Barro's model. As pointed out by Lucas (1976)
and others, counter-cyclical behaviour by the authorities will
also tend to invalidate the values of the coefficients in
Barro's model with which the simulations have been calculated.
In our model, by contrast, neither the private sector nor
the authorities have any scope for exploiting the term
structure of expectations as held at the beginning of period 3
(or at any other moment in time). Future fluctuations in the
growth rate of output or in the rate of inflation are never
foreseeable.

If Barro's model implies a term structure of expectations
that does not seem to be compatible with rational behaviour,
then the question arises how his empirical results can be explained. One possibility would be that he chose the wrong
transformation for the dependent variables in the analysis.
Barro worked with the logarithm of the rate of output and the
logarithm of the price level. Our alternative equations imply
the following effects of a monetary impulse $(\hat{M}-\hat{M}^e)$ on the levels
of y and p:

$$\log p_t = \log M_t - (\hat{M}-\hat{M}^e)_t - (\hat{M}-\hat{M}^e)_{t-1} - (\hat{M}-\hat{M}^e)_{t-2} +$$

$$- (\hat{M}-\hat{M}^e)_{t-3} - \ldots$$

$$\log y_t = 1.04(\hat{M}-\hat{M}^e)_t + 1.02(\hat{M}-\hat{M}^e)_{t-1} + 1.00(\hat{M}-\hat{M}^e)_{t-2} +$$

$$+ .98(\hat{M}-\hat{M}^e)_{t-3} + \ldots$$

In both cases the lags are infinite, which would explain the
long lags that Barro found in his empirical equations. If we
accept the alternative model then Barro's equations have
an incorrect dependent variable and suffer from mis-
specification.

3.6. SUMMARY

In this chapter Barro's recent empirical model of the influence
of money on output, unemployment, and prices has been compared to
our alternative model. There were three basic theoretical
differences between the two models. First, Barro uses the
equation of exchange for the actual levels of M, p, and y,
whereas in the alternative model the only postulated quantity-
theoretic relation is between the expected growth rates of money,
prices, and income. The second difference is that Barro makes
the assumption that income has a deterministic trend and therefore a fixed future rate of growth. The alternative assumption
is that there can be changes in the "level" of $\hat{y}^e$. The third
difference between the two models is that the alternative model
tries to deal explicitly with the term structure of
expectations. Assumptions are made about the stochastic processes
for money and income and about the functional form of the demand
for money equation. On the basis of these assumptions it is
possible to work with expectations that are rational in the
strong sense that knowledge about all future periods influences
current behaviour.

Barro's estimated equations show a good fit over the
sample period, and his coefficients are significant. The alternative equations are about equally successful in terms of $\bar{R}^2$ and
also satisfy all the theoretical coefficient restrictions of the
model in chapter 2. The basic differences between the two models
do not lead to a much better empirical fit in favour of one or
the other. Rather they appear in very different properties for
the term structures of expectations. In our model, there is
a constant term structure of expectations for the growth rate
of output, $\hat{y}$, and for the rate of inflation, $\hat{p}$, at all times.
If Barro's model is a true description of the economy, however,
agents will hold complicated term structures of expectations in
the first few years after a monetary impulse has occurred.
In particular, they can predict that the price level will remain
for some time below its long-term equilibrium level, after which

it will increase for the next six years. Such term structures of expectations are unstable in a rational world, for either the private sector or the authorities or both will try to exploit foreseeable fluctuations in output and prices, and thereby invalidate the predictions of the model. On the one hand Barro assumes that agents are rational, for they use the value of last year's monetary impulse when they forecast the growth in the money stock for the current period. But, on the other hand, he must assume that they neglect the opportunities to profit from foreseeable future changes in output and prices through intertemporal shifts in their production and spending plans.

Chapter 4

INFLATION IN THE NETHERLANDS

4.1. INTRODUCTION

In this chapter the theoretical model of chapter 2 will be tested
with annual data for the Dutch economy over the period 1954-1976.
As in the case of the U.S., we shall begin by developing time
series for $\hat{M}^e$, the anticipated growth rate of money, and $\hat{y}^e$,
the anticipated growth rate of g.d.p. In the previous chapter
the required expressions were very simple: expectations about
future money growth were based only on the history of the money
supply, and changes in output were accounted for by the monetary
impulse and just one other variable, the unanticipated growth
in government expenditure. In the case of the Dutch economy,
both of these equations are given a rather richer specification,
with some 3-4 variables in the equations for $\hat{M}$ and $\hat{y}$, but care
will be taken that the transfer functions are specified in such
a way that the requirements

$$_t\hat{EM}_{t+1} = {}_t\hat{EM}_{t+2} = \ldots. \text{ and } {}_t\hat{Ey}_{t+1} = {}_t\hat{Ey}_{t+2} = \ldots.$$

are satisfied.

When that has been done in sections 4.2. and 4.3., the
series for $\hat{M}^e$ and $\hat{y}^e$ will be combined to give an expression for
$\hat{p}^e$, the anticipated rate of growth of the g.d.p. deflator.
Simultaneously we shall investigate the corresponding estimates
of the prediction errors $(\hat{p} - \hat{p}^e)$. An important fraction of the
differences between $\hat{p}$ and $\hat{p}^e$ can be accounted for by unanticipated movements in some impulses; our preferred inflation

equation will contain three impulses that together explain about
half of the unanticipated movements in the price index.

In section 4.5. the results will be compared to those of
Korteweg (1978b). The discussion will be centered around
a question that is also at issue in the next section: how does
one model the money supply in a small, open economy with a fixed
or quasi-fixed rate of exchange? In the case of the U.S., we
assumed that unexpected changes in the rate of money growth
were caused by unforeseeable shifts in Central Bank Policy.
Consequently, we modelled the growth rate of the U.S. money
supply by way of a univariate Box-Jenkins process. But, we shall
see that this statistical approach is inadequate in the case of
the Netherlands. Since the Dutch guilder was on a fixed or quasi-
fixed rate of exchange during the period under review, the Dutch
money stock could not be determined in a completely autonomous
fashion by the Dutch monetary authorities, but depended on money
growth and economic developments abroad.

One way to model these foreign influences is to assume that
agents base their expectations about money growth on more than just
past rates of domestic money growth; in section 4.2. we shall
show that better estimates of $\hat{M}^e$ can indeed be obtained by using
a multivariate model. Another possibility is to make the expected
rate of domestic inflation, $\hat{p}^e$, a weighted average of expected
domestic money growth, $\hat{M}^e$, and an index of expected world
inflation, $\hat{p}^{*e}$, with both $\hat{M}^e$ and $\hat{p}^{*e}$ proxied by simple, univariate models. This second route has been chosen by Korteweg
(1978a, b); a comparison between the two approaches will be made
in section 4.5. In section 4.6. we compare the predictions of
our model to the official price forecasts of the Central Planning
Bureau, an agency of the Ministry of Economic Affairs. Finally,
the chapter ends with a non-technical summary in section 4.7.

4.2. MONEY GROWTH IN THE NETHERLANDS

Annual data for money growth in the Netherlands are in the first

column of table 4.1. A univariate analysis of this time series
leads to the simple ARIMA (0,1,0) model:

$$\Delta \hat{M}_t = a_t$$

with a_t uncorrelated noise.

This model was used by Korteweg (1978a, b). It implies high
values for the unforeseen monetary impulse in some years.
Particularly near the end of the sample period, large errors are
made, notably a forecasting error of 14 percentage points for
1975, when the expected rate of money growth was only 2.6% (the
previous year's value) as against an actual value of 16.9%.

In this study, we shall work with a series for expected
money growth that is based on more economic variables than just
past growth rates of money. This series for $\hat{M}^e$ changes much
more smoothly over time than the $\hat{M}_{t-1}$-series, used by Korteweg.
The data in the third column of table 4.2. show that the change
in $\hat{M}^e$ from one year to the next is never greater than 2.5%, which
is comparable to the variation that was found for the U.S. money
supply.

A casual comparison between the series for $\hat{M}^e$ and the
inflation data in columns 4 and 5 of the table suggests that $\hat{M}^e$
does trace the broad pattern of inflation in the Netherlands,
with moderate inflation in the mid-fifties, a slow-down from
1958 to 1963, moderate inflation again during the remaining
years of the 1960's and high inflation in the 1970's. The
statistical tests in section 4.4. will confirm that anticipated
monetary growth can indeed explain the course of inflation.

Because of the multivariate modelling of $\hat{M}^e$, we are able
to use expected changes in the narrowly defined money stock, M1,
as the principal determinant of Dutch inflation. Others have
shifted emphasis from M1 to some other aggregate when the
variability in M1 increased, or have advocated the use of
an average of growth rates for a number of monetary series.
Fratianni (1977), for example, uses an arithmetic average of
the growth rates of M2 and the domestic component of the mone-

Table 4.1.   DUTCH DATA

YEAR	$\hat{M}$	$\hat{M}_{Ge}$	$\hat{M}^e$	$\hat{p}_{gdp}$	$\hat{p}_c$
1954	7.0	11.3	8.2	4.7	4.5
1955	6.9	11.2	7.9	4.9	2.2
1956	2.5	8.5	7.7	3.4	2.7
1957	- 2.5	9.6	6.4	5.7	5.1
1958	4.0	12.0	4.0	2.3	1.5
1959	9.2	12.5	3.6	2.2	1.2
1960	5.0	8.9	5.2	3.1	2.4
1961	7.5	8.9	5.1	2.4	2.4
1962	5.6	10.4	5.7	3.5	2.6
1963	9.2	7.0	6.2	4.6	3.7
1964	8.2	8.1	7.4	8.0	6.6
1965	10.3	8.5	8.1	5.9	3.9
1966	7.0	4.2	8.8	5.7	5.3
1967	6.7	3.3	8.7	4.0	2.9
1968	8.2	7.3	7.9	3.8	2.5
1969	9.1	7.8	7.7	5.9	6.1
1970	10.0	6.0	8.8	5.3	4.4
1971	15.4	11.5	9.4	8.1	7.8
1972	16.2	12.3	10.8	8.5	8.1
1973	7.8	5.9	12.2	7.9	8.6
1974	2.6	4.1	12.2	8.3	9.2
1975	16.9	12.8	9.7	10.5	9.8
1976	11.5	10.3	11.2	8.0	8.8
1977	12.8	8.0	–	7.1	6.6

Notes:

$\hat{M}$: growth rate of the narrowly defined money stock;

$\hat{M}_{Ge}$: growth rate of the narrowly defined money stock in West Germany;

$\hat{M}^e$: expected rate of growth of the money stock (see text);

$\hat{p}_{gdp}$: growth rate of the price deflator for gross domestic product;

$\hat{p}_c$: growth rate of the price deflator for private consumption.

All growth rates are calculated as logarithmic first differences, multiplied by 100.

tary base. Koot (1975, 1977) applies factor analysis to
a collection of time series on money, time deposits, and other
financial stocks in order to extract a series that is less
vulnerable to irrelevant temporary deviations. Parkin (1977b)
suggests that for the U.K., the movements in M1 have become so
erratic, that it would be better to shift attention to the
monetary base.

The alternative of sticking to only one aggregate has
the advantage that the analysis remains directly relevant for
monetary policy. If inflation is a function of the expected
growth rate of M1, then it is clear that the authorities should
control M1. If, instead, inflation is shown to be closely
related to an average of the growth rates of several financial
stocks, then the policy prescription is much less obvious.
For this reason, we have preferred to work with a single
monetary aggregate and look for an economic explanation of
certain patterns in its growth rate over time. The decision that
this aggregate be M1, the narrowly defined money stock, was
taken in order to make the price and output equations
comparable to those of Korteweg (1978a, b). (When the latter
did investigate the explanatory power of wider monetary
aggregates in Dutch inflation equations, he invariably found it
to be less than that of M1.)

The purpose, then, of this section is to construct
a measure of expected money growth that satisfies:

$$_t\hat{EM}_{t+1} = {}_t\hat{EM}_{t+2} = \ldots.$$

Our theoretical requirement about the term structure of
expectations could easily be met when U.S. money growth was
modelled in chapter 3. However, in the case of the Netherlands,
the data suggest a more complicated pattern. We shall assume
that the actual rate of money growth in each year is composed
of two parts. First, an "underlying" growth rate that changes
in the same way as the growth rate of the U.S. money stock and
as postulated in our theoretical model:

$$\Delta \hat{M}_t = (1-\theta B)\, a_t$$

Second, we assume a purely temporary element in the growth rate
of M that is due to sudden shifts in the demand for money which
are known to be of a reversible nature.

Such temporary demand shifts can arise in the following
way: assume that the rate of return, r, on some near-money
asset that is sold by banks (e.g. time deposits or foreign
currency) increases suddenly by a substantial amount relative to
the rate of return on money. Further assume that the monetary
authorities do nothing to neutralize the resulting shift in the
demand for money, since it is generally expected that the surge
in r will be a short-term phenomenon only. In that case, there
will be a temporary fall in the money stock if the substitute is
a bank liability. However, we assume that agents will know that
this does not imply a decrease in the underlying rate of growth
of the money supply. On the contrary, they are assumed to be
capable of recognizing the purely temporary nature of the demand
shift. They will not change their assessment of the underlying
growth rate of the money stock, but will simply expect a
temporary increase in $\hat{M}$ when the interest rate drops again to its
normal level, and the short-term disturbance comes to an end.

In our theoretical model, such temporary demand shifts did
not occur, since that model contains one interest rate only, and
we have assumed that agents consider at all times that the
current interest rate is the optimal predictor of all future
interest rates. However, we shall argue that temporary demand
shifts did occur in the Netherlands, since the rates of return
on two short-term substitutes for money did not satisfy the
martingale property. First, we shall consider the rate of return
on foreign money, and after that the domestic interest rate on
three-month time deposits.

SHORT-TERM CURRENCY SUBSTITUTION

Consider the following form for the demand for money in an open
economy:

$$M/p = Cy^{\alpha_1} \exp^{-\alpha_2 r_1} \exp^{-\alpha_3 r_2} (f/e)^{-\alpha_4}$$

Here r_1 and r_2 are rates of interest on alternative domestic assets. (The rate of interest on demand deposits is not included, as it has never varied much and has been proved insignificant in empirical work on Dutch money demand.) f is the forward rate of exchange and e the spot rate, defined as the domestic price of foreign currency. (f/e) influences the demand for money because of substitution between domestic and foreign money. C is a constant and α_1, α_2, α_3 and α_4 are positive coefficients. Writing this demand for money function in terms of relative rates of growth, we get:

$$\hat{M}_t = \hat{P}_t + \alpha_1 \hat{y}_t - \alpha_2 \Delta r_{1,t} - \alpha_3 \Delta r_{2,t} - \alpha_4 \{\ln (f/e)_t +$$

$$- \ln (f/e)_{t-1}\}$$

In our empirical work, the expression $\{\ln(f/e)_t - \ln(f/e)_{t-1}\}$ is modelled by the first difference of the forward premium, ΔFP, so that we get:

$$(4.1) \qquad \hat{M}_t = \hat{P}_t + \alpha_1 \hat{y}_t - \alpha_2 \Delta r_{1,t} - \alpha_3 \Delta r_{2,t} - \alpha_4 \Delta FP_t$$

Under flexible exchange rates, the current value of the forward premium may well be the best predictor of all future values of the forward premium, in which case there are no foreseeable future changes in the forward premium. However, if the forward premium suddenly became significantly different from zero during the fixed-rate period, i.e. deviated from zero by more than could be explained by transaction costs, etc., then rational agents would not expect this to be a permanent phenomenon, since that would imply systematic profits from arbitrage in the foreign-currency markets. Therefore, they would expect the forward premium to be close to zero again in the near future. In that case, changes in the forward premium cause temporary and reversible shifts in the demand for money, which we want to

eliminate before estimating the "underlying" growth rate of
the money supply. For that purpose money was regressed both on
$FP_{US/NL}$, the forward premium of the U.S. dollar which is used
for the years 1954-1972 when there was a fixed dollar-guilder
rate, and on $FP_{Ge/NL}$, the forward premium of the D-Mark for
the complete period. $FP_{US/NL}$ was more significant in the regressions, but that may be because changes in $FP_{Ge/NL}$ were
correlated with a different type of short-term disturbance in
the demand for money to be discussed in a moment.

The estimated coefficients in the regression of the
money stock on the forward premium (over the fixed-rate period)
indicate the size of the corrections that have to be made in
order to eliminate the temporary effects of currency substitution. In making these corrections we assume that short-
term currency substitution under fixed exchange rates does not
induce the monetary authorities to alter the original underlying growth rate of the money supply, so that expectations
about $\hat{M}$ for all those years in the more distant future after
the speculative activity has ended, do not change. We reckon
that everybody believes in the temporary character of currency
substitution under fixed exchange rates, and that economic
agents assume that the associated short-run, reversible shifts
in the demand for domestic money do not have any lasting effects
on the economy. Hence, the expected rate of money growth that
people use when they make their production and consumption
plans, is not affected at all by these short-term disturbances
in the demand for money.

The forward premium $FP_{US/NL}$ is taken exogenous here. In
a one-country model, that is correct when speculation is induced
mainly by events abroad. Obviously, there were also cases when
the speculation was primarily based on a change in the market's
assessment of the Dutch economy -- as in the autumn of 1963
when the market felt for some time that a revaluation might be
considered by the Dutch authorities in order to reduce the
demand for Dutch exports. In such cases, to avoid simultaneity
problems (De Grauwe, 1975), we have to assume that the resulting

changes in the forward premium were not due primarily to the
current rate of growth of the money stock.

SHORT-TERM ANOMALIES IN THE SPECTRUM OF DOMESTIC INTEREST RATES

Apart from changes in the forward premium during the fixed-rate
period, a second short-term influence on the demand for money will
be specifically taken into account in our equation for the
expected growth rate of $\hat{M}$. Since 1971, there have been certain
periods when the policy of the Dutch Central Bank caused interest
rate anomalies of a clearly temporary nature, often in response
to speculative activity in the foreign exchange market. During
such periods, the rate on three-month time deposits (r_{T3}) deviated
from the rate on three-month savings deposits (r_{S3}) by more than
can be attributed to the different characteristics of these two
types of assets. r_{T3} sometimes rose far above r_{S3}, which caused
temporary increases in time deposits and corresponding falls in
savings and demand deposits, which are part of the narrowly
defined money stock. Fase (1975, 1977, 1978) has used the
difference between these two rates to calculate the size of the
ensuing "disturbances" in the stocks of time and savings
deposits, which is where the effects are most visible.

We will use the same interest differential to explain the
corresponding short-term, reversible shifts in M1. A problem with
this approach may be the assumed exogeneity of $\Delta(r_{T3}-r_{S3})$. Here,
the same restriction must be imposed as in the case of the
forward premium: the current rate of growth of the Dutch money
supply must not be a determining factor of $(r_{T3}-r_{S3})$. This
condition is satisfied, of course, if $(r_{T3}-r_{S3})$ is a function
of $FP_{Ge/NL}$ plus a white noise residual, with $FP_{Ge/NL}$ dependent
on events in West Germany. The fact that both interest rates
refer to assets with the same term to maturity should give some
confidence, too, in the exogeneity of changes in their differential
vis-à-vis current money growth. It would obviously not have been
correct to include the difference between a short and a long
interest rate in a model for $\Delta\hat{M}$, because such a differential
would certainly be dependent on current monetary conditions.

ESTIMATION OF THE REVERSIBLE SHIFTS IN THE DEMAND FOR MONEY

We estimate the size of the short-term reversible shifts in the demand for money by regressing the money stock on the forward premium (for the fixed-rate period) and on the interest rate differential, $r_{T3}-r_{S3}$. Since the demand shifts are super-imposed on the underlying trend in the money stock, which we shall model in the usual way as a (noisy) random walk for $\hat{M}$, we have taken the second differences of the logarithm of M and of the two variables that explain the size of the temporary demand shifts:

$$\Delta\hat{M}_t = C - \alpha_3\Delta\Delta FP_{US/NL,t} - \alpha_2\Delta\Delta(r_{T3} - r_{S3})_t$$

It has been stressed that there may be simultaneity pro-blems with this equation. For that reason, we have added another highly significant explanatory variable to the equation, because simultaneous equations bias in a regression is less severe if the fit of the equation increases. This additional variable is the unanticipated growth in the German money stock, so that the equation becomes:

$$\Delta\hat{M}_t = C - \alpha_3\Delta\Delta FP_{US/NL,t} - \alpha_2\Delta\Delta(r_{T3}-r_{S3})_t + \beta(\hat{M}_{Ge}-\hat{M}^e_{Ge})_t$$

A close association between Dutch and German money growth should cause no surprise. In the first place, the two economies have strong economic ties. Secondly, the Dutch monetary authorities have chosen to tie the Dutch guilder specifically to the German mark after the DM revaluation in 1969, and that situation has pre-vailed until now (see Schlesinger, 1978). In doing this, they have concurred with the general advice of many international eco-nomists (see, for example, Kenen, 1976, and Kindleberger, 1976), who reckon that a small, open economy with a diversified export sector should not have an independent exchange rate policy (but see Giersch, 1977a, for an example of the opposite opinion which avers that a flexible exchange rate remains always advantageous, as it reduces the impact of foreign disturbances). A specific further argument for the Dutch authorities that has never been officially stated in Holland has been voiced by the President of the German Bundesbank: they "wanted to benefit from German discipline" (Emminger, 1977, p. 48). The unexpected change in the growth rate of the German money supply is found after corrections for irrelevant temporary shifts in German money demand. We regress $\hat{\Delta M}_{Ge}$ on $\Delta\Delta FP_{US/Ge}$ where $FP_{US/Ge}$ represents the forward premium of the U.S. dollar in Germany for the fixed-rate period, and 0 after 1972:

$$\hat{\Delta M}_{Ge,t} = -.05 - .62 \ \Delta\Delta FP_{US/Ge,t}$$
$$(.63) \ (.30)$$

The residuals of this equation are now used in our equation for Holland. Note that $(\hat{M}_{Ge} - \hat{M}^e_{Ge})$ has been added only to increase the fit of the Dutch equation and therefore to sharpen the estimates of the coefficients of $\Delta\Delta FP_{US/NL}$ and $\Delta\Delta(r_{T3} - r_{S3})$. The demand shifts will be estimated by

$$\alpha_3 \ FP_{US/NL} + \alpha_2 \ (r_{T3} - r_{S3});$$

an expression that does not include the unexpected growth in the German money supply.

The estimated equation is as follows:

$$(4.2) \quad \hat{\Delta M}_t = .17 - 1.33 \ \Delta\Delta FP_{US/NL,t} - .67 \ \Delta\Delta(r_{T3} - r_{S3})'_t + .77 \ (\hat{M}_{Ge} - \hat{M}^e_{Ge})_t$$
$$(.58) \quad (.44) \qquad\qquad (.29) \qquad\qquad\qquad (.25)$$

$$\bar{R}^2 = .68, \qquad \sigma_u = 2.8, \qquad D.W. = 2.5, \qquad years: \ 1954-1976$$

with:

$FP_{US/NL}$: forward premium on the U.S. dollar until 1972 and 0 thereafter, when there was no longer a fixed exchange rate between the two currencies.

$\Delta(r_{T3}-r_{S3})'$: residuals of a regression of the first difference

in the interest differential on $FP_{US/NL}$:

$$\Delta(r_{T3}-r_{S3})_t = + .06 + .94 \Delta FP_{US/NL,t}$$
$$\quad\quad\quad (.31) \quad (.34)$$

$\hat{M}_{Ge}-\hat{M}^e_{Ge}$: residuals of a regression of $\Delta\hat{M}_{Ge}$ on $\Delta\Delta\hat{FP}_{US/Ge}$,

where $FP_{US/Ge}$ stands for the forward premium on the

U.S. dollar in terms of the Deutschmark until 1972

and 0 thereafter:

$$\Delta\hat{M}_{Ge,t} = - .05 - .62 \Delta\Delta FP_{US/Ge,t}$$
$$\quad\quad\quad (.63) \quad (.30)$$

The use of $\Delta(r_{T3}-r_{S3})'$ instead of $\Delta(r_{T3}-r_{S3})$ in equation (4.2)
does not of course affect the residuals, but reduces the multi-
collinearity in the equation.

One bothersome issue still remains with equation (4.2).
It is generally believed that the spectacular shifts in
$\Delta(r_{T3}-r_{S3})$ during the last few years largely reflect changes in
$FP_{Ge/NL}$, the forward premium of the D-Mark. There is indeed
a positive correlation between the two variables and one also gets
the correct sign when $\Delta FP_{Ge/NL}$ takes the place of $\Delta(r_{T3}-r_{S3})$ in
equation (4.2), but $\Delta(r_{T3}-r_{S3})$ happens to contribute more to an
explanation of $\Delta\hat{M}$ than $\Delta FP_{Ge/NL}$, and the coefficient of $\Delta FP_{Ge/NL}$
in equations for money growth shows lack of stability over time.
Regrettably, the use of yearly averages of $FP_{Ge/NL}$ and $r_{T3}-r_{S3}$
prevents us from investigating the nature of the causal structure
between these two variables (and their ultimate determinants),
since speculative phenomena are very short-lived.

The estimated coefficients of equation (4.2) now serve to
calculate a series $\hat{M}'$, that indicates the course the money stock
would have taken, if the temporary and reversible disturbances
in the demand for money had not occurred:

(4.3) $\quad\quad \hat{M}'_t = \hat{M}_t + 1.33 \Delta FP_{US/NL,t} + .67 \Delta(r_{T3}-r_{S3})'_t$

The autocorrelations of $\hat{M}'$ and $\Delta\hat{M}'$ as well as the characteristics

of the residuals from a moving average model for $\Delta M'$ show that
the model

$$(4.4) \qquad \hat{\Delta M}'_t = (1 - .65\ B)\,a_t$$
$$\qquad\qquad\qquad (.15)$$

is appropriate. The residuals a_t measure the unanticipated
monetary impulses that will be used in the next section, whereas
the corresponding series for anticipated money growth will appear
in the inflation regressions. We shall omit the prime and use
the notations $(\hat{M} - \hat{M}^e)$ and $\hat{M}^e$ for these two series in the remainder of this chapter.

4.3. THE DETERMINATION OF OUTPUT

According to the theoretical model presented in chapter 2, the
expected growth rate of output, $\hat{y}^e$, and the differences between
$\hat{y}^e$ and the actual rate of growth $\hat{y}$, are both functions of a set
of impulses. This section will be devoted to an investigation to
determine which impulses have a significant effect on the growth
of Dutch output, as measured by the growth rate of gross
domestic product. The resulting time series for $\hat{y}^e$ will then be
used in the next section, where we shall estimate inflation regressions of the type:

$$\hat{p} = 1.\hat{M}^e - (1 - \delta_1)\hat{y}^e + \text{other terms}$$

THE INFLUENCE OF WORLD TRADE

The most important impulse to influence the growth rate of
output in the very open Dutch economy is the course of world
trade. (We use an index for the volume of world trade, calculated
by the Dutch Central Planning Bureau, that applies different
weights to the imports of Dutch trading partners according to
their importance for the Netherlands.) Exports make up about
50% of g.d.p. and are much less predictable than, for example,

consumption. Therefore fluctuations in the foreign demand for Dutch goods do have a large effect on the domestic economy. According to the model of chapter 2, the ultimate determinants of unexpected changes in world trade would be monetary, fiscal, and other impulses in the various trading partners, together with "international" factors such as changes in tariffs. In the case of Dutch-weighted world trade, the impulses that emanate from West Germany and the U.S. should be particularly important.

Two simple examples of regressions for world trade are:

$$(4.5) \qquad \hat{\Delta m}_{w,t} = \underset{(.26)}{.79} (1 - B)(\hat{M}_{Ge} - \hat{M}^e_{Ge})_{t-1} +$$

$$+ \underset{(.47)}{.28} (1 - B)(\hat{M}_{US} - \hat{M}^e_{US})_{t-1} + (1 - \underset{(.17)}{.77} B)a_t$$

$$\bar{R}^2 = .49 \qquad \sigma_u = 4.1 \qquad \text{years: } 1954 - 1976$$

$$(4.6) \qquad \hat{\Delta m}_{w,t} = \underset{(.26)}{.77} (1 - B)(\hat{M}_{Ge} - \hat{M}^e_{Ge})_{t-1} + (1 - \underset{(.16)}{.80} B)a_t$$

$$\bar{R}^2 = .50 \qquad \sigma_u = 4.0 \qquad \text{years: } 1954 - 1976$$

Here, $\hat{M}_{Ge}$ and $\hat{M}_{US}$ are the growth rates of the money stocks in West Germany and the U.S. The series for $(\hat{M}_{Ge} - \hat{M}^e_{Ge})$ is that which was used in equation (4.2) and the series for $(\hat{M}_{US} - \hat{M}^e_{US})$ was developed in chapter 3.

The two equations (4.5) and (4.6) have been estimated with a Box-Jenkins transfer function program, which subtracts the means from each variable before the estimation so that the equations do not contain a constant term. As mentioned in chapter 1, the values of $\bar{R}^2$ are indicative of the proportion between the variance of the dependent variable and the residual variance, but they do not possess the properties of the coefficient of correlation in a linear regression model.

It has been assumed that the monetary impulses have

a purely temporary effect on the growth of world trade, so that
they enter the equation premultiplied by $\alpha_1(1-B)$ instead of the
more general $(\alpha_1-\alpha_2)B$. This is plausible on theoretical grounds;
it also reduces the number of free parameters in an equation
which fits only moderately well. The U.S. monetary impulse has
the right sign, but is not significant, so that the equation
(4.6) has been used in what follows. Equation (4.5) may serve as
a simple illustration of the type of transfer function in which
world trade depends on monetary impulses in two major nations
together with an error model.

On the assumption that traders act as if they know
equation (4.6) but do not possess information about the current
residual shock a_t and the German monetary impulse, a measure for
$(\hat{m}_w-\hat{m}_w^e)$ can be calculated. If the deviations of the growth rate
of world trade from its mean are used instead, this makes little
difference to the output regressions below -- and is, of course,
a simpler procedure than working with a transfer function. The
reason that the simple mean-corrected $\hat{m}_w$ series was rejected in
favour of the series calculated from the transfer function is
that $\hat{m}_w$ minus its mean is not white noise. Also, using $\hat{m}_w$ minus
its mean value as a measure of unanticipated growth in world
trade implies that the annual growth rates of world trade
fluctuate around a constant mean and that the value of this
average growth rate for the post-war period was known already
in the early fifties.

OTHER IMPULSES IN THE OUTPUT EQUATION

The impulse in the output equation that comes second in order of
importance is the domestic monetary impulse, $(\hat{M}-\hat{M}^e)$, as developed
in the previous section. Just as in Korteweg (1978b), the best
results for this impulse were obtained when it was lagged one
year. A remarkable property of the monetary impulse is its high
positive correlation with $(\hat{m}_w-\hat{m}_w^e)$, which was noted also by
Korteweg with his proxies of both impulses. The correlation is
interesting because of the fact that $(\hat{M}-\hat{M}^e)$ is lagged one period
whereas $(\hat{m}_w-\hat{m}_w^e)$ is not; however, the Dutch monetary impulse can

hardly be a significant influence on world trade and neither can
unanticipated growth in world trade be allowed to determine money
growth in the previous year. The likely explanation is that
current money growth in the Netherlands is very much determined
by monetary developments in other countries, as we were able to
illustrate in equation (4.2) vis-à-vis Germany, and that the
foreign monetary impulses influence foreign demand and, with
a further lag, the growth of world trade (equations (4.5) and
(4.6) show something of this mechanism). The two remaining
impulses that appear in our regressions for the growth rate of
gross domestic product, $\hat{gdp}$, are:

$(\hat{glg}-\hat{glg}^e)$: the unanticipated rate of growth of total direct
government expenditure in constant prices;

$(\hat{y}_{ag}-\hat{y}^e_{ag})$: the unanticipated rate of growth of agricultural
production.

One impulse that has not been included is the unexpected
change in foreign prices. This variable, for which both a (dollar)
index for the rate of inflation in the O.E.C.D. -- less the Netherlands -- and a (guilder) index of Dutch import prices were tried,
had the correct, positive, sign, but was not significant.

The complete transfer function for $\Delta\hat{gdp}$ has to be of the form:

$$\Delta\hat{gdp}_t = (\alpha_1-\alpha_2 B)(\hat{m}_w-\hat{m}^e_w)_t + (\alpha_3-\alpha_4 B)(\hat{glg}-\hat{glg}^e)_t +$$

$$+ (\alpha_5-\alpha_6 B)(\hat{y}_{ag}-\hat{y}^e_{ag}) + (\alpha_7-\alpha_8 B)(\hat{M}-\hat{M}^e)_t + (1-\theta B)a_t,$$

in order to obtain:

$$_t E\ \hat{gdp}_{t+1} = {}_t E\ \hat{gdp}_{t+2} = \ldots.$$

It is hazardous to estimate nine coefficients with only 23
data points. One plausible coefficient restriction is to require
that unanticipated changes in agricultural production, presumably
dominated by the weather, do not have a permanent influence on

the growth rate of $\hat{g}dp$. It so happens that estimation of the remaining 8 coefficients results in plausible values for all of them, so that equation (4.7) will be used for the determination of $\hat{g}dp^e$ and $\hat{g}dp\text{-}\hat{g}dp^e$:

$$(4.7) \quad \Delta\hat{g}dp_t = \underset{(.09)\,(.06)}{(.28 - .30\,B)}\,(\hat{m}_w - \hat{m}_w^e)_t + \underset{(.13)\,(.11)}{(.55 - .36\,B)}\,(\hat{glg} - \hat{glg}^e)_t +$$

$$+ \underset{(.04)}{.15\,(1-B)}\,(\hat{y}_{ag} - \hat{y}_{ag}^e)_t + \underset{(.10)\,(.11)}{(.39 - .30\,B)}\,(\hat{M} - \hat{M}^e)_{t-1} + \underset{(.23)}{(1 - .73\,B)}\,a_t$$

$$\bar{R}^2 = .89, \qquad \sigma_u = 1.1, \qquad \text{years: } 1954 - 1976.$$

Almost identical results are obtained when additional constraints are imposed on the coefficients of the unanticipated growth in world trade, government expenditure, and money:

$$\hat{g}dp_t = \underset{(.06)}{.29\,(1 - B)}\,(\hat{m}_w - \hat{m}_w^e)_t + \underset{(.12)}{.42\,(1 - B)}\,(\hat{glg} - \hat{glg}^e)_t +$$

$$+ \underset{(.03)}{.14\,(1 - B)}\,(\hat{y}_{ag} - \hat{y}_{ag}^e)_t + \underset{(.09)}{.33\,(1 - B)}\,(\hat{M} - \hat{M}^e)_{t-1} + \underset{(.20)}{(1 - .54\,B)}\,a_t$$

$$\bar{R}^2 = .89, \qquad \sigma_u = 1.1, \qquad \text{years: } 1954 - 1976.$$

The transfer function (4.7) can now be used to develop measures for the anticipated growth rate of output, $\hat{g}dp^e$, and for the unanticipated changes, $\hat{g}dp\text{-}\hat{g}dp^e$. We get:

$$(4.8) \quad \hat{g}dp_t^e = \hat{g}dp_{t-1} - .30\,(\hat{m}_w - \hat{m}_w^e)_{t-1} - .36\,(\hat{glg} - \hat{glg}^e)_{t-1} +$$

$$- .15\,(\hat{y}_{ag} - \hat{y}_{ag}^e)_{t-1} - .30\,(\hat{M} - \hat{M}^e)_{t-2} - .73\,a_{t-1}$$

$$(4.9) \quad (\hat{g}dp\text{-}\hat{g}dp^e)_t = .28\,(\hat{m}_w - \hat{m}_w^e)_t + .55\,(\hat{glg} - \hat{glg}^e)_t +$$

$$+ .15\,(\hat{y}_{ag} - \hat{y}_{ag}^e)_t + .39\,(\hat{M} - \hat{M}^e)_t$$

The resulting series for $\hat{gdp}^e$ is much smoother than the $\hat{gdp}$ series itself, and empirically it does not make much difference whether we include $- \hat{y}^e$ in the price equation, as postulated by the quantity theory, or whether we subsume $- \hat{y}^e$ in the constant term of the equation. In this respect, the inflation regressions, to which we turn now, will be similar to the results obtained for the U.S. in chapter 3 (cf. Fourcans, 1978, for the same finding with respect to the French economy).

4.4. THE PRICE EQUATION

Having derived measures for anticipated money growth, $\hat{M}^e$ and expected output growth $\hat{y}^e$, we can now investigate whether an equation of the type:

$$\hat{p}^e = 1.\hat{M}^e - (1 - \delta_1)\hat{y}^e$$

is capable of tracing out the broad pattern of inflation in the Netherlands. After that, we can explore whether the unexpected impulses that caused $\hat{y}$ to deviate from $\hat{y}^e$ are also of use in explaining the difference between $\hat{p}$ and $\hat{p}^e$.

The rate of price change will be measured by the logarithmic first differences of the price index of g.d.p. This choice is dictated by our use of the quantity theory because the price and quantity indices in

$$\hat{M}^e + \hat{V}^e = \hat{p}^e + \hat{y}^e$$

must refer to the same economic aggregate. However, we shall also present a regression for $\hat{p}_c$, the deflator of private consumption and for $\hat{p}_{gdpb}$, the price deflator of private business output. $\hat{p}_{gdpb}$ is the dependent variable in Korteweg (1978b), whereas from the point of view of the individual asset holder, $\hat{p}_c$ is the most appropriate measure of inflation, as consumption remains the ultimate purpose of wealth accumulation (Fisher, 1930). This theoretical argument, coupled with the practical fact that consumption price indices are published more frequently and are much more discussed than the gdp deflator, are reasons for looking also at the time series for $\hat{p}_c$, which is to be found in table 4.1., together with the data for $\hat{p}_{gdp}$.

Our equation for expected inflation is:

$$(4.10) \qquad \hat{p}^e_{gdp,t} = 1.75 + 1 \times (\hat{M}^e - \hat{gdp}^e)_{t-.5}$$
$$\qquad\qquad\qquad (.30) \ (-)$$

$$\bar{R}^2 = .60 \quad \text{(with respect to the variance of } \hat{p}_{gdp})$$
$$\sigma_u = 1.4, \qquad D.W. = 1.8, \qquad \text{years: } 1954 - 1976.$$

The variation in $\hat{p}_{gdp}$ is predominantly explained by the movements in $\hat{M}^e$, not by changes in $- \hat{gdp}^e$. An equally good result is obtained when $\hat{p}_{gdp}$ is regressed on $\hat{M}^e_{-.5}$ only:

$$(4.11) \qquad \hat{p}^e_{gdp,t} = - 1.1 + .84 \ \hat{M}^e_{t-.5}$$
$$\qquad\qquad\qquad (1.1) \ (.13)$$

$$\bar{R}^2 = .63 \quad \text{(with respect to the variance of } \hat{p}_{gdp})$$
$$\sigma_u = 1.4, \qquad D.W. = 1.6, \qquad \text{years: } 1954 - 1976.$$

Both in equation (4.10) and in equation (4.11) $\hat{p}^e$ is determined by the average of the current and once lagged values of $\hat{M}^e$ and $\hat{gdp}^e$. In the case of the U.S., there was no difference empirically between using $\hat{M}^e_t$ or $.5(\hat{M}^e_t + \hat{M}^e_{t-1})$; for the Netherlands, one has to work with the average of current and immediate past values for $\hat{M}^e$.

When the equation (4.10) is augmented with terms that explain the difference $(\hat{p}_{gdp} - \hat{p}^e_{gdp})$, we obtain a relation for the current rate of price change:

$$(4.12) \qquad \hat{p}_{gdp,t} = 1. \hat{p}^e_{gdp,t} + 1.33 \text{ shift } 68/69 + .22(\hat{M} - \hat{M}^e)_t +$$
$$\qquad\qquad\qquad (-) \qquad\qquad (.74) \qquad\qquad (.07)$$

$$+ .44 \; ((\hat{TRF}/G) - (\hat{TRF}/G)^e)_t$$

$$(.11)$$

$$\bar{R}^2 = .81, \quad \sigma_u = 1.0, \quad D.W. = 1.9 \text{ (when an -- insignific-}$$
ant -- constant term is added) years: 1954 - 1976.

Here, $\hat{p}^e_{gdp}$ is taken from equation (4.10) and $(\hat{M}-\hat{M}^e)$ is the monetary impulse that also proved to be important in the output equation. The other two terms are new.

The first one, shift 68/69, is also used by Korteweg (1978a, b). It takes account

> "in a somewhat ad hoc fashion of a once-for-all institutional change in 1969 when the existing excise tax system was transformed into a value-added regime on January 1, 1969. The announcement of this change in tax regime prompted entrepreneurs to postpone price increases during the last part of 1968 in order to have them concur with the transition period when all price tags would have to be changed anyway. To catch the timing effects produced by the transition, we inserted a dummy variable in the equations (shift 68/69) assuming the value of -1 in 1968, +1 in 1969, and zero otherwise".

(Korteweg, 1978a, p. 39).

The remaining variable in equation (4.12) is $((\hat{TRF}/G) - (\hat{TRF}/G)^e)$ with (TRF/G) the proportion of transfer payments in total government expenditure. Quite similar results are obtained when we use Korteweg's (1978b) variable $((\hat{TSP}/Y) - (\hat{TSP}/Y)^e)$, the unanticipated growth in taxes and social premiums as a proportion of national income. $(\hat{TRF}/G)$ has been preferred here, as it is a more direct measure of unforeseen increases in nominal demand than $(\hat{TSP}/Y)$, which refers to what government receives, rather than to what it spends.

Let us now consider whether the same set of impulses appears in both the output and the price equations. Of the four impulses in the output equation (4.7), one, the monetary impulse, is also present in the price equation. A measure for government expen-

diture is included also in both equations, but two different
variables are used. Faced with the choice between maximizing
the contribution of some measure of the government impulse in
the two equations, even if this meant using two different
variables, or working with one single variable and accepting
low significance in either the output or the price equation,
we opted for the first possibility. Public expenditure is far
from homogeneous in the real world, so that a single variable
may not be adequate to describe both the impact on g.d.p. and
the effect on prices. Admittedly a superior way to take account
of the diversity in public expenditure would be to specify
a number of indices of government outlays in both the output
and the price equations; however, the small number of degrees
of freedom that are available precludes this solution.

The agricultural impulse appears in the output equation
only. As discussed in section 2.8., this impulse leads to shifts
of both the demand and the supply curves, so that the effect of
a positive agricultural impulse on $(\hat{p}-\hat{p}^e)$ is uncertain; the
absence of a term $(\hat{y}_{ag}-\hat{y}^e_{ag})$ in the price equation should not
count as an indictment of the model.

The statistical tests do provide evidence against the
model, however, through their rejection of a term $(\hat{m}_w-\hat{m}^e_w)$ in
the price equation. Unexpected increases in world trade should
not only influence output, but also the rate of price change.
However, the simple correlation coefficient between $(\hat{p}-\hat{p}^e)$ and
$(\hat{m}_w-\hat{m}^e_w)$ is (insignificantly) negative, and $(\hat{m}_w-\hat{m}^e_w)$ is never
significant in the regressions for $\hat{p}$. Measurement bias in our
proxy for $(\hat{m}_w-\hat{m}^e_w)$ can hardly explain this negative result, for
the same series did perform satisfactorily in the equation for
the actual growth in output that was discussed in the previous
section. Furthermore, different proxies for the unanticipated
rate of price change and for the unanticipated change in world
trade also fail to show a positive correlation between the two.
For, the series of discrepancies between the predicted rates of
inflation, as forecast by the Dutch Central Planning Bureau,
and the actual rates of price change are not correlated with

the forecast errors in the growth in world trade made by the same organization (see the next section for more details about the Planning Bureau and its forecasts). It remains unclear why errors in forecasting world trade, however measured, have a definite effect on the current rate of output, but do not appear to help explain the discrepancy between expected and actual prices.

A few further observations about the price equation follow. First, when $(\hat{M}^e - \hat{gdp}^e)_t$ and $(\hat{M}^e - \hat{gdp}^e)_{t-1}$ are included separately, the coefficients are .39 (.17) and .35 (.17) so that the restriction on the two coefficients is justified. Second, in a test of the coefficient restriction on $\hat{gdp}^e_{t-.5}$, we included $\hat{M}^e_{t-.5}$ and $\hat{gdp}^e_{t-.5}$ separately in the price equation. The coefficients were .92 (.11) and -.52 (.41), respectively, so that we do not have to reject the hypothesis -- implicit in equation (4.10) that these two coefficients are equal in magnitude and of opposite sign. Third, in order to see whether the use of transfer function models for the formation of expectations does result in a better explanation of inflation, a price equation was estimated with $\hat{M}^e_{t-.5}$ replaced by the simpler expression $\hat{M}_{t-1.5}$, as used by Korteweg, which is the optimal univariate model for expected money growth, lagged .5 years. The coefficient on expected money growth drops from .92 to .53 which indicates support for our economic model for $\hat{M}^e$. As regards the model for $\hat{gdp}^e$, it has already been pointed out that replacing $\hat{gdp}^e$ by a constant does not significantly reduce the explanatory power of the equation. But, if the expected rate of growth of g.d.p. is alternatively modelled by the own lagged growth rate, then the fit deteriorates significantly.

Fourth, we tested whether the treatment in section 4.2. of changes in the forward premium and in the interest rate differential $(r_{T3} - r_{S3})$ has not eliminated part of what should be monetary impulses. The differences between the original $\hat{M}$ and $\hat{M}'$ (see equation (4.3) above) proved insignificant in the equations for output and prices, which provides support for the hypothesis that reversible short-term changes in $FP_{US/NL}$ and

$(r_{T3}-r_{S3})$ should neither affect $\hat{M}^e$, nor be part of the monetary
impulse. Fifth, we tested for an influence of the unexpected
increase in foreign prices on the acutal rate of price change in
Holland. But, as in the case of the output equation, although
the coefficient for this variable was positive, it did not achieve
statistical significance in the equation (t-value equal to .7).

Finally, the specification of equation (4.12) also works
with the other two measures of inflation:

$$(4.13) \qquad \hat{P}_{gdpb,t} = \hat{P}^e_{gdpb,t} + 1.26 \text{ shift } 68/69 + .24(\hat{M}-\hat{M}^e)_t +$$
$$\qquad\qquad\qquad\qquad (.68) \qquad\qquad\qquad (.07)$$

$$+ .42((\widehat{TRF/G}) - (\widehat{TRF/G})^e)_t$$
$$(.10)$$

$$\bar{R}^2 = .84, \quad \sigma_u = .94, \quad \text{D.W.} = 1.7, \quad \text{years: } 1954\text{-}1976.$$

Here, $\hat{P}_{gdpb}$ is the rate of change of the deflator for private
business output.

$$(4.14) \qquad \hat{P}_{c,t} = \hat{P}^e_{c,t} + 2.15 \text{ shift } 68/69 + .15(\hat{M}-\hat{M}^e)_t +$$
$$\qquad\qquad\qquad\qquad (.83) \qquad\qquad\qquad (.08)$$

$$+ .38((\widehat{TRF/G}) - (\widehat{TRF/G})^e)_t$$
$$(.13)$$

$$\bar{R}^2 = .82, \quad \sigma_u = 1.1, \quad \text{D.W.} = 1.3, \quad \text{years: } 1954\text{-}1976.$$

The dependent variable now is the rate of change of the consumption deflator.

In these equations, $\hat{P}^e_{gdpb,t}$ and $\hat{P}^e_{c,t}$ are computed in the
same way as $\hat{P}^e_{gdp,t}$ in equation (4.10) above. The D.W. statistic
in the equation for $\hat{P}_c$ suggests positive residual autocorrelation,
but otherwise the equations are satisfactory.

4.5. FOREIGN INFLUENCES ON DUTCH PRICES

According to our model, economic subjects do not require any
further foreign data for forming their expectations about future
domestic inflation, when the terms $\Delta\Delta FP_{US/NL}$ and $\Delta\Delta(r_{T3}-r_{S3})$ have
been incorporated in the model for money growth, equation (4.2).
In this section we shall compare our results to those of
Korteweg (1978b), who worked with a simpler formula for $\hat{M}^e$, but
did extend the basis for $\hat{p}^e$ to include not only his $\hat{M}^e$, but also
$\hat{p}^{*e}$, as a measure of world inflation. Korteweg's preferred
inflation regression is:

(4.15)
$$\hat{p}_{gdpb,t} = .63 + .32 \, \hat{M}^e_{t-.5} + .43 \, \hat{p}^{*e}_{t-.5} + .12(\hat{M}-\hat{M}^e) +$$
$$\quad (.59) \ (.08) \qquad\qquad (.07) \qquad\qquad (.05)$$

$$+ 1.27 \text{ shift } 68/69 + .33((\widehat{TSP/Y})-(\widehat{TSP/Y})^e)_t$$
$$\quad (.68) \qquad\qquad\qquad (.10)$$

$$\bar{R}^2 = .84, \qquad \sigma_u = .94, \qquad \text{years: } 1954 - 1976.$$

Here, $\hat{M}^e$ is proxied by the optimal univariate model $\hat{M}^e_t = \hat{M}_{t-1}$,
and $\hat{p}^*$ is the growth rate of a dollar index of prices in the
O.E.C.D.-area (with the Netherlands excluded); $\hat{p}^{*e}_t$ is modelled
by the lagged growth rate $\hat{p}^*_{t-1}$. Equation (4.15) should by
compared to equation (4.13) above, which has the same dependent
variable:

(4.13)
$$\hat{p}_{gdpb,t} = 1.08 + (\hat{M}^e-\hat{gdp}^e)_{t-.5} + .24(\hat{M}-\hat{M}^e)_t +$$
$$\qquad\qquad (.29) \qquad\qquad\qquad (.07)$$

$$+ 1.26 \text{ shift } 68/69 + .42((\widehat{TRF/G})-(\widehat{TRF/G})^e)_t$$
$$\quad (.68) \qquad\qquad\qquad (.10)$$

$$\bar{R}^2 = .84, \qquad \sigma_u = .94, \qquad \text{years: } 1954 - 1976.$$

The explanatory power of the two equations is the same, which is

also illustrated by the fact that $\hat{p}^{*e}_{t-.5}$ has an insignificant
coefficient when it is added to the R.H.S. of our equations
(4.12) – (4.14). The rate of inflation in the Netherlands can be
equally well predicted by either using both $\hat{p}^{*e}$ and a naive
statistical model for expected money growth, or by working with
a more economic model for $\hat{M}^e$.

ECONOMETRIC ISSUES

Both methods have their drawbacks. As far as statistical issues
are concerned, our model for expected money growth is vulnerable
to the criticism of simultaneous equations bias. We use changes
in the forward premium (during the fixed-rate period) and changes
in the interest differential $(r_{T3}-r_{S3})$ as explanatory variables in
the multivariate model for $\hat{\Delta M}$. If there are links between the
current rate of Dutch monetary growth and these two variables,
then the coefficients in the equation for $\hat{\Delta M}$ are biased.

Korteweg's univariate model for $\hat{M}^e$ avoids simultaneity
problems; however, his equation $\hat{M}^e_t = \hat{M}_{t-1}$ results in a series for
$\hat{M}^e$ that has very substantial forecasting errors in some years
(recall table 4.1). We should not over-react to this, however,
for two reasons. First, Korteweg's series for $\hat{M}^e$ may be
a slightly imperfect proxy for expected money growth, but this
is compensated for by the fact that expected inflation in his
model also depends on the expected rate of change in world prices,
$\hat{p}^{*e}$. Equation (4.15) indicates that the coefficient on $\hat{p}^{*e}$ is
larger than that on $\hat{M}^e$ (and also has a higher t-value); this
remains true for different estimation periods. In equation (4.15),
for example, the coefficient on expected money growth is .32
only, so that measurement errors in the proxy for $\hat{M}^e$ have a much
smaller effect on the computed values of $\hat{p}^e$ than measurement
errors in our multivariate expression for $\hat{M}^e$, which enters
equations (4.12) – (4.14) with a coefficient of unity. Second,
really serious and ubiquitous measurement errors in Korteweg's
series for $\hat{M}^e$ would contaminate the corresponding proxy for
$(\hat{M}-\hat{M}^e)$; the fact that his $(\hat{M}-\hat{M}^e)$ series performs well in the
output and price equations suggests that such errors, although

possibly large in a few years, cannot be too serious on average.

TWO ASSUMPTIONS THAT UNDERLIE KORTEWEG'S EQUATION

More important than such statistical points are the different
economic assumptions that underlie Korteweg's and our inflation
models. The usefulness of Korteweg's equation for forecasting
purposes depends on two conditions, both of which were ful-
filled during the sample period. One condition has to do with
the measurement of world inflation, the other with the stability
of the coefficients in the price equation. Let us consider them
in order.

The first condition that must be satisfied in order for
Korteweg's model to be valid, is the existence of a meaningful
index of world inflation (Genberg, 1977). This would be a trivial
problem if all exchange rates were fixed permanently, for then
any currency could be used for the calculation of a weighted
index of world inflation. Even if we have fixed exchange rates
with occasional parity changes, we can redefine the "world" as
those countries that remain on a fixed parity with the country
that is being investigated, or we can disregard certain years
during which parity changes took place (Genberg, 1975). But the
situation becomes quite different when we consider a world with
floating exchange rates. It now becomes vital which currency we
use when the money stock and the rate of inflation for the world
are calculated (Johnson, 1977b, p. 652). If there were one
currency that could indeed be regarded as a benchmark, or as
a standard for the world, together with a number of other less
important currencies, then there would be a case for using such
a dominant currency as the unit for world money and world
inflation. During the transition to floating exchange rates,
some people believed that the dollar would continue to perform
this anchor function. McKinnon (1976) declared that

> "speculators need a haven, a relatively riskless asset,
> from which they can operate".
>
> (p. 90).

One should read this statement not as expressing a truth about

speculation, which it clearly is not, but as typical of what
many expected that a floating world would look like: one stable
dominant currency, the dollar, surrounded by a number of other
currencies. At any moment in time, some currencies might
appreciate against the dollar and others would go down, with
speculators trying to switch in and out of these currencies at
the right moment. There would be no systematic positive
correlation between contemporaneous movements of the different
exchange rates, so that one would speak only about re- or
devaluations of the mark, the lira, the guilder, etc., but not
about an (expected) change in the value of the dollar. If such
is the situation in the real world, then one can still work with
a dollar-denominated index of world prices and world money.

Until the time of writing (April 1979), the exchange rate
of the dollar has indeed remained within a fairly narrow band.
Morgan Guaranty's index of the trade-weighted rate of exchange
shows a drop of 2% only between March 1973 (when the Smithsonian
agreement broke down) and March 1979; the highest and lowest
values during the six intervening years were less than 10% away
from the March 1973 rate. Also, Korteweg uses a two-year moving
average of world prices in his regressions for Dutch inflation
$(.5\hat{p}^{*}_{t-1} + .5\hat{p}^{*}_{t-2})$, so that the short-run fluctuations in the
dollar's exchange rate that did occur in the 1973-1979 period
do not significantly affect his proxy for $\hat{p}^{*}_{t-.5}$. Until now,
the first of the two conditions which his inflation model
requires -- an empirically useful index of world inflation --
has been satisfied. The dollar is still the dominant currency
in the world (the share of dollar-denominated assets in official
foreign exchange reserves even increased slightly from 78% in
1971 to 81% in 1977), and a dollar index can indicate the broad
movement of world prices. Difficulties might arise only if one
attempted to construct an index for world inflation on, say,
a quarterly basis, for in that case the temporary movements in
the exchange rate of the dollar could contaminate the index.

The second condition which Korteweg's model requires is
stability of the coefficients on $\hat{M}^{e}$ and $\hat{p}^{*e}$. Stable coefficients

can be obtained as long as the Dutch guilder is not floating in
a completely free way, but moves more or less in step with other
currencies, or, equivalently, as long as inflation in the Netherlands is broadly similar to inflation in the rest of the world.
To see this, consider what would happen if Dutch inflation
increased to, say, 50% per annum. In that case the guilder would
depreciate at a similar rate and the coefficients on $\hat{M}^e$ and $\hat{p}^{*e}$
in Korteweg's equation would become approximately 1 and 0,
respectively.

The rate of growth of world prices and that of the Dutch
money supply cannot be completely independent in Korteweg's
model. For, if that were the case, one should be able to simulate
the effects of a permanent increase in either one of these two
variables. But that leads to unacceptable results: a permanent
increase in $\hat{M}$ with $\hat{p}^*$ fixed implies that the velocity of money
goes to zero; a permanent increase in $\hat{p}^*$ with $\hat{M}$ held fixed is
equally impossible. However, the precise nature of the connections between $\hat{M}$ and $\hat{p}^*$ is not spelled out, so that it does not
appear possible to formulate precisely by how much Dutch
inflation can differ from world inflation before Korteweg's
equation breaks down. It is clear, though, that the stability
of the coefficients has not yet become a problem.

ASSUMPTIONS UNDERLYING THE PRESENT MODEL FOR INFLATION

Having discussed the economic background of Korteweg's equation
in detail, we can be much more concise about the conditions under
which our alternative model for inflation is appropriate. One
condition necessary for the present approach is a stable demand
for money function in which all relevant rates of return on
substitutes for money must satisfy the martingale property. If,
on the contrary, there are temporary interest anomalies, such as
those discussed above, then there must be an acceptable way of
calculating the magnitude of the corresponding temporary shifts
in the demand for money, so that corrections can be made to the
raw figures for the rate of money growth. Also, the assumptions
made in chapter 2 about the velocity of money must be appropriate.

If there are sudden large changes in the way money is used, the rate of growth of the money stock will not be indicative of the expected rate of inflation during the shift in the demand for money. Such shifts in the demand for money have not marred our regression results for the U.S. and the Netherlands; whether this will remain true for the future cannot be predicted. It helps, of course, that the growth rate of money is connected to the rate of growth of prices, so that permanent shifts in the demand for money have a temporary effect only on the residuals of our equation for the rate of inflation. In Barro's equation for the level of prices and the stock of money, permanent shifts in the demand for money can cause more serious problems.

The second condition required by our model is that the expected rate of growth in the stock of money be not determined on the demand side. This condition may be satisfied in a number of different contexts, the most obvious being that of a freely floating rate of exchange. But the present model may be acceptable also under fixed or quasi-fixed rates of exchange: first, if there can be significant short-run deviations from purchasing power parity, so that the monetary authorities have a degree of autonomy in deciding upon the growth rate of the money stock and thus on the domestic rate of inflation. Second, if changes in the growth rates of money abroad affect the domestic rate of growth of money before they become visible in higher rates of inflation in foreign countries. For, in that case, the expected rate of growth of the domestic money stock remains a useful leading indicator of future domestic inflation.

The regressions in section 4.4. have shown that there exists a stable demand for money function in the Netherlands, and the statistical tests in section 2.6. indicated that the rate of growth of money in Holland is not determined completely on the demand side. Apparently, both conditions required by our model were satisfied during the estimation period. By contrast, the model will not be of use if applied, for example, to a situation in which the exchange rate is fixed, the domestic price level hardly deviates from P.P.P. and the demand for money

function is rather loose. In such a case, indices of inflation
in other countries cannot be dispensed with as indicators of
future domestic inflation.

4.6. THE OFFICIAL DUTCH FORECASTS OF INFLATION

*"It is sometimes difficult to tell the difference between
a forecast and a prayer."*
(Bosworth, 1978).

THE CENTRAL PLANNING BUREAU AND ITS ANNUAL ECONOMETRIC MODEL

After the last war, the Dutch Parliament established a Central
Planning Bureau (C.P.B.) as an agency of the Ministry of Economic
Affairs. The name "Planning Bureau" still reminds one of Social-
Democratic aspirations for a planned economy, but the role of the
C.P.B. has always been limited to analysis and forecasting.
A majority in Parliament was opposed to actual planning powers
for the government, either as a matter of principle or -- in the
case of the Catholic Party -- because of a preference for
corporatist organisation.

A main activity of the C.P.B. consists of publishing, during
the first few months of each calendar year, a "Central Economic
Plan" (C.E.P.), a book-length report on the Dutch economy that
includes a set of forecasts for the current year. In addition,
the C.P.B. tenders confidential or public advice to the Government throughout the year, particularly during the summer months
when the next budget is being prepared. Since 1960, a report has
been published together with the budget proposals in mid-
September (called "Macro-Economische Verkenning", abbreviated
to M.E.V.) with a set of preliminary forecasts for the next year.
As in the case of the C.E.P., the forecasts are made for one year
ahead and refer to the yearly average value of the variables.

Until 1975 the regular forecasts were made with a short-
term annual model. Versions of this model have been published in
1955, 1956, 1958, 1961, 1963, 1970 and 1977. Although the model

has changed over the years, some general points made by Arrow (1958) in his review of a theoretical volume by Tinbergen (1956), the first Director of the C.P.B., remain characteristic of the whole series. In the first place there is the heavy emphasis on the wage level as an "instrument of policy" (Tinbergen, 1956). Later versions of the model did contain an endogenous wage variable, but the forecast has nearly always been inserted as an exogenous variable. Only in the C.E.P.'s of 1966, 1972, and 1973 was the rate of change of wages endogenous. We return to this issue below, when the systematic under-prediction of prices and wages will be discussed.

A second feature of the models is that they are clearly short-run models. Little attention is given to the supply side of the economy, and government expenditure is the main regulator of employment. That this followed from acceptance of Keynes' interpretation of the Thirties, was seen at an early stage by Drees (1957): "the model is a depression model. The outcomes which it produces can easily lead to inflationary policy advice" (p. 13). Even the latest version of the model has been termed "Keynesian with its inherent limitations" by its authors (Verdoorn and Post, 1976).

The third point made by Arrow is the consistent neglect of the monetary sector: "Classical monetary policy is not considered seriously" (p. 92). Tinbergen only specifies a monetary sector in two out of twenty-one theoretical models in his book, and both of these two assume a fixed price level. He remarks that the monetary relations have been "so far neglected by statistical and econometric research ...." and that "little is known about their true shape" (p. 111). In spite of these *empirical* problems, Tinbergen used to stress monetary developments in the text that accompanied the forecasts. In the very first C.E.P., dated September 1946, he writes of inflation-ary effects of the government budget deficit if it is financed by an increase in the money stock (p. 59). Similar statements are to be found in his 1956 book, for example on p. 73: with "money creation, the danger of potential inflation may come up" (see also Appendix A to the 1955 C.E.P. about "potential inflation").

Monetary factors were not only neglected in the models but also received less and less attention in the text of the Plans until, finally, the C.P.B. merely indicated the monetary implications of the forecasts (C.E.P. for 1967, p. 91). An appendix to each C.E.P. contained a simple set of flow-of-funds accounts, but these were apparently of no importance and only a *consequence* of the forecasts, not an input in the forecasting process. There has always been a remarkable contrast between the C.P.B. models on the one hand and the monetary model developed by the Dutch Central Bank (Holtrop, 1972, and Selden, 1975) on the other.

With this neglect of the monetary side of the economy, it will come as no surprise that the C.P.B. has never worked with a monetary theory of inflation. The price equations in the models have always been of the form:

$$\hat{p} = \alpha(\hat{w} - \hat{H}) + \beta \hat{p}_m + \text{other terms}$$

with:

$\hat{p}$ the rate of change of prices

$\hat{w}$ the rate of change of wages

$\hat{H}$ the rate of change of labour productivity

$\hat{p}_m$ the rate of change of import prices.

At the same time, the model contained a wage equation of the type:

$$\hat{w} = \gamma\hat{p} + \delta\hat{H} + \text{other terms.}$$

THE FORECASTS

The main function of the annual model has been to aid in the preparation of the two sets of forecasts that are published each year. Table 4.2. contains the inflation predictions together with the preliminary realisations taken from the next C.E.P. and the definitive figures based on national accounts data. The table also shows C.E.P. forecasts and preliminary realisations for the three main explanatory variables in the consumption price equation:

wages, labour productivity, and import prices. The final variable
in the table, $\hat{m}_w$, the growth rate of Dutch-weighted world trade,
does not appear directly in the price equation. It is, however,
the most important exogenous variable in the model, and some
versions of the model had an excess-demand term in the price
equation of the form

$$\hat{(m} - \hat{v)}$$

with: $\hat{m}$ growth rate of real imports,
and $\hat{v}$ growth rate of real expenditure.

Both the growth rate of imports and that of expenditure are
largely determined by $\hat{m}_w$.

The forecasts in table 4.2. have been made with, not by,
the model. This is clear from the fact that there is significant
bias in the predicted changes in consumption prices, wages,
productivity, and world trade. For, the one excuse for biased
model forecasts -- a model in levels of variables and forecasts
that are given as percentage changes, or vice versa -- does not
apply. All versions of the model, except for the very first, have
been specified in relative rates of growth, so that this cannot
have been the cause of systematic bias in the forecasts.

As our measure of the average bias in the forecasts we
take the differences between the preliminary realisation and
the forecast, so that underestimation results in positive errors.
We relate the forecasts to the preliminary realisations in the
next year's C.E.P. and not to the definitive values, since this
makes a more proper test possible of hypotheses about the way
the forecasts are made. If, for example, a first-order error-
learning process adequately described the way in which the C.P.B.
reacts to its own forecasting errors, that should affect the
correlation between

$$(\hat{x}^0 - \hat{x}^F)_t \qquad \text{and} \qquad (\hat{x}^0 - \hat{x}^F)_{t-1}$$

Table 4.2.

PREDICTIONS AND REALIZATIONS

YEAR	p_c^{FF} (1)	$\hat{p}_c^{F}$ (2)	$\hat{p}_c^{0}$ (3)	$\hat{p}_c^{R}$ (4)	$\hat{w}^{F}$ (5)	$\hat{w}^{0}$ (6)	$\hat{H}^{F}$ (7)	$\hat{H}^{0}$ (8)	$\hat{p}_m^{F}$ (9)	$\hat{p}_m^{0}$ (10)	$\hat{m}_w^{F}$ (11)	$\hat{m}_w^{0}$ (12)
1953	1.5	- 2.3	0.0	- 0.4	2.2	2.4	5.2	4.9	-12.0	-11.0	7.0	3.8
1954	3.8	2.0	4.0	4.6	7.1	10.6	1.6	4.0	- 7.0	- 5.0	0.0	9.3
1955	0.2	1.7	1.0	2.3	5.0	6.5	0.4.	4.2	0.0	2.0	4.0	11.9
1956	- 0.3	1.0	1.5	2.7	5.0	10.0	2.5	2.0	1.0	4.0	7.5	7.1
1957	4.7	4.5	6.0	5.3	6.7	6.5	0.7	1.0	4.0	5.0	5.0	7.2
1958	2.2	1.0	1.4	1.6	3.0	3.0	- 1.4	1.0	- 2.0	- 6.5	3.0	- 0.8
1959	- 1.0	- 1.0	1.0	1.2	3.0	3.0	2.0	3.5	- 1.0	- 3.0	3.5	9.4
1960	2.5	2.0	2.0	2.5	7.5	8.7	4.0	5.8	2.0	0.0	6.0	15.0
1961	1.5	1.5	1.5	2.4	5.0	5.3	2.5	1.0	- 1.0	- 2.0	6.0	3.8
1962	2.0	2.0	2.5	2.6	6.0	8.0	2.0	2.0	0.0	- 1.5	4.0	6.1
1963	2.0	2.5	3.5	3.8	7.5	8.0	3.0	2.5	0.0	1.5	4.0	8.0
1964	2.0	7.0	6.5	6.8	16.0	17.0	4.5	6.5	1.5	3.0	9.0	10.0
1965	4.5*	4.5	4.5	4.0	9.0	11.0	3.5	4.0	1.0	0.5	7.0	8.0
1966	4.5	4.5	6.0	5.4	9.5	10.5	5.0	4.0	0.0	1.0	6.0	6.0
1967	4.5	4.5	3.5	3.0	8.0	8.0	4.0	6.0	0.5	- 0.5	5.0	4.0
1968	3.0	3.0	3.0	2.6	5.0	6.5	3.5	6.0	- 1.0	- 2.0	5.0	10.0
1969	4.0	5.0	7.0	6.3	8.5	10.5	3.5	4.5	1.0	4.0	9.0	14.0
1970	3.8	4.0	3.5	4.5	8.0	12.5	4.0	5.5	4.0	7.0	10.0	10.0
1971	5.3	6.0	7.0	8.1	12.0	13.5	3.5	4.5	1.0	4.5	6.0	6.5
1972	7.0	6.5	8.0	8.4	12.0	12.5	3.5	5.5	- 0.5	- 1.0	6.0	9.0
1973	7.5*	7.5	9.0	9.0	13.5	15.0	4.0	5.5	3.5	8.5	10.0	11.5
1974	8.0	11.5	10.0	9.7	14.5	15.0	3.0	2.5	25.0	35.0	3.0	2.5
1975	9.5	9.5	10.5	10.3	12.5	13.5	2.0	0.0	3.0	4.0	0.0	- 4.0
1976	8.5	8.8	9.0	9.2	8.9	10.7	5.0	5.0	5.0	6.0	6.0	12.0
1977	7.0	6.5	7.0	6.8	7.5	8.0	4.5	3.0	4.0	3.5	7.0	4.0
1978	6.0	4.5	4.5	--	7.0	7.3	3.0	3.0	0.0	- 2.0	5.0	5.0

FF : September forecast (M.E.V.)

F : Forecast in C.E.P.

0 : Value as given in the next C.E.P.

R : Definitive value

p_c : price index

w : wage rate in enterprises

H : labour productivity

p_m : import price index (guilders)

m_w : Dutch weighted index of world trade

Note: All entries are percentage rates of change.
      Values for 1976 and earlier years are those used in the statistical analysis.
      Numbers for 1977 and 1978 have been added to show the most recent trends.
    * Not available: taken to be equal to the C.E.P. forecast.

With the forecast errors defined this way, we get:

$$\hat{p}_c^0 - \hat{p}_c^{FF} = .82 \qquad \sigma_u = 1.3 \qquad R.M.S.E. = 1.5$$
$$(.26)$$

$$\hat{p}_c^0 - \hat{p}_c^F = .59 \qquad \sigma_u = 1.0 \qquad R.M.S.E. = 1.2$$
$$(.21)$$

$$\hat{w}^0 - \hat{w}^F = 1.25 \qquad \sigma_u = 1.2 \qquad R.M.S.E. = 1.8$$
$$(.25)$$

$$\hat{H}^0 - \hat{H}^F = .80 \qquad \sigma_u = 1.4 \qquad R.M.S.E. = 1.6$$
$$(.29)$$

$$\hat{p}_m^0 - \hat{p}_m^F = .93 \qquad \sigma_u = 2.6 \qquad R.M.S.E. = 2.7$$
$$(.52)$$

$$\hat{m}_w^0 - \hat{m}_w^F = 1.84 \qquad \sigma_u = 3.6 \qquad R.M.S.E. = 4.1$$
$$(.74)$$

Here, R.M.S.E. indicates the root mean square of the forecast errors. The tests cover the period 1953-1976, but omitting the last few years makes no difference to the results. Our choice of starting point conforms to other studies of the C.P.B. forecasts and is caused by the fact that several sets of forecasts were given for 1952 without an indication of the Bureau's preference for one particular set. It would be incorrect to work with such a long, undivided sample period if the forecast errors had a tendency to become smaller over time. However, this is not the case with the official Dutch forecasts (neither with the official U.S. forecasts in the "Economic Report of the President" nor for the forecasts by the O.E.C.D., according to Smyth and Ash (1975) and Goldstein (1977)).

THE BIAS IN THE FORECASTS

The consistent bias in the predictions has often been noted,

even by the C.P.B. itself (C.P.B., 1954, Verdoorn, 1964, and
Van den Beld, 1965). Van de Panne (1959) notes that the forecasts
have been "unduly pessimistic" (p. 105), and Ter Heide (1970)
writing as general secretary of the largest trade union
federation also refers to the "over-pessimistic" views of the
C.P.B. (p. 49). Foreign observers, too, were struck by the
"systematic tendency toward under-estimation" of the economy's
prospects (Lundberg, 1968, p. 299). We emphasize the number of
times that the bias in the forecasts has been observed, because
it is important for an answer to the question as to *why* the
forecasts were biased.

One reason why inflation forecasts may be too low on
average has been pointed out by Carlson (1977). He argues that
unforeseen events that cause discrepancies between forecast and
realisation -- poor harvests, natural disasters, strikes, adverse
weather -- will more often than not have an upward effect on
the rate of price change:

> "unpredictable events came along .... primarily on the side
> of accelerating inflation"
>
> (p. 42).

Granted that this will be correct for most periods, it
would mean that rational forecasters have to allow for the fact
that unforeseeable shocks will occur from time to time. However,
it is difficult to attach a probability, for example, to the
occurrence of an earthquake, or an oil embargo. It follows that
tests for the rationality of price forecasts should exclude
periods when "unique" events have a major and unforeseen
influence on prices. It would not be realistic, for example,
to expect that a large forecasting error in 1974 is compensated
for by a series of small opposite errors in all preceding and
subsequent years, because economic subjects considered there
was a small likelihood of an oil embargo taking place.

A careful recent analysis of price forecasts (Mullineaux,
1978) found, in contrast to most earlier studies, that the forecasts of U.S. inflation six and twelve months ahead by a group
of professional American forecasters (the Livingston data) were

indeed rational -- which implies lack of bias -- over the years 1959-1969. The forecasts were irrational only for particular eventful periods outside these years. Fackler and Stanhouse (1977) reached a similar conclusion for a series of forecasts, based on surveys of public opinion, that is collected by the University of Michigan (see also Carlson 1975, De Menil, 1977, Wachtel, 1977). However, their analysis and many earlier studies of the Livingston series that rejected the hypothesis of unbiasedness, used inappropriate statistical procedures (see Granger and Newbold, 1973, and Mullineaux, 1978, for the reasons why one should investigate the time series of the forecast errors and not the separate series of forecasts and realisations).

The evidence from the U.S. is ambiguous as regards inflation forecasts by the public; it is clear, however (Moore, 1969, 1972, Zarnowitz, 1978), that official inflation forecasts in the "Economic Report of the President" tend to underestimate inflation, just as in the Dutch case. Official U.S. forecasts were made only from 1962 onwards, so that it is not (yet) possible to test statistically whether the underestimation is more severe in one of the two countries. However, the data do suggest that there is a difference of degree. When inflation accelerates, the authorities in both countries tend to underestimate it by about one percent. During periods with little change in the underlying rate of inflation (1962-1968 in the U.S., 1959-1963 and 1972-1976 in the Netherlands), forecast errors in the U.S. are about .4 percentage points, whereas the C.P.B. still underestimates $\hat{p}_c$ by two thirds of a percentage in the C.E.P. and by one percentage point on average in the M.E.V. In any case, the U.S. data provide additional support for rejecting the hypothesis that official forecasts of inflation are biased downwards by chance only.

There are two plausible hypotheses about the reason for the bias in the official Dutch forecasts. First, it may be caused by systematic errors in one or more of the other variables needed for the inflation forecasts. This hypothesis is

rejected by the data. There are no connections between the errors
in the inflation forecasts and the errors in the forecasts of
wages, productivity, import prices or world trade. The lack of
a positive correlation between

$$(\hat{p}_c^{\,0} - \hat{p}_c^{\,F}) \qquad \text{and} \qquad (\hat{w}^0 - \hat{w}^F), \qquad \text{in particular,}$$

indicates that the problem is not a general failure of predicting movements in nominal variables, since the C.P.B. is
quite capable of heavily underpredicting the rate of inflation
in a given year without making a corresponding error in the prediction of the change in nominal wages. It also means that the
errors in $\hat{p}_c^{\,F}$ are not due to systematic low predictions for the
rise in nominal wages that are subsequently inserted in the price
equation of the C.P.B. model. We shall need two separate theories,
one about the bias in the inflation forecasts, another about
the errors in predicting nominal wages. Similarly, the fact that

$$(\hat{p}_c^{\,0} - \hat{p}_c^{\,F}) \qquad \text{and} \qquad (\hat{m}_w^{\,0} - \hat{m}_w^{\,F})$$

are not correlated, means that the errors in predicting $\hat{m}_w$ --
emphasized by Rutten (1978) as a main source of error in the
forecasts -- also fail to explain the *underprediction* of inflation.

The alternative hypothesis about the bias in the inflation
forecasts must be that underprediction is done on purpose by the
Planning Bureau. The forecasts can be systematically wrong,
because the aim of the C.P.B. is not primarily to produce the
best possible forecasts: the Bureau is

"not directly interested in accuracy at all. From its point
of view, announced forecasts are merely means to ends, and
the most efficacious forecasts may be wildly and
deliberately inaccurate. This evidently raises ethical
issues similar to those involved in the suppression of
unfavourable war news or of unpromising medical diagnoses.
It also poses a technical dilemma: to achieve economic objectives it may be necessary to repeatedly hoodwink the

public, but the possibility of hoodwinking derives from
gullibility, and even the most gullible will not be
deceived indefinitely by the same confidence trick"
(Kemp, 1962, p. 496).

This quotation appears in a general discussion of forecasting by
the authorities, but it is applicable to the Dutch situation,
when we make the following pair of assumptions:

1.   When the bias in the forecasts is systematic, this will be
      noticed by the public, but the weight attached to the fore-
      casts remains greater than zero. The public continues to
      attach some value to the price forecasts, either because
      everybody knows how to correct for the bias, or because
      people assume that the advantages of economies of scale in
      forecasting which the C.P.B. possesses outweigh the dis-
      advantage of the known bias (Muth, 1961, points out that
      public forecasts will be useful when the authorities
      dispose of an informational advantage; see also Chiang, 1963).

2.   There are important feedback effects from the forecasts to
      the behaviour of the economic subjects. This does not make
      accurate public forecasting impossible (Grunberg and
      Modigliani, 1954, and Devletoglou, 1961), but it means that
      "if these feedback effects are significant, then the
      accuracy of the forecasts is not only important .... fore-
      casts may become important tools of economic control"
      (Galatin, 1976).

These two assumptions are necessary to explain that systematic bias can occur. We need additional assumptions to explain
why it occurs in the particular case of the inflation forecasts.
The following tentative theory is proposed:

1.   The C.P.B. believes that wages are set by specific negotia-
      tions rather than determined by an anonymous market process.

2.   The wage negotiations are primarily about the increase in
      real wages.

These two assumptions are sufficient to explain why the rate of price increase is systematically underpredicted: the C.P.B. hopes to exercise a favourable influence upon the negotiations about the real wage.

This explanation for the systematic underpredictions of inflation can then be combined with a well-known theory about the bias in the wage forecasts, which maintains that the C.P.B. tends to give too low a figure for $\hat{w}^F$, because the forecast is considered by the unions as an indication of the minimum increase to be achieved in the negotiations. We have argued already that such an assumption about the ritual significance attachted to $\hat{w}^F$ cannot be used to explain the underpredictions of $\hat{p}_c$ as well, because there is no positive correlation between $(\hat{w}^0 - \hat{w}^F)$ and $(\hat{p}_c^{\,0} - \hat{p}_c^{\,F})$.

COMPARING DIFFERENT FORECASTS OF INFLATION

To get an idea of the accuracy of these biased inflations forecasts, we can compare the R.M.S.E.'s to the residual errors in some estimated price equations:

R.M.S.E.

1.5 $(\hat{p}_c^{\,0} - \hat{p}_c^{\,FF})$ M.E.V. forecast in September compared to the preliminary realisation 1½ years later.

1.2 $(\hat{p}_c^{\,0} - \hat{p}_c^{\,F})$ C.E.P. forecast in the first quarter of the forecast year compared to the preliminary realisation in the next C.E.P.

1.3 $(\hat{p}_c^{\,R} - \hat{p}_c^{\,F})$ C.E.P. forecast in the first quarter of the forecast year compared to the definite value.

1.4   residuals 1953-1972 of the reduced form of the annual model (Hasselman et al., 1977).

1.0   residuals 1951-1972 of the structural equation in the annual model (Hasselman, 1976).

S.E.E.

1.1   residuals 1954-1976 of our consumption price
                       equation (4.14) (same value for 1954-1972).

0.9   residuals 1954-1976 of Korteweg's price
                       equation, equation (4.15).

A direct comparison between the performance of the C.P.B.
model and that of the C.P.B. *staff* is impossible, since the model
is estimated with national accounts data, whereas the forecasters
have to work with preliminary data or even forecasts of the
exogenous variables. Whether the forecasters improve upon the
computer output through hand-made adjustments and, if so, by
how much, is impossible to say. But a comparison can be made
between the C.P.B. model and the various monetarist equations.
The figures show that the C.P.B. model has somewhat larger
residuals, when we consider the reduced form of the model, and
that the structural residuals of the C.P.B. price equation are of
the same size as the residuals of our relation. Korteweg's
residuals are the smallest of all. It should be remembered that
the main variable in the C.P.B. equation is the *current* rate of
wage change as against the *lagged* growth rate of money in the
monetarist equations. Also, the C.P.B. model does contain
a variable for "autonomous" changes in p_c, which has a favourable
effect on the size of the residuals.

To conclude this section, a test is presented that
summarizes the relative strengths of the competing approaches
to inflation forecasting. It is only natural to assume that the
C.P.B. has a comparative advantage in the assessment of various
special factors that influence the short-term rate of price
change. Moreover, the Planning Bureau can exploit the information
contained in the recent movements of the index for wholesale
prices, which tends to lead p_c by a few months (Moore, 1969).
On the other hand, the monetarist equation should be useful for
capturing the longer-term sustained rate of inflation. This
hypothesis is supported by the following pair of regressions:

$$\hat{p}_{c,t} = 2.15 + .69 \ (\hat{p}_c^{\ F})_{t-1} \qquad \bar{R}^2 = .48 \quad D.W. = 2.1$$
$$\qquad\qquad (.74) \ (.15) \qquad\qquad\qquad \sigma_u = 2.0 \quad \text{years: } 1955\text{--}1976$$

$$\hat{p}_{c,t} = .95 + 1.03 \ (\hat{M}^e - \hat{gdp}^e)_{t-1.5} \qquad \bar{R}^2 = .59 \quad D.W. = 1.3$$
$$\qquad\qquad (.80) \quad (.18) \qquad\qquad\qquad \sigma_u = 1.8 \quad \text{years: } 1955\text{--}1976$$

Here the forecasts are compared with the actual rate of inflation in the year after the one for which the forecasts are made. Whereas we have seen that $\hat{p}_c^{\ F}$ and the forecasts from the monetarist equation are nearly equal in their usefulness in predicting the current rate of price change, the monetarist forecast is somewhat more informative about inflation in the future.

4.7. SUMMARY

The aim of this chapter was to investigate the usefulness of the theoretical model of chapter 2 in determining inflation and output growth in the Netherlands. The order in which the various equations of the model were discussed, was the same as in the two previous chapters. In section 4.2. we looked at the time series for the growth rates of the Dutch money stock, $\hat{M}$, narrowly defined as the sum of currency and demand deposits. In contrast with the model for the U.S. in chapter 3, the equation for expected money growth $\hat{M}^e$, was not based solely on past rates of money growth; instead, it was assumed that economic agents use information that is available in the financial markets in order to distinguish between two types of unforeseen changes in the money stock. First, there are unanticipated changes in the rate at which the monetary authorities supply new money; these unforeseen supply shifts correspond to the shock terms a_t in the model of chapter 2. Second, there are unforeseen shocks to the demand for money that are expected to be of a temporary and reversible character: agents know that the effects of such shocks will not be permanent when they form their estimates of the expected future rate of monetary growth. Two shifts in the demand for money are discussed extensively in section 4.2.; they are related to short-term substitution between Dutch and foreign money balances.

What the multivariate model for money growth tries to do is to interpret the money stock data with due regard for the fact that the Netherlands is an open economy which maintained a fixed or quasi-fixed exchange rate during the estimation period.

Both the time series for expected money growth and the series for the unanticipated monetary impulse are shown to be important for the Dutch economy. Expected money growth, either just by itself, or with expected output growth subtracted, is capable of explaining two thirds of the variation in the rate of inflation. When some other variables are added, the degree of explanatory power further increases and the residual errors are not larger than 1% on average.

Whereas anticipated money growth determines inflation, un-anticipated money growth is highly significant in regressions for the discrepancy between planned and actual growth of output. As a further illustration of this fact, one regression will be quoted here, to convey the message in a simple way:

$$(4.18) \qquad \hat{gnp}_{NL,t} - \hat{gnp}_{Ge,t} = -2.65 + .35 \{ (\hat{M}_{NL} - \hat{M}_{NL}^e)_t +$$
$$\qquad\qquad\qquad\qquad\qquad (.59)\ (.08)$$

$$- (\hat{M}_{Ge} - \hat{M}_{Ge}) \}_{t-1} + .20\ \text{TREND}$$
$$\qquad\qquad\qquad\qquad\qquad (.04)$$

$$\bar{R}^2 = .65, \qquad \sigma_u = 1.4, \qquad \text{D.W.} = 2.3, \qquad \text{years: } 1954-1976.$$

Here, $\hat{gnp}_{NL}$ and $\hat{gnp}_{Ge}$ represent the real growth rates of gross national product in the two countries, $\hat{M}$ and $\hat{M}^e$ the actual and expected growth rates of money, and TREND a linear trend variable which assumes the value 1 in 1954, 2 in 1955, and so on.

This equation is not concerned with the growth rate of Dutch output, as in the main text, but with the *difference* between the growth rates in the Netherlands and West Germany.

Some factors that are important in both countries can therefore
be left out, which makes equation (4.18) the simplest possible
illustration of the effects of unanticipated money growth. We see
that the differences between the indices of unanticipated money
growth in the two countries are highly significant in explaining
the differential in the growth rates of g.n.p. Regressions for
the growth of output in the Netherlands alone have to contain
more variables, but show a similar influence of unanticipated
money on output.

   After the regressions for production and inflation have
been discussed in sections 4.3. and 4.4., the chapter continues
with a comparison of the results to the related analysis in
Korteweg (1978a, b). Korteweg uses a simpler model for expected
money growth, but includes the expected growth rate of a dollar
index of world prices, $\hat{p}^{*e}$, together with his univariate model
for $\hat{M}^e$ as a second determinant of expected Dutch inflation. His
equations fit the sample period very well, and he avoids the
simultaneous equations bias that may be present in our multivariate model for expected money growth.

   As regards the future, Korteweg's equation should continue
to perform well if the dollar remains a dominant currency in the
world and if Dutch inflation does not diverge too widely from
world inflation, for otherwise the coefficients $\hat{M}^e$ and $\hat{p}^{*e}$ will
start to change. If either condition suddenly failed to apply,
then our equation might be a preferred alternative. On the other
hand, the one-to-one link between domestic money growth and
domestic inflation that is postulated in our equation will break
if the demand for money function becomes very unstable or if
the Dutch monetary authorities follow an exchange rate policy
through which Dutch inflation is determined by the average rate
of inflation in a number of foreign countries. If the recent
creation of the European Monetary Union proves to be a permanent
institution, then this could well mean that the expected growth
rates of the individual money supplies in the participating
countries lose much of their value as a predictor of domestic
inflation.

Section 4.6., finally, is concerned with an analysis of the price forecasts by the Dutch Central Planning Bureau. These forecasts are somewhat less accurate than those of the rational expectations models in Korteweg and in this chapter, although based on more inputs. Furthermore, the official forecasts are systematically biased. We investigate the possible sources of the bias and conclude that the most likely explanation is that the Dutch authorities underpredict inflation with the hope of exercising a moderating influence on wage negotiations.

Chapter 5

STRUCTURAL MODELS AND RATIONAL EXPECTATIONS

"A huge lie is less than a small truth"
D.H. Lawrence: Women in love.

5.1. INTRODUCTION

Throughout this study great emphasis has been laid on the correct modelling of expectations. Both in the theoretical model of chapter 2 and in the empirical work of chapters 3 and 4 it has been assumed that rational behaviour implies rational expectations: economic agents behave as if their subjective forecasts are identical to the forecasts that can be derived from the model. More concretely, let $\hat{y}$ be the growth rate of some variable y, then we assume that the forecasts $\hat{y}_t^e = {}_{t-1}E\hat{y}_t$ are based on all the relevant information available at the end of period t-1, so that forecast errors $(\hat{y}-\hat{y}^e)_t$ are due only to events taking place during period t that were not anticipated. Furthermore, requirements were imposed on the so-called term structure of expectations: for many endogenous variables, notably money, prices, and output, we assumed that the expected rate of growth in the next period would be equal to the expected growth rate in all subsequent periods. To assume otherwise would mean that strings of expectations have to enter the behavioural equations in the model, and that was something we tried to avoid.

The statistical tests in chapters 3 and 4 have confirmed that these theoretical notions can be imposed in practical work. A small model, which satisfied both rational expectations and

the requirement of a constant term structure of expectations for
a number of endogenous variables, was estimated successfully with
annual data for two different countries. Now that we have seen
that rational expectations models are feasible, it seems useful
to ask whether the strict adherence to rational expectations has
not been achieved at too great a cost: the models are tiny when
compared to many traditional macro-econometric models and moreover,
the estimated equations are of the reduced-form type. Both for
the U.S. and the Netherlands a variety of large structural models
have been estimated; even if the modelling of expectations in
them does not conform to rational expectations, would it not be
preferable to improve on the way in which these non-rational
expectations are modelled rather than to build an alternative
model that may be strong on expectations but is so much smaller
and less powerful than the existing structural models?

Systematic evaluation of the merits and demerits of
different types of models (large versus small, structural versus
reduced-form, rational versus non-rational) would require
consideration of the different uses to which econometric models
are put. Some models are designed with the aim of preparing
unconditional forecasts, i.e. what will happen in the future if
there are no changes in economic policy; other models are constructed for conditional forecasting, i.e. simulations of changes
in economic policy. (This dichotomy is sufficient, since a third
use of econometric models that springs to mind, namely to
enable tests of competing economic hypotheses is subsumed in
those two functions.) Also, one would have to relate the usefulness of different types of models to the resources that have to
be spent in their construction. Finally, it is important to know
whether models are suitable for "diagnostic checking", in the
terminology of Box and Jenkins (1970). If a model is so large and
complicated that its dynamic characteristics can be investigated
only through simulations and are no longer derivable from the
properties of the model equations, then it may become very hard
to determine which equations should be changed if the dynamics
of the model and its long-run properties need to be altered.

In the analysis that follows we shall limit ourselves to just one of these issues: the use of different classes of econometric models for simulations of economic policy. There are two sound reasons for concentrating on the calculation of conditional forecasts. First, the rationale for large structural models must be that they have greater potential than small reduced-form models for showing the consequences of changes in policy. This in view of the finding that structural models tend not to emerge with much honour from comparisons with reduced forms or even univariate Box-Jenkins models when unconditional forecasts are compared (see Nelson, 1972, for the first comparison). If big structural models have a comparative advantage, it is presumably in the field of simulations (Bryant, 1975, p. 345).

The second reason for focussing on the formation of conditional forecasts is that the question of rational versus non-rational expectations is more vital for simulations than for the calculation of unconditional forecasts. Many different types of models may produce a good fit over some sample period; therefore we cannot discriminate between "true" and "false" models by comparing the unconditional forecasts. But simulations of economic policy with a variety of models will often produce significantly different results for the same change in policy (the reasons for this will be explored below). We therefore compare the merits of different classes of econometric models in the calculation of policy simulations. This choice of battle ground should avoid the charge that the contest is unfair to the large, structural, models; it ties in also with our interest in alternative ways of calculating expectations.

CONTENTS OF THE REMAINING SECTIONS

In section 5.2. we show that adherence to rational expectations limits the kind of policy changes that can be simulated properly with econometric models. Many policy experiments just cannot be made with econometric models, even if such models do conform to the notion of rational expectations. However, some policy experiments are, in principle, amenable to analysis. For these "admissible" simulations the question arise whether a structural model that is not based on the assumption of rational expectations would give results that differ significantly from the outcomes of a rational expectations model. The issue will be discussed in general terms in section 5.3., where we shall review the well-known phenomenon that a model although generating unbiased forecasts over the estimation period, at the same time produces strings of serially correlated errors when it is simulated to show the effects of changes in economic policy. If that is the case, then the outcomes of the simulation will be systematically wrong, unless we assume that people are irrational and do not try to trim their sails to the wind.

In the next two sections we consider whether it is feasible to take an existing non-rational model and impose rational expectations on it in order to eliminate systematic forecast errors. In the literature, a procedure to achieve this has been proposed by Anderson (1979); if his technique were acceptable, then we could simply adjust available models instead of having to construct new rational expectations models. It will be submitted, however, that Anderson's procedure provides no solution.

After that, a further two sections are concerned with an application of the theoretical analysis to a recent macro-economic model of the Dutch economy. It will be impossible to impose rational expectations on this model, but it so happens that some instances of systematically irrational behaviour can easily be eliminated. Two alterations to the model are discussed in section 5.6. We then investigate in section 5.7. whether a number of experiments performed with this model are admissible in the sense of section 5.2., and proceed to re-calculate the admissible simulations with two versions of the model in which some systematically irrational behaviour has been removed.

The chapter ends with a summary of the main points in section 5.8.

5.2. EXPECTATIONS ABOUT THE EXOGENOUS VARIABLES

In this section and the next we shall attempt to discuss some
consequences of rational expectations for the simulation of
changes in economic policy. The analysis is simply an attempt
to explain in precise terms what is meant by saying that the past
can help to predict the future only if the future does not differ
too much from the past. By way of introduction, suppose we
consider the conduct of economic policy as a game played between
the government and the private sector. In the past, the government actually played many games at the same time: in every period
there were changes in monetary policy, in government expenditure,
possibly in taxation, etc. Our econometric model aims to unscramble these different policies, so that we can separate the
effects of changes in monetary policy from the consequences of
fiscal policy, and so on. Normally, the purpose of a simulation
is to show what happens when, for example, monetary policy is
changed and all other instruments of economic policy are held
fixed. However, such simulations make sense only if the following
two conditions are met:

   First, the government must not start playing a completely
new game, for then the reactions of the private sector cannot
be predicted with an old model (the policy experiment has to be
"admissible"). This is further discussed in the present section,
which elaborates on the argument originally put forward by
Lucas (1976). Second, the government must be the first player in
each game and once it has revealed to the private sector which
game it intends to play, then the model must be such that
economic agents solve their decision problems rationally. There
may be surprise effects at the start of the game, but once everybody knows the rules of the game that is being played, then any
further (unnecessary) forecasting errors by the private sector
would be contrary to our assumption of rational behaviour
(cf. Hansen and Sargent, 1978, p. 5). The reason why systematic
forecasting errors often appear will be discussed in section 5.3.,
together with the consequences for the simulations when such

systematic errors are generated.

Whether a simulation is "admissible" or not in the sense
that will become clear presently, depends on whether the behaviour
of the exogenous variables continues to conform to the patterns
observed in the past. Exogenous variables are present in every
econometric model, for these models are designed as open-loop
systems; some (exogenous) variables have an influence on other
(endogenous) variables, but are not in turn subject to feedback.
Although the model usually fails to provide information about
the future of these exogenous variables, this does not mean that
rational economic agents will not try to anticipate imminent
changes in world trade, tax schedules, or foreign interest rates --
to mention only a few variables that often are exogenous in
macro-econometric models.

Lucas (1976) and subsequently Sargent (1977b) and Prescott
(1977) have pointed out the consequences of assuming that agents
form expectations about future values of the exogenous variables:
many interesting policy experiments just cannot be simulated with
given econometric models. Even if a model is available in which
expectations about the endogenous variables are constructed without fault, then such a "rational expectations" model still cannot
be used for policy experiments that are not "admissible" as
defined below.

DIFFERENT STOCHASTIC MODELS FOR A POLICY INSTRUMENT

We shall attempt to illustrate the argument with a lengthy
example where an imaginary rational expectations model is
simulated to show the effects of several different policies that
can be modelled by means of changing an exogenous policy variable.
Many changes in policy will be seen to be "inadmissible"; our
econometric model cannot predict their numerical effects.

Let us assume for our example, that the rate of corporation
tax, T, is an exogenous variable in some hypothetical model.
T is a determinant of after-tax profits, and it will be assumed
that expected net profits are one of the factors that determine
present investment. Economic subjects have a strong incentive

to try to guess any future changes in the corporation tax rate, because such changes will influence the profitability of present investment projects. In the model, changes in T dot not depend on changes in any other variable; for the real economy, the equivalent assumption is that agents can only base their fore-casts of future changes in T on the past record of changes in corporation tax.

Three simple models for past T are illustrated in the first three lines of table 5.1. In each case, it has been assumed that the rate is presently (year 0) fixed at 45 per cent and that the most recent change in policy took place in year -3. The top line of the table represents the case that an ARIMA (0,0,0) model is appropriate for past T:

$$T_t = 45 + a_t, \text{ with } a_t \text{ uncorrelated noise.}$$

Occasionally, the rate is changed, but all such changes have been temporary, and after one year the rate goes back to 45 per cent. The second line illustrates the ARIMA (0,1,0) model for past T:

$$\Delta T_t = a_t$$

Sometimes the government changes T, and then the new rate remains in effect until a further, as yet, unforeseeable change is effectuated. Changes in policy have always consisted of a per-manent increase or decrease in the level of T, in contrast to the first case when a change in policy was a temporary one-year change in T. The third line stands for yet another pattern over time. Now, each change in T is followed by subsequent changes in the same direction:

$$\Delta (\Delta T)_t = a_t.$$

In this case, a change in tax policy has always meant that the government decides upon some ideal new level for T, and embark on a program of regular yearly changes in the value of T in order

Table 5.1.

Hypothetical experiments with the rate of corporation tax, T

combination	past model for T:	change in year 1:	-5	-4	-3	-2	-1	0	1	2	3	4
				past rate of T					hypothetical future values of T			
(1)	(0,0,0)		45	45	47	45	45	45	44	45	45	45
(2)	(0,1,0)	(a)	41	41	45	45	45	45	44	45	45	45
(3)	(0,2,0)		41	41	42	43	44	45	44	45	45	45
(4)	(0,0,0)		45	45	42	45	45	45	44	44	44	44
(5)	(0,1,0)	(b)	42	42	45	45	45	45	44	44	44	44
(6)	(0,2,0)		25	25	30	35	40	45	44	44	44	44
(7)	(0,0,0)		45	45	50	45	45	45	44	43	42	41
(8)	(0,1,0)	(c)	40	40	45	45	45	45	44	43	42	41
(9)	(0,2,0)		37	37	39	41	43	45	44	43	42	41

Notes:

(a) : temporary change in the level of the tax rate (corresponds to a (0,0,0) model)

(b) : permanent change in the level of the tax rate (corresponds to a (0,1,0) model)

(c) : first of series of yearly changes in the tax rate (corresponds to a (0,2,0) model)

The stochastic model for T remains unchanged for combinations (1) (5) and (9); these combinations are admissible. If the new policy can be viewed as a sequence of two c.q. three unexpected shocks, then combinations (2), (3) and (6) are admissible also. Combinations for which T or ΔT were stationary in the past, but would no longer be stationary in the future are inadmissible; this holds for (4), (7) and (8) (see text for further elaboration).

to gradually achieve the desired rate of corporation tax.

Assume that one of these three basic models for T is the
true one and that economic agents form their expectations of
future T according to this true model.

Let us consider three hypothetical changes in policy that
could occur in year 1; first, a temporary cut in corporation tax;
second, a permanent cut in the tax rate; finally, a systematic
lowering of corporation taxes, so that the tax rate is decreased
by, for example, 1 per cent each year. On the right in table 5.1.,
the three different policies have been illustrated. In the top
three lines of the table, the new policy is assumed to consist
of a one-time decrease in the tax-rate. Similarly, lines 4-6
and 7-9 show the other two proposed policies, once again in
combination with the three stochastic patterns that might have
held for the past. This gives a total of 3 x 3 = 9 different
combinations of past and future.

On the surface, it would appear straightforward to calculate
the effects of all three policies with the help of the model,
since the rate of corporation tax is one of the exogenous
variables. Analysis of the experiments, however, will reveal
difficulties in those cases where a change in policy has to be
simulated with the help of a systematic sequence of shocks in the
stochastic model for T. Whether or not this is the case depends
on the amount of information provided by the government in the
initial year of the new policy. First we shall discuss the
situation in which the government does not try to deceive people,
but announces its intentions for the future when it decides on
a change in policy in year 1. After that, we shall consider the
contrasting case in which the authorities leave it to the market
to guess what their future intentions are.

EXAMPLE OF AN INADMISSIBLE SIMULATION

If the government announces new rates of corporation tax for the
whole future in year 1, then our imaginary model cannot deal with
many combinations of past and future, for example, the combination
in the fourth line of the table. The proposed change in policy is

to lower the tax rate permanently by one percentage point from
45% to 44%. In the past, however, changes in the corporation tax
have always been transitory and have never generated expectations
of a permanently higher after-tax rate of return on investment.
From time to time (most recently in year -3) the government
changed the tax rate, so that the private sector had to revise
its calculations for the current year, but each change was
temporary and reversed in the following years: the change in
year -3 for example, did not mean that investment plans for
years -2, -1 and beyond had to be quickly revised, for the tax-
rate was firmly expected to be set again at 45% from year -2
and beyond.

But consider the change of policy in year 1. Once again,
the private sector has made an expectational error: it expected
the tax rate to remain at 45%, whereas the government decides
on a lower rate. Furthermore, the authorities announce that the
tax rate is to remain at 44 percentage points. Not only did the
private sector make an error for year 1, but its plans for the
more distant future will also require urgent revision in the light
of this permanent change in policy. However, as noted above, this
is the first time that a change in the rate of corporation tax
has implications for subsequent years. As a consequence, the
coefficients of the tax rate in the investment equation of the
model cannot be used to evaluate the effects of this policy
whereby tax rates are permanently lowered to a more favourable
level. For, although the proposed change in year 1 is three times
as small as the changes that occurred in years -3 and -2,
rational firms may well respond much more vigorously to a small
permanent change than to a large but temporary one; it seems
highly implausible that the effect of the permanent change in
year 1 will be three times as small as that of the temporary
change in year -3.

THE REMAINING SIMULATIONS

For similar reasons our imaginary model is useless for combinations (7) and (8). In these two cases also, the government is

contemplating a policy that is qualitatively different from
the policies executed during the estimation period of the model.
In combination (7), there were large, but purely temporary
changes in the past, whereas now a series of small but cumulative
decreases in the tax rate is considered. In experiment (8) the
proposed change for year 1 is also different in nature from the
change that took place in year -3, because in the past changes
in the tax rate did not herald further changes in the same
direction, whereas the new policy will consist of yearly
decreases in the burden of corporation tax. The government
intends to play a different game, thus invalidating the decision
rules for the private sector that are incorporated in the
equations of the model.

Next consider combination (2). We have assumed that the
private sector will be informed in year 1 of the government's
intentions for years 2 and beyond. Therefore, this combination
cannot be analysed either, for we just do not know from the past
how agents will react to the new phenomenon of a change limited
to one year only. Similarly, no existing model provides answers
for the combinations (3) and (6). The only cases that can be
analysed with the model are combinations (1), (5) and (9), in
which the stochastic nature of the series for T does not change.
In combinations (1), (5) and (9) a single shock in the stochastic
model for T in year 1 is sufficient to obtain all future values
of T (until further -- as yet unplanned -- changes in policy take
place). In contrast, all the other combinations require two or
more shocks in the respective models for T, and this means that
there are future shocks which agents can foresee. These
simulations are "inadmissible" for the following reason: it has
been assumed that all shocks that occurred in the past were
unforeseen, and therefore the model cannot be used to calculate
the consequences of something which has never happened yet,
namely a foreseeable shock in the model for T. Policy has to
change in the same way as in the past, otherwise the effects
cannot be calculated with a model that has been estimated over
the past period.

Note that we have neglected any effects on investment of the greater certainty which the government creates by making its intentions known for years 2, 3 etc. If the government announces its intentions for more than one year, and if the private sector trusts such an announcement, then the resulting decrease in uncertainty could have important effects on the economy. The effects of such an announcement, if they were significant, would also invalidate the simulation results even for the admissible combinations (1), (5) and (9); they are disregarded here.

Let us proceed to consider the case in which the private sector is informed only about the current change in the tax rate and has to draw its own inferences about the future. The combinations (1), (5) and (9) remain amenable to analysis. Although the government has not made known its plans for years 2 and beyond, private agents can make a correct guess on the basis of the past, so that a simulation of these three cases with a model estimated over the past is possible. But, on the assumption of uncertainty in year 1 about the value of T in year 2 and subsequent years, the combinations (2), (3) and (6) can also be analysed. Combination (2), for example, now has to be interpreted as a sequence of two shocks: a fall in the tax rate in year 1, and an unexpected increase in year 2. Here, and in combinations (3) and (6), the future pattern of tax rates can be simulated by a finite and unpredictable sequence of unanticipated shocks.

The remaining combinations, (4), (7) and (8), however, still cannot be analysed with the help of the model. In combination (4) a tax rate which is assumed to be stationary is now permanently decreased. Tax rate changes in the past have always been transitory, so that the change in year 1 at first does not generate anticipations of a permanently lower rate that should boost the long-run rate of return on investment. Behaviour in year 1 is still described correctly by the model, but as time goes by, agents must come to realize that an infinite series of shocks

$$a_t = -1 \ (t = 1,2, \ \ldots.)$$

is taking place. Then they will realize that the new policy is
qualitatively different from the way the rate of corporation tax
was manipulated in the past, and predict further negative values
for a_t. When that happens, investment will react more vigorously
to the new tax rate than it used to when taxes were decreased
just for one year. At the same time, the old model loses its
predictive power.

CONCLUSION

The general conclusion from our example must be that simulations
which involve changes in an exogenous variable are not meaningful
in the absence of explicit assumptions about the stochastic behaviour of that variable in the past. When such an assumption has
been made, then one can decide which simulations are admissible
and which future policies can never be simulated, because they
imply a break in the time series model for that exogenous variable.
More accurately: if expectations about future values of some
exogenous variable x are important for the determination of
current behaviour, then simulations that imply changes in x are
admissible only if the proposed future path of x can be described
by a single shock or an unsystematic sequence of shocks a_t in the
univariate Box-Jenkins model that described the evolution of x
in the past. For, a change in policy that must be modelled as
a systematic (e.g. infinite) series of shocks a_t means that
after some time agents can predict values of a_t that have not yet
occurred. At that moment, they will stop behaving in the way they
did when there were no foreseeable future shocks. In particular,
a simulation is inadmissible if it involves a permanent increase
in an x that used to be stationary, or permanent non-zero growth
in an x that was modelled correctly in the past as a random walk.

For this definition of "admissible" to be operational, there
are two requirements. First, a time-series analysis is required
for all those exogenous variables that are changed in the course
of the simulations. Second, the model must discriminate between

the effects of expected changes in the policy instruments on the
one hand and unexpected shifts in these variables on the other.
Rational expectations models, for example those in chapter 3 and 4,
or the models of Korteweg (1978a, b) satisfy both conditions; for
these models it is easy to judge whether a simulation is admissible
or not. In contrast, most if not all structural econometric models
fall short of the two requirements, which means that simulations
with such models, however plausible they may appear, could well
be inadmissible.

5.3. THE MODELLING OF EXPECTATIONS INSIDE THE MODEL

> *"Economic planning is not a game against nature but, rather,
> a game against rational agents."*
> (Kydland and Prescott, 1977).

Whereas section 5.2. was concerned with the formation of expectations about the future of the exogenous variables, in this section
we consider the forecasts of the endogenous variables. All econometric models contain proxies for the expectations of some endogenous
variables: consumption, for example, will depend on expected income, investment on expected profits, wages on expected inflation,
etc. Two aspects of these expectational variables will be discussed:
first, assuming that a certain variable $\hat{y}$ depends on the expected
growth rate of another endogenous variable z, how does one model the
expected growth rate $\hat{z}^e$? Second, granted that in empirical work the
growth rate of y cannot depend on expectations about all the other
endogenous variables in the model, what are the implications of
omitting the expectations about many endogenous variables from the
behavioural equations of a model? Both issues are, once again, considered only in the context of simulated changes in economic policy,
assumed to be admissible in the sense defined in the previous section.

IRRATIONAL EXPRESSIONS FOR EXPECTATIONAL VARIABLES

First, let us discuss the way in which expectations are modelled.
Assume that a model has been specified with due regard for the

fact that unanticipated changes in economic variables can have
effects different from those of an anticipated change in the
same variable. Further assume that expectations for each endogenous variable y are modelled in such a way that the time series
of one-period forecast errors $(y-y^e)$ are uncorrelated white noise
over the estimated period of the model. Even these strong
conditions are insufficient to guarantee that admissible policy
simulations with the model will not lead to systematic prediction errors for one or more endogenous variables. To eliminate
such errors, the model must satisfy a much stronger condition
with respect to the way in which expectations are modelled: we
have assumed that the forecast errors were serially uncorrelated
in the past; we must assume also that the information set on
which the forecasts are based includes every variable that can
contribute to the predictions.

By way of an illustration, suppose that somwehere in an
econometric model the expected growth rate of real g.n.p., $\hat{y}^e$ is
required. In chapter 2 we used the expected growth rate of $\hat{y}$ in
the demand for money function; other plausible possibilities
would be equations for the demand for imports, the rate of real
consumption, the rate of inventory investment and so on. Assume
that in one or more of these equations a distributed lag on past
y is used to model the expected growth of g.n.p.:

$$(5.1) \qquad \hat{y}^e_t = (1-\psi)\,\hat{y}_{t-1} + \psi(1-\psi)\,\hat{y}_{t-2} + \psi^2(1-\psi)\,\hat{y}_{t-3} + \ldots$$

with $0 \leq \psi < 1$

As reviewed in section 2.2., if $\hat{y}$ can be modelled by an ARIMA
(0,1,1) model, then eq. (5.1) is the correct univariate prediction formula. More realistically, if the final-form equation
for $\hat{\Delta y}$ would be

$$\hat{\Delta y}_t = (\beta_1 - \gamma_1 B).(\hat{x}_1 - \hat{x}^e_1)_t + (\beta_2 - \gamma_2 B)(\hat{x}_2 - \hat{x}^e_2)_t + \ldots (1-\theta B)a_t$$

with $\hat{x}_1$, $\hat{x}_2$, $\ldots$ the growth rates of the exogenous variables that influence g.n.p., then a value for ψ can be found for which the univariate model (5.1) produces serially uncorrelated forecasts, for the sum of two or more moving average processes is again a moving average process (section 2.3.).

Assume for concreteness that the final-form equation for $\Delta \hat{y}$ is:

(5.2) $\Delta \hat{y}_t = \beta_1 (1-B) \ (\hat{M}-\hat{M}^e)_t + (1-\theta B) a_t,$

with $\beta_1 > 0;\ 0 < \theta < 1$

Here, $(\hat{M}-\hat{M}^e)$ represents the unanticipated growth in money which has a purely temporary effect on output. The serially uncorrelated errors a_t stand for all other influences on output, which do have some lasting effect on the growth rate $\hat{y}$, so that the average "level" of $\hat{y}$ can change over time.

In this particular, simple case, the correct value of $(1-\psi)$ would be a weighted average of 0 and $(1-\theta)$ with weights that depend on the variances of the two series of innovations $(\hat{M}-\hat{M}^e)_t$ and a_t (Box and Jenkins, 1970, p. 121). Forecasts of $\hat{y}$ with the univariate model (5.1) are sub-optimal but unbiased as long as the relative "mix" of monetary and non-monetary shocks does not change. Therefore, eq. (5.1) may well be adequate for unconditional forecasts, i.e. predictions of what would happen when the future is nothing but an extrapolation of the past with no changes in economic policy. But the univariate model does not exploit the fact that the monetary disturbances have a temporary effect on $\hat{y}$, whereas non-monetary shocks influence the "level" of $\hat{y}$ with a proportionality factor $(1-\theta)$. Instead, it is now assumed that every shock influences future income growth with a proportionality factor $(1-\psi)$, which is too high for monetary shocks and too small (for $1-\theta > 1-\psi$) for non-monetary disturbances.

For unconditional forecasting, it may be appropriate to assume that agents do not know exactly which shocks have just occured when they form expectations for the next period or,

alternatively, that they economize on effort when they forecast future income growth and do not bother to investigate the
precise "mix" of shocks that have hit the economy in the most
recent period. In both cases, agents will predict future income
growth on the basis of past income growth only. However, a model
which assumes univariate income forecasts may become systematically wrong for simulations of changes in policy (i.e. conditional
forecasting). A monetary shock, for example, can no longer be
simulated, for the univariate expectations of future income
growth will always be too high. Market participants must come
to realize this, for it has been assumed that they pay attention
to past income growth when they form their expectations, and they
will be quick to change their behaviour, once they have noted the
systematic element in their forecast errors.

In our hypothetical example, the reduced-form equation for
$\Delta\hat{y}$ contained just one exogenous variable, $\hat{M}$, plus an error term,
so that the obvious remedy against these biased forecasts of $\hat{y}$
would be to replace the univariate formula (5.1) by the correct
expression for $\hat{y}^e$:

$$\hat{y}^e_t = \hat{y}^e_{t-1} + (1-\theta)a_{t-1}$$

(see section 2.3.). However, in a more realistic setting, the
true final-form equation for as important a variable as g.n.p.
could involve a great number of explanatory variables, so that it
would be not feasible to proxy $\hat{y}^e$ by the optimal forecasts that
could be derived from the model itself. It follows that the
proxy for $\hat{y}^e$, however well it performs over the past, is wrong
for all policy simulations that involve changes in one or more
of the variables that appear in the final-form for $\Delta\hat{y}$ (which
simply means that the forecasts of $\hat{y}^e$ will usually be unacceptable for all simulations).

OMITTED EXPECTATIONAL VARIABLES

The discussion so far has been based on the assumption that the
model fully reflects rational behaviour and that the only aspect

in which it is deficient is the modelling of expectations of the
endogenous variables. However, there is a second consequence of
the assumption of rational behaviour: we have raised the issue
whether an expectation, say $\hat{z}^e$, in a given equation has been
modelled correctly, but there is also the prior problem whether
it is rational to assume that economic agents consider the future
growth of $\hat{z}$ only and neglect the expected future course of all
those other variables that are excluded from the equation. Is it
reasonable to assume, as many structural models do, that exporters
base their actions on the expected growth rate of world trade,
whereas entrepreneurs look at the future course of profits only,
and consumers are only interested in their own future earnings?
After all, many goods can be exported, invested or consumed, so
that even if we make a conceptual distinction between exporters,
entrepreneurs and consumers, all three categories of transactors
still have to meet in the same markets. Many econometric models,
however, appear to assume that there is a strict compartmenti-
zation between the different classes of transactors.

    Such differentiation between various groups of transactors
obscures the fact that exporters, investors and consumers will
frequently trade in the same markets. Price and quantity in each
market will be functions of all the relevant information possessed
by all agents who operate in it (Liu, 1960, Sargent and Sims,
1977). It is profoundly irrational to compartmentalize like this
in the formation of expectations. Once we realize this fact, we
can hardly use the results of simulations with such a model to
criticize reduced-form models that assume rational expectations.
We have to view with particular suspicion evidence taken from
simulations with large, structural models when such evidence
claims that a change in, for example, monetary policy affects
various markets consecutively (first the financial markets, then
the market for consumption goods, finally the market for investment goods). The issue is of more than academic interest, for
much policy advice is based on simulations with large structural
models. If such models indicate that the economy takes many years
to adjust after an external shock, then there clearly is more

scope for economic activism, than if simulations show that the
economy quickly reaches a new equilibrium path. In the latter
case, the argument for "Keynesian" monetary and fiscal policy
would be much weaker.

CONCLUSIONS

In this section we have considered two types of problems that
arise with expectations about the future of the endogenous
variables. A first batch of problems is concerned with the way
in which a given expectation was modelled. We saw that a non-
rational proxy (for example a univariate model) may work well
over the sample period, but will be wrong when the model is used
to calculate the effects of changes in economic policy.

A second set of problems arises when we consider whether
each behavioural equation of a given model contains the proper
number of expectational variables. It appears doubtful to assume
-- as many models do -- that the behaviour of suppliers in a
market is based on the expected growth of some z_1, whereas the
demanders in the same market neglect $\hat{z}_1^e$, but base their actions
on the expected future course of z_2 (Miller, 1976, Sims, 1979).

Both sets of problems are interesting and important; however, the first type is much more suited for empirical investigation. If a certain expectation has been modelled in a non-
rational way, then we can attempt to replace the irrational
proxy by another, more rational, expression. This type of local
surgery will be discussed and executed in the remaining sections
of the present chapter.

The second type of problem is far more intractable, as noted
by Liu (1960). On the one hand, if we extend the behavioural equations of a non-rational model and include all the expectational
variables that should be relevant on theoretical grounds, then
there will be severe identification problems. On the other hand,
limiting the number of expectational variables to just a few
in each equation will imply irrational behaviour, if not for the
past, then certainly for the simulations. It is easy to point out
that many existing econometric models embody this kind of

irrationality, but hard to devise ways of countering it short of
altering the original model beyond recognition. For that reason
only -- not because the issue is unimportant -- we shall limit
the empirical analysis that follows to the first set of problems:
how to improve on the non-rational modelling of expectations in
a given equation that is acceptable in all other respects as
a valid decision rule for rational economic agents.

5.4. RATIONAL FORECASTS FROM NON-RATIONAL MODELS?

We have seen in the previous two sections that policy simulations
with econometric models can easily imply irrational behaviour,
even if the model generates unbiased expectations over the
estimation period. First, information is required about the
stochastic behaviour of the relevant exogenous variables before
one can decide whether a proposed simulation is at all admissible
(section 5.2.). Second, expectations that are calculated in the
model have to be based on all the available information since
expectations based on a sub-optimal information set (for
instance: on past values of the variable to be forecast only)
can be systematically wrong when changes in policy are simulated
(section 5.3.).

Many existing econometric models fall short of these
requirements: information about the stochastic properties of the
exogenous variables is typically not provided, and various non-
rational proxies are used to express expectations about future
values of the endogenous variables.

The question thus arises whether it is possible to take
an existing econometric model and make it conform to rational
expectations. If there is a method for imposing rational expectations on non-rational models, then we can profit directly
from the accumulated knowledge that is embodied in existing
models and there is no need to go to the trouble of constructing
new models. The rational expectations models of chapters 3 and 4
may retain some interest as expository devices, but it is clear

that these tiny structures will be no match for a rational
expectations version of a large structural model.

This section and section 5.5. will be concerned with the
difficulties encountered when one tries to impose rational expectations on a given non-rational model. Our conclusion will be
that it is impossible to go all the way towards rational expectations, but that it may be feasible to remove some instances of
irrationality from a non-rational model. Obviously, it would be
preferable to study the bias in a non-rational model by constructing a new version of the model that did fully conform to
rational expectations. That being an impossibility, however, we
have to rely on a more limited type of experiment that can be
executed successfully.

This would be a more modest enterprise, but still well worth
undertaking, since it enables one to test hypotheses about the
extent and the nature of the bias inherent in simulations with
a non-rational model. For, consider the hypothesis that a cavalier
attitude towards the formation of expectations does no great harm,
so that a large structural model with sub optimal formation of expectations is worth more than models as those of chapters 3 and 4
in which strict adherence to rational expectations has been given
priority over the estimation of structural equations and the de-
tailed modelling of allocative processes. If this hypothesis is
correct, then it follows that a limited number of improvements in
the modelling of expectations in a given large structural model
must not make a significant difference to the outcomes of simulations performed with that model. We shall test the hypothesis (and
reject it) for a structural model of the Dutch economy in
section 5.7.

The alternative hypothesis, viz. that the way in which expectations are modelled does matter, was, of course, the central
assumption that underlay the work in chapters 2-4 above. This hypothesis will obtain some support from the experiments in section 5.7.

ANDERSON'S TWO-STEP PROCEDURE FOR IMPOSING RATIONAL EXPECTATIONS
Let us first consider why the more ambitious task of constructing

a rational expectations version of a given econometric model
will be impossible. It will be convenient to organize the discussion around a proposal by Anderson (1979) who purports to
alter non-rational models so that they can be simulated under
the assumptions of rational expectations. Anderson's procedure
has two stages: first, an analysis of simulations with a model
in order to determine whether it generates expectations that are
non-rational; second, a method for altering non-rational models,
so that they conform to rational expectations.

The test procedure is as follows: suppose that one or more
equations in a model contain the expected growth rate of some
endogenous variable y. In order to determine whether the expectations of $\hat{y}$ are modelled in conformity with rational expectations, we perform one or more arbitrary simulations with
the model. If the values of $\hat{y}_t^e$ are not systematically different
from the actual values of $\hat{y}_t$ as calculated by solving the model,
then we conclude that the series for $\hat{y}^e$ is in agreement with
rational expectations. If, however, there are systematic discrepancies between the expectations $\hat{y}_t^e$ and the model's own
solution path for $\hat{y}_t$, then we conclude that $\hat{y}^e$ has been proxied
by an expression that is contrary to rational expectations.

If the test procedure has led to the conclusion that an
expectational variable $\hat{y}^e$ is unacceptable from the point of
view of rational expectations, then Anderson proposes that we
make the following alteration to the model. We replace $\hat{y}_t^e$ with
the actual growth rate $\hat{y}_t$ in all those equations in which $\hat{y}_t^e$ is
present. Thus forecast errors are completely eliminated; the
value for the expected growth rate of y is equal to the realized
value of $\hat{y}$ as calculated by the complete model.

Assume, for instance, that the equation for the increase
in nominal wages contains the expected rate of inflation proxied
in the original model by a distributed lag on actual rates of
price change. Anderson substitutes the actual rate of price
change for this distributed lag so that wage increases are now
based on a correct assessment of the current rate of inflation.
If the model requires many expectational variables, then

"rationality in the forecasting of other important variables can be handled in the same way" (p. 78).

This is a systematic procedure, which ostensibly opens a practical way of imposing rational expectations on existing econometric models. But Anderson's method has two disadvantages: first, it neglects the distinction of section 5.2. between admissible and inadmissible simulations; second, it constitutes an attempt to do too much, namely to impose perfect foresight rather than rational expectations.

TESTS OF ANDERSON'S PROCEDURE

In the remainder of this section, we shall discuss these consequences of the procedure by applying it to a model that conforms already to rational expectations. Admittedly, this is an unrealistic context, but one that is nevertheless well suited to bring out the difficulties with Anderson's approach. For, we can investigate whether the test for irrationality and the proposed alterations to non-rational models have the property of leaving a model unaltered if it already satisfies the requirement of rational expectations. The tests that follow are reminiscent of those performed sometimes with smoothing procedures of seasonal adjustment filters, where if $A(x)$ represents a filter that is applied to some time series x, one often requires:

$$A(A(x)) = A(x)$$

In words: if we apply a method for seasonal adjustment to a deseasonalized series, then it should leave the (already adjusted) series unaltered. Does Anderson's procedure also have this invariance property when it is applied to a model that conforms already to rational expectations?

ANDERSON'S PROCEDURE APPLIED TO A RATIONAL EXPECTATIONS MODEL

Consider the following equation, that was estimated in chapter 3:

$$(5.3) \qquad \hat{p}_t = .036 + 1.0(\hat{M}_t^e - \hat{y}_t^e) + .085(\hat{g} - \hat{g}^e)_t$$

This is our inflation equation (3.11) for the U.S., with $\hat{p}^e$ replaced by its determinant according to the equation of exchange, and $\hat{y}^e$ assumed to be constant for the sake of simplicity. $\hat{p}$ represents the rate of change of the g.n.p. deflator, $\hat{M}^e$ the expected rate of growth of the domestic U.S. money stock, $\hat{y}^e$ the (constant) expected rate of growth of real g.n.p. and $\hat{g}$ the annual rate of growth of real expenditure on goods and services by the federal government. When this equation is combined with the expectational models for $\hat{M}^e$ and $\hat{g}^e$ that were estimated in chapter 3, then the resulting three-equation model constitutes a small rational expectations model for the determination of inflation in the U.S.

We shall perform a number of simulations with this model, apply Anderson's test to these simulations and change the model if the test shows systematic differences between the actual and the expected values of $\hat{M}$, $\hat{g}$, and $\hat{p}$. Four tests will be performed: two admissible and two inadmissible simulations with respect to $\hat{g}$ and $\hat{M}$. Whether simulations are admissible depends on the stochastic model for the relevant exogenous variable; these models were (see chapter 3 for further details):

$$\hat{g}_t = \hat{g}_{t-1} + a_{1,t} \rightarrow \hat{g}^e_t = \hat{g}_{t-1}$$

$$\Delta\hat{M}_t = (1 - .59B)a_{2,t} \rightarrow \hat{M}^e_t = .41\hat{M}_{t-1} + .41x.59\hat{M}_{t-2} +$$

$$+ .41x(.59)^2\hat{M}_{t-3} + ...$$

Our first simulation consists of a permanent increase in the growth rate of g by one percentage point that takes place in year 1. This experiment can be modelled by a single, unexpected shock $a_{1,1} = 1$; it is therefore admissible. Both $\hat{g}$ and $\hat{p}$ will be underpredicted for year 1, but after that no further forecast errors occur. The second simulation concerns a single unexpected monetary impulse of one percentage point in year 1. This change in monetary policy will lead to a permanently higher growth rate of the money stock. The new growth rate of $\hat{M}$ is predicted

correctly from year 2 onwards and equation (5.3) will give the
corresponding rational forecasts of inflation.

In neither of these simulations do we get strings of
serially correlated prediction errors, so that there is no
reason to question the correctness of the forecast models for
$\hat{g}$, $\hat{M}$ or the endogenous variable $\hat{p}$. The test procedure has shown
-- correctly -- that there is no need to alter the equation.

Let us next consider two inadmissible simulations with
eq. (5.3) (Anderson does not distinguish between admissible and
inadmissible simulations; therefore inadmissible simulations may
well be conceived). Once again we follow Anderson's method: first
we perform the simulations with the original model and the original
formulas for the calculation of expectations; then if systematic
forecast errors occur, we replace the ostensibly non-rational
forecasts by the actual realisations and perform the simulation
again, this time with a "rational expectations" version of
the original model.

As a first example, consider what happens when we simulate
yearly decreases in the rate of growth of government expenditure.
Assume, for example that $\hat{g}$ was 10% in year 0 and that it is
proposed to lower g to 0 per cent per annum over a period of
ten years. When this inadmissible simulation is performed, both
$\hat{g}$ and $\hat{p}$ are overpredicted for all years of the simulation. Consequently, Anderson's procedure would lead to substituting $\hat{g}_t$
for $\hat{g}_t^e$, which would mean dropping the term $(\hat{g}-\hat{g}^e)_t$ from the
price equation. There is now perfect foresight with respect to $\hat{g}$
and changes in $\hat{g}$ no longer affect the rate of price changes:

$$\hat{p}_t = .036 + 1.0(\hat{M}_t^e - \hat{y}_t^e)$$

This would be a "rational expectations" version of equation (5.3).
Note that the original equation has been altered, not because
there is anything wrong with the modelling of expectations in
the U.S. model, but because an inadmissible simulation has been
performed.

Our second inadmissible simulation is concerned with

a systematic decrease in the rate of money growth, spread out over a number of years. Let $\hat{M}$ be 10% in year 0 and assume that the effects are simulated of lowering $\hat{M}$ to 9% in year 1, to 8% in year 2 and so on, until $\hat{M}$ reaches 2% in year 8 after which money growth is held constant. This simulation results in strings of negative forecast errors for both $\hat{M}$ and $\hat{p}$; the forecasts for $\hat{M}$ are too high for all future periods (also after year 8) and inflation is thus overpredicted in every period.

According to Anderson, we should eliminate these forecast errors by replacing $\hat{M}_t^e$ with the actual realized rate of money growth $\hat{M}_t$. Equation (5.3) would become:

$$(5.4) \qquad \hat{p}_t = .036 + \hat{M}_t - \hat{y}_t^e + .085(\hat{g} - \hat{g}^e)_t$$

Combining this second alteration with the substitution of $\hat{g}_t$ for $\hat{g}_t^e$, we would get:

$$(5.5) \qquad \hat{p}_t = .036 + \hat{M}_t - \hat{y}_t^e$$

Equation (5.5) is the "rational expectations" version of our U.S. inflation regression. This equation can now be used for every imaginable simulation of changes in $\hat{M}$ and $\hat{g}$ and will never generate any forecasting errors. But one can no longer claim that the equation is derived from empirical work on U.S. data, nor that it is grounded in economic theory. One variable, $(\hat{g} - \hat{g}^e)$, which was significant in the past, has been deleted from the equation, and the lag of one year in the effect of changes in money growth on inflation has been replaced by a one-to-one contemporaneous effect of $\hat{M}_t$ on $\hat{p}_t$, something which has not been observed during the estimation period.

CONCLUSION

On the basis of the four simulations that have been considered, we can now evaluate Anderson's suggestion to replace $_{t-1}E(\hat{y})_t$ by the model solution for $\hat{y}_t$ in all those cases where a simulation with the original model produces correlated forecast errors for

a variable $\hat{y}^e$. Clearly, there is the danger that unwarranted
changes might be made in the model, namely if an inadmissible
simulation is used to test whether the original model produces
serially correlated errors. This happened in the second pair of
simulations that we performed with the U.S. inflation equation.
This equation, although fully consistent with rational expectations, gives serially correlated forecast errors, if the
simulation is inadmissible. The conclusion must be that only
admissible simulations can be used to investigate whether the
original model produces forecasts that are systematically biased
and must be eliminated through alterations in the model.

5.5. MAKING CHANGES IN NON-RATIONAL MODELS

In the previous section we applied Anderson's two-step procedure
to a model that did conform already to rational expectations,
in order to investigate its properties. We found that the test
for irrationally can only be used in the case of admissible
simulations. In this section we shall assume that one or more
admissible simulations have been performed with a given econometric model and that systematic forecast errors have been
observed. In that case, we must conclude that the model does not
conform to rational expectations.

Assume for the sake of simplicity that a certain simulation
consisted of a single unexpected change in a policy variable x
that occurred in the initial period of the simulation. According
to Anderson, in that case all the non-rational expectations, $\hat{y}_t^e$,
need to be replaced by the actual values $\hat{y}_t$, as calculated with
the complete model. However, it appears preferable not to do this
for the initial period of the simulation, when the change in x
must come as a surprise to all economic agents, but to substitute
$\hat{y}_t$ for $\hat{y}_t^e$ beginning with period 2 of the simulation. In that case,
we have achieved rationality for period two and beyond, and the
single forecast error in the initial period is not contrary to
rational expectations, but represents the unavoidable error that

is made when government policy differs from what was expected
before the start of that period.

However, two problems remain that will invalidate the claim
that we are now performing the simulation under rational expectations. One problem concerns the term structure of expectations;
the second problem arises when the distinction between expected
and unexpected changes in economic variables is neglected, as it
tends to be in many non-rational models. We discuss both
arguments in order.

THE TERM STRUCTURE OF EXPECTATIONS

Expectations for periods in the distant future are relevant,
because what is usually required in a behavioural equation is
not the expected growth rate for the current period, but rather
some weighted average of the complete term structure of expectations. Many existing econometric models are not explicit on this
issue, so that one does not know whether some distributed lag on
past $\hat{y}$ is meant as a proxy of $_{t-1}E\hat{y}_t$ or whether it represents
a discounted average of $_{t-1}E\hat{y}_t$, $_{t-1}E\hat{y}_{t+1}$, $_{t-1}E\hat{y}_{t+2}$, ... etc.
In the latter case, one may well make matters worse if one re-
places a distributed lag on past $\hat{y}$ by the single term $\hat{y}_t$ for
the simulations. For example, how should one model a rational
expectation of the level of profits in an investment equation?
A distributed lag on past profits can lead to systematic forecasting errors. Substituting current profits for expected profits
(Anderson's approach) would only be correct with perfect foresight and with a term structure of expectations about future
profits in which current profits can represent the discounted
present value of future profits.

In the rational expectations models of chapters 3 and 4,
this difficulty did not arise, because all the expectations
$_{t-1}E\hat{y}_t$, $_{t-1}E\hat{y}_{t+1}$, $_{t-1}E\hat{y}_{t+2}$, ... etc. were always identical.
This simple term structure of expectations was achieved by
specifying reduced form equations (more precisely: final form
equations) which satisfied certain formal properties that were
discussed in section 2.3. above. By contrast, structural econo-

metric models are generally constructed without regard for the
term structure of expectations for the endogenous variables,
so that simulations with such models will produce complicated
patterns over time for some if not all endogenous variables.
Only under very restrictive assumptions about the term structure
of expectations, will the current value $\hat{y}_t$ represent the
(properly weighted) average of all the expectations for the
future, and no structural models seem to exist that satisfy these
requirements. It follows that rational expectations cannot be
imposed on these models by simply substituting the actual current
values as proxies for expectations.

UNSCRAMBLING MIXTURES OF EXPECTED AND UNEXPECTED EFFECTS

A second difficulty with improving the formation of expectations
in non-rational models arises when an equation of the model
contains a distributed lag on some variable $\hat{x}$, that is a mixture
of expected and unexpected influences of changes in x. The first
of the two models discussed in Anderson (1979) provides an
illustration. In the original model, only one expectation is
mentioned explicitly, namely the expected rate of inflation, $\hat{p}^e$.
Anderson imposes rational expectations with respect to prices and
replaces the proxy for $\hat{p}^e_t$ by the actual value $\hat{p}_t$ (we assume that
the simulation is admissible and disregard difficulties arising
from the term structure of expectations; we also neglect the
question, discussed earlier, whether $\hat{p}^e_t$ can be equal to $\hat{p}_t$ for
the initial period of the simulation).

No further changes are made in the model, which is now
assumed to satisfy rational expectations with respect to prices.
But, in one of the other (unchanged) equations of the model,
the change in nominal national income is a function of current
and lagged changes in the money stock (and other variables disregarded here). The shape of the lag function has been estimated
over a period during which economic agents did not possess perfect
foresight regarding changes in money and there is no basis for
assuming that the lag will remain the same when perfect foresight
is assumed. For the relative change in nominal income is the sum

of the relative changes in real income and in prices, and the
analysis in chapters 2-4 has shown that expected and unexpected
changes in money differ in their effects both on real income
and on prices.

   The model is now inconsistent. On the one hand, Anderson
has rejected the original rule for forecasting inflation, and
replaced it by a different forecasting scheme: the model solution
for the current value of $\hat{p}_t$. That can only be correct if agents
know the correct values of $\hat{M}_t$, the current rates of change in the
money stock. At the same time, the solution for $\hat{p}_t$ is calculated
with the help of an equation that represents a decision rule for
economic agents that is valid only under uncertainty over recent
money growth, viz. the equation for nominal national income. Having
altered the rule for the formation of inflationary expectations,
Anderson should also have eliminated all the effects of unexpected
increases in money on real income and prices from the equation
for nominal national income. But this is not done in Anderson
(1979), simply because the original model does not distinguish
between expected and unexpected changes in the money stock.

   The problem is, of course, that if the original model
includes distributed lags on explanatory variables that represent
both expected and unexpected influences, then there is no way to
separate these two effects afterwards. To see this, consider the
following equation, a simplified version of Korteweg's inflation
regression for the Netherlands:

(5.6) $\hat{p}_t = .32\ \hat{M}^e_{t-5} + .12\ (\hat{M}-\hat{M}^e)_t + \ldots$

In eq. (5.6) the terms in $\hat{M}^e$ and $(\hat{M}-\hat{M}^e)$ are as in eq. (4.15)
above; the constant term and all the other explanatory variables
have been omitted. In Korteweg's model, $\hat{M}^e_t$ is given by the univariate model

$$\hat{M}^e_t = \hat{M}_{t-1}$$

Substitution gives:

(5.7) $\hat{p}_t = .12\ \hat{M}_t + .04\ \hat{M}_{t-1} + .16\ \hat{M}_{t-2} + \dots$

However, without the information that $\hat{M}^e$ is proxied by $\hat{M}_{t-1}$, eq. (5.7) could equally well stand for a number of other combinations of $\hat{M}^e$ and $(\hat{M}-\hat{M}^e)$, for example:

(5.8) $\hat{p}_t = .57\ \hat{M}^e_t + .12\ (\hat{M}-\hat{M}^e)_t + \dots$

with $\hat{M}^e_t$ given by

(5.9) $\hat{M}^e_t = .089\ \hat{M}_{t-1} + .356\ \hat{M}_{t-2}$

Substituting eq. (5.9) in eq. (5.8) also gives eq. (5.7); to reject eq. (5.8) one needs to know the correct stochastic model for $\hat{M}$.

In this example what was involved was a distributed lag on an exogenous variable, so that a univariate Box-Jenkins analysis would be sufficient to calculate expressions for the expected and unexpected changes. However, if a model contains a distributed lag on some endogenous variable in which the distinction between expected and unexpected effects has been neglected, then it will become much more difficult to unscramble the two.

There is regrettably no short cut to rational expectations. It will be necessary to analyse the stochastic structure of all the exogenous variables that play a part in the simulations. This is the only way to find out whether a proposed simulation is admissible or not, and whether expected changes, unexpected changes or some mixture of the two should appear in the behavioural equations of the model. Only after this has been done, does it become possible to remove from the model some irrationality in the formation of expectations. We shall attempt to illustrate this in the next two sections. However, the goal of imposing full rationality remains elusive, because of the difficulties encountered with the term structure of expectations: the problems have been solved for small reduced form models, but not (yet) for large structural models.

5.6. IRRATIONALITY IN A MODEL OF THE DUTCH ECONOMY

It will generally be impossible to take an existing non-rational
structural model and impose rational expectations on it. But, to
quote Macaulay (1829): "If we cannot set up truth, it is something
to pull down error". A partial attempt to make an existing non-
rational model more rational will not teach us much about the real
world, but can teach us something about the traditional structural
models which play an important part in policy making and in
shaping opinions on how the real economy works. At least the experiments by Anderson (1979) and in this chapter show how
sensitive the outcomes of such models are to changes in the way
expectations are modelled.

For our experiments we shall employ the most recent and
complete model of the Dutch economy (Knoester, 1979). This model
may be less known than those of the Central Planning Bureau, but
it has the important advantages, first, of being estimated with
recent data and second, of incorporating a monetary sector.
Knoester's model contains 18 stochastic equations, estimated
with annual data for 1953-1975 and a further 40 identities and
defintions. A listing of the model can be found in Knoester
(1979); more information about the individual equations is available in Knoester (1974, 1975) and Knoester en Buitelaar (1975).

Although the importance of expectations for economic
behaviour is repeatedly stressed, nevertheless when the author
models an expectational effect, he always proceeds as follows:
the rate of increase of some variable y is claimed to depend,
other things being equal, on the expected change in a variable x,
but no evidence to support this claim is presented, apart from
the fact that current and/or lagged values of x contribute to
the statistical fit of the equation for y. If now x were an
exogenous variable, then one could develop time series for $\hat{x}^e$
and $(x-\hat{x}^e)$ and respecify the equation for $\hat{y}$ with the single
distributed lag on $\hat{x}$ replaced by some combination of $\hat{x}^e$ and
$(x-\hat{x}^e)$. However, in all instances where Knoester mentions the
influence of expectations, they always concern expectations of

an endogenous variable. We have seen in section 5.3. how difficult it is to derive series for the expected and unexpected changes in endogenous variables. Furthermore, it is not clear to which period the expectations refer, so that all the problems with the term structure of expectations that were discussed in section 5.5. are present. Increases in investment, for example, are said to depend on the expected increase in profits, but what does that mean in the case of a simulation (to be described below) in which there is an initial increase in profits, followed by a subsequent fall below the original level? It is clear that what matters is discounted profits over the complete lifetime of the investment, but what is the correct discounting factor in a model with endogenous real interest rates that change in a significant way when the model is simulated?

UNEXPECTED CHANGES IN THE MONETARY BASE

The model also contains instances where only the unexpected changes in a certain variable have an effect. In such a case it will prove to be easier to impose more rationality on the model. Some equations in Knoester's model contain the following expression as one of the explanatory variables:

$$((\hat{B}^r - \hat{V})_t - .5(\hat{B}^r - \hat{V})_{t-1})_{-1}$$

with B^r the monetary base and V total final sales in current prices. Because $\hat{B}^r$ fluctuates much more than $\hat{V}$, one can regard changes in this so-called monetary disequilibrium indicator (in short: indicator) as being proximately determined in the monetary sector of the model. Knoester's inclusion of the indicator in the equations for consumption and investment thus provides a transmission mechanism between the monetary and the real sectors of the model.

The author stresses that it is unexpected changes in $(\hat{B}^r - \hat{V})$ that influence consumption and investment (Knoester and Buitelaar, 1975, p. 499, footnote 30). This is confirmed by a Box-Jenkins analysis of the time series for $(\hat{B}^r - \hat{V})$, which shows that the indicator is a univariate proxy for the unexpected change in $(\hat{B}^r - \hat{V})$, lagged one period. A first-order auto-regressive model

$$(1-\psi B) \ (\hat{B}^r - \hat{V})_t = a_t,$$

with a_t white noise, results in a value for ψ close to 0.5, which Knoester presumably has found by attempting to maximize the con-tribution of the indicator in the four equations in which it is included. When these equations are re-estimated with the uni-variate models for both

$$((\hat{B}^r - \hat{V})^e)_{t-1} \ \text{and} \ ((\hat{B}^r - \hat{V}) - (\hat{B}^r - \hat{V})^e)_{t-1}$$

instead of the original monetary disequilibrium indicator, then the coefficients of

$$((\hat{B}^r - \hat{V}) - (\hat{B}^r - \hat{V})^e)_{t-1}$$

are indeed very similar to the coefficients of the indicator in Knoester's original equations, and the coefficient of

$$((\hat{B}^r - \hat{V})^e)_{t-1}$$

is never significant. These findings strongly suggest that, in contrast with the case where both expected and unexpected changes in some variable x have an influence on y (section 5.5.), we now have the simpler situation that unexptected changes only in x have an effect on y. We reject the implausible (but theoretically possible) alternative that actual changes in $(\hat{B}^r - \hat{V})$ influence consumption and investment with a peculiar lag pattern (see Sargent, 1976a, b, and Neftci and Sargent, 1978, for the way in which a definitive test might be conducted).

It was noted in section 5.3. that univariate models for the expected or unexpected changes in endogenous variables may be quite adequate for the period over which the model is estimated,

but will be wrong for almost all simulations, the reason being
that the univariate model is no longer an unbiased simplified
version of the true multivariate model from which the expectations should be derived. This is also the case with the expression

$$(\hat{B}^r - \hat{V})_t - .5 \ (\hat{B}^r - \hat{V})_{t-1}$$

that represents unexpected changes in $(\hat{B}^r - \hat{V})$. During the
estimation period, this univariate model produces unbiased errors.
But, when the simulations are conducted, we must assume that
rational economic agents will make forecast errors only in those
years in which they are surprised by changes in economic policy
or other unanticipated events. In the absence of unforeseen
events, rational agents will be capable of correctly predicting
all endogenous variables.

All the simulations in Knoester (1979) are concerned with
a single innovation in economic policy, assumed to have taken
place in 1976. Depending on the nature of the change in policy,
there can be large or small forecasting errors in $(\hat{B}^r - \hat{V})$ for
1976, the initial year of the simulation. We can use the uni-
variate expression for $(\hat{B}^r - \hat{V}) - (\hat{B}^r - \hat{V})^e$ to calculate these
forecast errors. But the univariate formula can no longer be used
after year one (when no further shocks take place). It will not
produce the zero forecast errors which we require for these years,
unless $(\hat{B}^r - \hat{V})$ happens to follow a first-order autoregressive
scheme in the simulation. The actual values for $(\hat{B}^r - \hat{V})$ do not
satisfy this particular ARIMA process for any of the simulations,
and application of the univariate model leads to an unending
series of forecast errors $(\hat{B}^r - \hat{V}) - (\hat{B}^r - \hat{V})^e$. Inspection of the
simulation results in Knoester (1979) shows that for all the
simulations the forecast errors in $(\hat{B}^r - \hat{V})$, as calculated with
the univariate model, fail to fade out quickly, so that these
irrational errors continue to have a significant influence on
the behaviour of the other endogenous variables in the model,
many years after a change in policy has occurred.

In our first alteration to the model, we have used the

univariate model for $(\hat{B}^r - \hat{V}) - (\hat{B}^r - \hat{V})^e$ for the initial year of
the simulation, and have assumed that agents can forecast
$(\hat{B}^r - \hat{V})^e$ correctly in all those subsequent years in which no
further surprises or shocks affect the economy: the forecast errors
$(\hat{B}^r - \hat{V}) - (\hat{B}^r - \hat{V})^e$ have been put equal to zero for 1977, 1978
and beyond, since no unexpected events occur after the first year
of the simulations. The one-year lag in the influence of the
indicator on the real sector means that changes in base money
therefore have no effect on real consumption and real investment
from 1978 onwards.

A SECOND ALTERATION IN THE MODEL

Although Knoester does not mention other instances in his model
of only unexpected changes in some variable x having an effect
on a variable y, we shall argue that there is at least one other
place in the model where this is the case. Consider the equation
for inventory investment:

$$\Delta\left(\frac{i_{invs}}{v}\right)_t = -.10 + .23\,\hat{v}_{t-1} - .99\left(\frac{i_{invs}}{v}\right)_{t-1} - .11\,\Delta(r_c - \hat{p}_v)_{t-.25} +$$
$$\phantom{\Delta\left(\frac{i_{invs}}{v}\right)_t =}\;(.38)\;(.05)\qquad\quad(.16)\qquad\qquad(.06)$$

$$+\;.41\;\left((\hat{B}^r - \hat{V})_t - .5(\hat{B}^r - \hat{V})_{t-1}\right) + .043\,\hat{y}_{ag,t}$$
$$(.022)\qquad\qquad\qquad\qquad\qquad(.019)$$

$$\bar{R}^2 = .82,\qquad \sigma_u = .55,\qquad D.W. = 1.4,\qquad \text{years: } 1953-1975.$$

Meaning of symbols:

i_{invs} = investment in inventories in real terms;

v = total final sales (domestic and foreign) in real terms;

r_c = call money rate;

p_v = price deflator of total final sales;

B^r = redefined monetary base;

V = total final sales in current guilders;

y_{ag} = volume of agricultural production.

Unexpected changes in the monetary disequilibrium indicator have a temporary effect on inventory investment. So do changes in the real rate of interest and in the current rate of growth of agricultural production. Both these variables will be largely unpredictable. By contrast, the term in $\hat{v}_{t-1}$ is claimed to represent expectations about the current growth of sales (see Knoester and Buitelaar, 1975, p. 508, where this is put forward twice as the only reason for including $\hat{v}_{t-1}$ in the equation). Inspection of the autocorrelation function of $\hat{v}$ shows that we have to reject the untested hypothesis that $\hat{v}_{t-1}$ can stand for $\hat{v}_t^e$ (see Pesando, 1976, for the relation between expectations formation and ARIMA models). The first autocorrelation coefficient does not differ significantly from zero, instead of being close to one, as required by the model $_{t-1}E\hat{v}_t = \hat{v}_{t-1}$.

An alternative explanation for the empirical contribution of $\hat{v}_{t-1}$ to the fit of this equation is provided by the high correlation between $\hat{v}$ and $(\hat{m}_w - \hat{m}_w^e)$, the unexpected growth in world trade, as calculated in chapter 4. When $(\hat{m}_w - \hat{m}_w^e)_{t-1}$ takes the place of $\hat{v}_{t-1}$ the residual standard error of the equation goes down from .55 to .47 and the D.W.-statistic improves from 1.41 to 1.99. We have seen in chapter 4 that $(\hat{m}_w - \hat{m}_w^e)$ is one of the main determinants of the unanticipated growth in output, and an increase in business activity may well lead to a higher level of work in progress which is expressed by a higher value for i_{invs}.

It is interesting to note parenthetically that replacing $\hat{y}_{ag}$ by the unexpected growth in agricultural production (another determinant of $(\hat{gdp} - \hat{gdp}^e)$ in chapter 4) leads to a further improvement in the fit of the equation, which now indicates how inventories change in response to a number of predominantly unforeseeable events. (Whether this alteration is made in the model or not is irrelevant, since $\hat{y}_{ag}$ is an exogenous variable that remains at zero in all the simulations.)

None of the simulation exercises in Knoester (1979) involves changes in world trade. The consequences of the proposed alteration in the equation for inventory investment are thus straightforward: $\hat{v}_{t-1}$ is replaced by a term in $(\hat{m}_w - \hat{m}_w^e)$ which is set equal to zero in all the simulations.

SUMMARY

We shall make two alterations in the model to make it conform better to rational expectations. First, the forecast errors with respect to $(\hat{B}^r - \hat{V})$ will be set equal to zero after the initial year of each simulation, the only year in which there is an unexpected change in economic policy. We assume that in the initial year economic agents use the univariate forecast formula for $(\hat{B}^r - \hat{V})^e$ that worked in the past, and thus make a forecast error in year one that is given by the value of the monetary disequilibrium indicator. But, after year one no further unexpected events occur, and therefore we assume that people use the complete model to forecast the future values of $(\hat{B}^r - \hat{V})$. In other words, we substitute the actual change $(\hat{B}^r - \hat{V})_t$ for the expected change $(\hat{B}^r - \hat{V})^e$ in year two and beyond, so that the forecast errors $(\hat{B}^r - \hat{V}) - (\hat{B}^r - \hat{V})^e$ automatically become zero for all these years in which no unexpected shocks take place. Second, we make a change in the equation for inventory investment in the model. All the explanatory variables in this equation stand for unexpected changes in the economic determinants of inventory investment, with one exception where Knoester claims that the expected rate of growth of sales has an influence on inventories. Statistical analysis of his proxy for the expected change in sales shows that this variable cannot possibly represent $\hat{v}^e$; we replace it by the unexpected change in world trade, $(\hat{m}_w - \hat{m}_w^e)$. This change improves the fit of the equation, and fits in with the fact that all its other explanatory variables represent unexpected changes also. Since none of the simulations involves changes in m_w, the effect of our alteration is that the terms $(\hat{m}_w - \hat{m}_w^e)$ will be set equal to zero for all years in every simulation.

5.7. SIMULATIONS WITH A SLIGHTLY ALTERED MODEL

In Knoester (1979) six policy experiments are presented and
discussed, all of them concerned with changes in monetary and
fiscal policy. (There is one further simulation, consisting of
systematic, annual devaluations of the Dutch guilder, but we
shall disregard it here, for it requires an (arbitrary) change
in one of the estimated coefficients of the original model
specified for fixed exchange rates.)

A description of the six simulations follows, together
with a discussion of the question whether they are admissible
in the sense of section 5.2. After that, we shall juxtapose the
results of three different implementations of the admissible
simulations: first with Knoester's original unaltered model;
second, with Knoester's model in which forecast errors in $(\hat{B}^r - \hat{V})$
have been set equal to zero after the initial year of each
simulation; third, with Knoester's model, but this time with the
term $\hat{v}_{t-1}$ in the equation for inventory investment replaced
by $(\hat{m}_w - \hat{m}_w^e)_{t-1}$. In the final part of the section, some interesting
patterns that emerge from this comparison are discussed, and an
attempt is made to formulate some tentative generalizations about
what will happen generally when we attempt to remove pockets of
systematic irrationality from structural models.

SIX SIMULATIONS

The simulations in Knoester (1979) are as follows:
Simulation (A) involves a single increase in the monetary base
of 2 billion guilders, equivalent to 10 per cent of the base in
1975. The growth rate of the monetary base, $\hat{B}^r$, is one of the
endogenous variables in the model and occurs in a number of
equations, including one equation in which $\hat{B}^r$ is explained as
a weighted average of the growth rates of some of its components
on the sources side. In this equation an error term represents
the remaining, unmodelled, components of the base. We can model
a single increase in the base by giving a positive value to this
residual term for the initial year of the simulation. The errors-

and-omissions term in the equation for $\hat{B}^r$ appears nowhere else
in the model, and a single nonzero value for it is no reason for
economic agents to revise their behaviour. The simulation is
admissible, since only if a systematic pattern of nonzero values
for this term were required to model the simulation, would we
have to assume that economic agents will start revising their
decision rules.

This happens in simulation (B), however, which is concerned
with systematic annual increases of 2 billion guilders in the
monetary base. Now, the errors-and-omissions term in the equation
for $\hat{B}^r$ will have to assume the same positive value for every year
of the simulation. The positive shock in 1976 does not occur in
isolation, but is one of an unending series of similar increases
in the monetary base. After a while agents will understand this,
and thus be able to forecast future shocks. It follows from the
definition of an inadmissible simulation in section 6.2. that
simulation (B) is inadmissible, unless expectations about the
future growth of the base are nowhere important in the model.
However, the monetary sector of the model contains several
equations in which the banking sector adjusts its balance sheet
when $\hat{B}^r$ changes. The model contains decision rules for the
banking sector that cannot remain correct now that the banks
know something they did not know before, namely that the increases in $\hat{B}^r$ are not random events but will be repeated every
year: the simulation is inadmissible.

Simulation (C) concerns a one-time change in the income
tax schedule, so that taxes on wages and salaries increase by
2 billion guilders in the initial year. The simulation can be
performed by a single nonzero shock in the equation that
determines the rate of growth of taxes on labour income: it is
formally similar to (A) and equally admissible.

In simulation (D), the volume of real government expenditure is increased permanently by 2 billion guilders.
Knoester assumes that the additional government outlays are
financed on the capital market which is not explicitly included
in his model. The growth rate of government expenditure is an

exogenous variable that occurs in one equation only, viz. the
relation that explains $\hat{v}$, the growth rate of total sales, as
the weighted sum of the growth rates of consumption, investment,
exports, government expenditure, etc. The data do not reject
the simple ARIMA model $\hat{g}_t = c + a_t$ with c a constant and a_t uncorrelated noise for $\hat{g}$, the rate of increase in government expenditure, so that this simulation can be modelled by a single
nonzero value of the error term a_t in the model for $\hat{g}$: the
simulation is admissible.

In the final two simulations, government expenditure is
increased in the same way as in experiment D, but now the
financing of the deficit is taken into account. In simulation (E),
the deficit is financed with base money and in simulation (F),
each deficit is financed with annual changes in the schedule of
income taxes. In order to model (E), one has to include the
(endogenous) variable for the government deficit in the equation
for the growth rate of the monetary base, and for simulation (F)
we must introduce the deficit in the equation that determines the
rate of growth of income taxes. When these changes have been
made, then the simulation is performed in the same way as simulation (D) namely as a single nonzero term for the innovation in
the stochastic model for the exogenous variable $\hat{g}$. We have seen
already that this is admissible.

Summarizing, we find that one of the six simulations with
Knoester's model has to be rejected a priori for being inadmissible,
whereas the remaining five simulations are admissible.

RESULTS OF THE SIMULATIONS

Different tables in Knoester (1979) show the consequences of each
change in policy for a number of economic variables after 1, 2, 3,
4, 5 and also after 10 years, which he considers representative
of the long-term results. In order to save space, we focus on five
central variables: the level of production, the rate of unemployment, the level of real consumption, the wage rate and the
current account of the balance of payments. (The model also
contains four different endogenous price indices, but all of them

Table 5.2.

CHANGE IN PRODUCTION

Experiment A - A single increase in base money

year	(1)	(2)	(3)	(4)	(5)	level after 10 years
original model	.0	1.2	-1.4	-.2	.9	.3
alteration (1)	.0	1.2	.0	-.1	.0	2.1
alteration (2)	.0	1.2	-1.4	-.0	.6	.2

Experiment C - A permanent increase in income taxes

year	(1)	(2)	(3)	(4)	(5)	level after 10 years
original model	-.4	-.1	.2	.2	.0	.4
alteration (1)	-.4	-.1	.1	.1	.1	-.0
alteration (2)	-.4	-.1	.2	.2	.1	.4

Experiment D - Additional government expenditure,
debt-financed

year	(1)	(2)	(3)	(4)	(5)	level after 10 years
original model	1.0	-.5	-.6	.1	.1	-1.0
alteration (1)	1.0	-.5	-.3	-.1	-.1	- .6
alteration (2)	1.0	-.5	-.4	-.0	-.1	-1.0

Experiment E - Additional government expenditure,
financed with money

year	(1)	(2)	(3)	(4)	(5)	level after 10 years
original model	1.0	.4	-.9	-.1	.6	.6
alteration (1)	1.0	.4	-.2	-.2	-.0	1.4
alteration (2)	1.0	.4	-.8	-.1	.2	.6

Experiment F - Additional government expenditure, financed with an increase in income taxes

year	(1)	(2)	(3)	(4)	(5)	level after 10 years
original model	.7	-.6	-.4	.3	.2	-.6
alteration (1)	.7	-.6	-.3	-.0	.0	-.7
alteration (2)	.7	-.6	-.3	.2	-.0	-.6

Note:

Entries for years (1) - (5) are percentage rates of change in
each year; the final entry on each line shows the cumulated percentage change in the level of production after 10 years.

Table 5.3.

CHANGE IN UNEMPLOYMENT

Experiment A - A single increase in base money

year	(1)	(2)	(3)	(4)	(5)	level after 10 years
original model	-.00	-.24	.19	-.06	.03	.03
alteration (1)	-.00	-.24	-.11	-.21	-.09	-.37
alteration (2)	-.00	-.24	.19	-.10	.07	.04

Experiment C - A permanent increase in income taxes

year	(1)	(2)	(3)	(4)	(5)	level after 10 years
original model	.16	.22	.13	-.04	-.15	-.31
alteration (1)	.16	.22	.16	-.02	-.14	-.16
alteration (2)	.16	.22	.14	-.04	-.16	-.32

Experiment D - Additional government expenditure,
debt-financed

year	(1)	(2)	(3)	(4)	(5)	level after 10 years
original model	-.13	.07	.05	.09	.04	.36
alteration (1)	-.13	.07	-.00	.10	.05	.22
alteration (2)	-.13	.07	.02	.09	.09	.38

Experiment E - Additional government expenditure,
financed with money

year	(1)	(2)	(3)	(4)	(5)	level after 10 years
original model	-.13	-.12	.05	-.03	-.02	-.01
alteration (1)	-.13	-.12	-.11	-.08	-.04	-.17
alteration (2)	-.13	-.12	.02	-.05	.01	.01

Experiment F - Additional government expenditure, financed with an increase in income taxes

year	(1)	(2)	(3)	(4)	(5)	level after 10 years
original model	.01	.28	.21	.08	-.09	.07
alteration (1)	.01	.28	.18	.13	-.05	.10
alteration (2)	.01	.28	.18	.09	-.07	.09

Note:

Entries for years (1) - (5) are annual changes in unemployment,
expressed as a percentage of the dependent labour force; the
final entry on each line shows the cumulated change after 10
years.

Table 5.4.
==========

CHANGE IN REAL CONSUMPTION

Experiment A - A single increase in base money

year	(1)	(2)	(3)	(4)	(5)	level after 10 years
original model	.0	1.5	-1.5	-.4	1.0	.5
alteration (1)	.0	1.5	.4	.1	.2	3.7
alteration (2)	.0	1.5	-1.5	-.2	.7	.3

Experiment C - A permanent increase in income taxes

year	(1)	(2)	(3)	(4)	(5)	level after 10 years
original model	-1.1	-.3	.1	.0	-.1	- .7
alteration (1)	-1.1	-.3	-.1	-.1	-.1	-1.4
alteration (2)	-1.1	-.3	-.0	-.0	-.0	- .6

Experiment D - Additional government expenditure, debt-financed

year	(1)	(2)	(3)	(4)	(5)	level after 10 years
original model	.3	-.3	-.6	.0	.2	-1.9
alteration (1)	.3	-.3	-.3	-.1	-.1	-1.2
alteration (2)	.3	-.3	-.4	-.0	-.1	-2.0

Experiment E - Additional government expenditure, financed with money

year	(1)	(2)	(3)	(4)	(5)	level after 10 years
original model	.4	.9	-.8	-.1	.8	.8
alteration (1)	.4	.9	.1	.0	.1	2.3
alteration (2)	.4	.9	-.6	-.0	.4	.9

Experiment F - Additional government expenditure, financed with an increase in income taxes

year	(1)	(2)	(3)	(4)	(5)	level after 10 years
original model	-.6	-.7	-.7	.0	.1	-2.8
alteration (1)	-.6	-.7	-.5	-.3	-.2	-3.0
alteration (2)	-.6	-.7	-.6	-.1	-.1	-2.8

Note:

Entries for years (1) - (5) are percentage rates of changes in each year; the final entry on each line shows the cumulative percentage change in the level of consumption after 10 years.

Table 5.5.

CHANGE IN WAGES

Experiment A - A single increase in base money

year	(1)	(2)	(3)	(4)	(5)	level after 10 years
original model	.0	.6	-.4	-.2	.4	.5
alteration (1)	.0	.6	.4	.4	.5	4.5
alteration (2)	.0	.6	-.4	-.1	.3	.5

Experiment C - A permanent increase in income taxes

year	(1)	(2)	(3)	(4)	(5)	level after 10 years
original model	.3	.4	-.2	-.3	-.3	.0
alteration (1)	.3	.4	-.2	-.4	-.4	-.7
alteration (2)	.3	.4	-.2	-.3	-.3	.0

Experiment D - Additional government expenditure, debt-financed

year	(1)	(2)	(3)	(4)	(5)	level after 10 years
original model	.5	.1	-.0	.0	.0	-.8
alteration (1)	.5	.1	.0	.0	-.0	-.2
alteration (2)	.5	.1	-.1	.0	-.1	-.8

Experiment E - Additional government expenditure, financed with money

year	(1)	(2)	(3)	(4)	(5)	level after 10 years
original model	.5	.6	-.0	.1	.5	2.3
alteration (1)	.5	.6	.4	.4	.4	4.0
alteration (2)	.5	.6	.1	.2	.4	2.3

Experiment F - Additional government expenditure, financed with an increase in income taxes

year	(1)	(2)	(3)	(4)	(5)	level after 10 years
original model	.8	.4	-.2	-.2	-.3	- .8
alteration (1)	.8	.4	-.2	-.3	-.4	-1.1
alteration (2)	.8	.4	-.2	-.2	-.2	- .9

Note:

Entries for years (1) - (5) are percentage rates of change in each year; the final entry on each line shows the cumulated percentage change in the level of wages after 10 years.

Table 5.6.
==========

CURRENT ACCOUNT BALANCE

Experiment A - A single increase in base money

year	(1)	(2)	(3)	(4)	(5)	level after 10 years
original model	-.1	-10.2	2.3	6.9	-2.9	- 8.0
alteration (1)	-.1	-10.2	-9.9	-6.0	-4.6	-57.1
alteration (2)	-.1	-10.2	5.3	2.1	-2.7	- 6.7

Experiment C - A permanent increase in income taxes

year	(1)	(2)	(3)	(4)	(5)	level after 10 years
original model	1.9	3.2	1.7	.6	1.4	16.4
alteration (1)	1.9	3.2	3.0	2.1	1.8	26.8
alteration (2)	1.9	2.3	2.0	1.5	1.3	16.6

Experiment D - Additional government expenditure, debt-financed

year	(1)	(2)	(3)	(4)	(5)	level after 10 years
original model	-5.7	-5.4	- .1	-2.0	-5.0	-27.2
alteration (1)	-5.7	-5.4	-2.5	-2.5	-3.3	-36.5
alteration (2)	-5.7	-3.1	-2.3	-3.5	-3.2	-27.9

Experiment E - Additional government expenditure, financed with money

year	(1)	(2)	(3)	(4)	(5)	level after 10 years
original model	-5.7	-13.6	- 4.6	-2.7	-9.4	-68.8
alteration (1)	-5.7	-13.6	-11.1	-8.2	-7.8	-89.9
alteration (2)	-5.7	-11.3	- 4.5	-6.0	-7.9	-67.8

Experiment F - Additional government expenditure, financed with an increase in income taxes

year	(1)	(2)	(3)	(4)	(5)	level after 10 years
original model	-4.0	-2.4	2.0	- .9	-3.7	- 9.7
alteration (1)	-4.0	-2.4	.8	.3	- .9	- 6.4
alteration (2)	-4.0	- .8	- .1	-1.8	-1.7	-10.0

Note:

Entries for years (1) - (5) are the annual values of the surplus or deficit, expressed as a percentage of the 1975 stock of base money; the final entry on each line shows the cumulated surplus or deficit after 10 years.

are closely related to the variable for nominal wages; for that
reason they have been omitted here.)

First consider the results calculated with the original
model. The figures represent annual changes for the first five
years of each simulation plus the cumulated change in the level
of production, unemployment etc. after 10 years. An exception is
formed by the current account figures in table 5.6., that represent the surplus or deficit as a percentage of the 1975 stock
of base money. The figures are based on a replication of Knoester's
simulations, which generally led to results that were little
different from the results in his tables. Correction of an error
in his two experiments involving changes in taxation, however,
meant some important changes for experiments (C) and (F).

The results obtained with the original Knoester model can
now be compared to those of the same set of simulations with two
alternative versions of the model.

"Alteration (1)" refers to the monetary disequilibrium
indicator. Rational expectations implies that agents will not
make forecasting errors in years where no shocks occur; therefore we have assumed that $(\hat{B}^r - \hat{V})$ is predicted correctly after
year 1. Forecasting errors in the growth of base money relative
to total nominal sales have a lagged effect on consumption and
investment; consequently the outcomes begin to differ for the
first time in year 3 if we assume that each change in policy
leads to a single forecasting error in year 1. The results in
table 5.2.-5.6. show that both the short-term effects of changes
in policy and the long-run effects are sensitive to the
assumptions made regarding the forecasts of the monetary disequilibrium indicator. Differences in the short-run effects
could be expected; it is remarkable that the outcomes even after
10 years depend heavily on what we assume about the speed with
which economic agents interpret the changes in economic policy.

"Alteration (2)" in each section in tables 5.2.-5.6. refers
to the change in the equation for inventory investment, where
the term $\hat{v}_{t-1}$ has been replaced with the unanticipated change in
world trade, $(\hat{m}_w - \hat{m}_w^e)_{t-1}$. Because of the one-year lag in both

expressions, the results are identical for the initial year of
the simulation, but may be different from year 2 onwards. This
time, the divergences with the original model are more modest:
the long-term results in particular are hardly changed. For
years 2-5, the size of the discrepancies depends on the
variable we are interested in and on the simulation performed.
The two extreme cases are wages (table 5.5.) that remain
virtually unchanged and the balance of payments (table 5.6.)
where some figures are quite different for all five simulations.
Overall, the differences from the original model are much less
marked than in the case of version (1), but still noticeable.

Before we proceed to present more evidence about the three
sets of simulations, let us try to draw some conclusions from
the data in tables 5.2.-5.6. Since the calculations have been
performed for one particular econometric model, these conclusions are best called hypotheses, to be confirmed or rejected
in subsequent work. Two specific hypotheses can be formulated
on the basis of the results in the tables:

Hypothesis 1: *Non-rational econometric models produce unreliable*
results when they are used for simulations. Alterations that
make the formation of expectations in the models less irrational,
can result in significant differences in the outcomes of the
simulations.

Anderson (1979) found this to be true for two U.S. models; in
this chapter we obtained similar results for a Dutch model.

Hypothesis 2: *Making the formation of expectations in non-*
rational models less irrational affects not only the short-run
outcomes of simulation exercises; the long-run results may be
also affected.

This can be seen most clearly in the case of alteration (1),
where both the short-term and the long-term results were
different for all variables in almost all simulations.

THE TERM STRUCTURE OF EXPECTATIONS

In some cases we can go beyond just pointing out how sensitive
the outcomes of simulations are to changes in the modelling of

expectations: we can reject simulations with a non-rational
model for being contrary to the assumptions that underlie the
individual equations of that model. Consider, for example, the
equation for business investment in Knoester's model. According
to this equation, one of the main determinants of the change in
investment is the expected growth in profits, $\hat{z}_t^e$. The expectation is modelled by the simple univariate model,

$$\hat{z}_t^e = \hat{z}_{t-1}$$

The assumption that the expected growth in profits can be
modelled by the acutal growth in the previous period has two
implications for simulations with the model. First, if there
are systematic discrepancies between $\hat{z}_t^e$ and $\hat{z}_t$ when an admissible simulation is performed, we should change the model,
for example by substituting the actual change $\hat{z}_t$ for the
expected change in profits in all those years where no unexpected shocks take place. Second, the complete future path
of profits, as calculated with the model, must be such that
the rate of growth of profits for the next period is representative of the expected growth in profits for all subsequent
periods. For, let us assume that rational agents use the model
for the preparation of their forecasts and foresee marked
fluctuations in profits for the future. In that case they will
stop behaving according to the model equation that connects the
change in investment only to the expected change in profits for
the current period.

In tables 5.7. and 5.8. the results for after-tax profits
are given for each of the first ten years of the six different
simulations. Let us look first at the results obtained with
Knoester's original model. Remember that all the simulations
involve a single change of policy in year 1, and no surprises
in subsequent years, so that at the end of year 1, rational
agents can utilize the model to form correct expectations for
years 2, 3 and beyond for all endogenous variables, including
profits.

Table 5.7.

ANNUAL PERCENTAGE CHANGE IN PROFITS -- ORIGINAL MODEL

year	1	2	3	4	5	6	7	8	9	10
Exp. A	.0	3.2	-5.1	.4	2.8	- .7	-1.7	.8	1.0	- .6
C	-1.9	.0	1.6	.4	- .3	- .1	.0	- .2	- .3	- .1
D	3.1	-2.1	- .9	1.1	.5	- .9	- .2	.6	.0	- .4
E	3.1	.5	-2.9	.6	1.7	-1.3	- .8	1.1	.2	- .7
F	1.4	2.3	.2	1.7	.6	-1.1	- .4	.5	- .1	- .6

- ALTERATION 1

year	1	2	3	4	5	6	7	8	9	10
Exp. A	.0	3.2	-1.1	- .8	- .4	- .3	- .2	- .1	.0	.1
C	-1.9	.0	1.1	.5	.1	- .2	- .2	- .2	- .2	- .1
D	3.1	-2.1	- .1	.2	.1	.1	.0	.0	.0	.0
E	3.1	.5	- .8	- .4	- .2	- .2	- .1	- .0	.1	.1
F	1.4	-2.3	.6	.7	.3	.0	- .2	- .3	- .2	- .2

- ALTERATION 2

year	1	2	3	4	5	6	7	8	9	10
Exp. A	.0	3.2	-5.2	.9	1.9	-1.0	- .2	.4	- .0	- .0
C	-1.9	.1	1.4	.5	.0	- .1	- .2	- .2	- .2	- .1
D	3.1	-2.1	- .5	.7	- .1	- .3	.1	.1	.0	.0
E	3.1	.5	-2.5	.5	.7	- .8	.0	.3	- .1	.1
F	1.4	-2.3	.6	1.3	.1	- .4	- .2	- .1	- .2	- .1

Table 5.8.
=========

CUMULATED CHANGE IN THE LEVEL OF PROFITS -- ORIGINAL MODEL

year	1	2	3	4	5	6	7	8	9	10
Exp. A	.0	3.3	-1.9	-1.5	1.3	.6	-1.1	- .2	.7	.1
C	-1.9	-1.9	- .3	.1	- .2	- .2	- .2	- .4	- .7	- .8
D	3.1	.9	.1	1.1	1.6	.7	.5	1.1	1.1	.8
E	3.1	3.6	.6	1.2	2.9	1.6	.8	1.9	2.1	1.3
F	1.4	- .9	- .7	1.0	1.6	.5	.1	.6	.5	- .1

- ALTERATION 1

year	1	2	3	4	5	6	7	8	9	10
Exp. A	.0	3.3	2.2	1.4	1.0	.7	.5	.5	.5	.6
C	-1.9	-1.9	- .8	- .3	- .2	- .3	- .6	- .8	-1.0	-1.1
D	3.1	.9	.8	1.0	1.1	1.2	1.2	1.3	1.3	1.3
E	3.1	3.6	2.7	2.3	2.1	1.9	1.8	1.8	1.9	2.0
F	1.4	- .9	- .3	.4	.8	.8	.6	.5	.1	- .0

- ALTERATION 2

year	1	2	3	4	5	6	7	8	9	10
Exp. A	.0	3.3	-1.9	-1.0	.9	- .1	- .3	.1	.1	.0
C	-1.9	-1.9	- .5	.0	.0	- .1	- .3	- .4	- .6	- .7
D	3.1	.9	.5	1.1	1.0	.8	.8	.9	.9	.9
E	3.1	3.5	1.0	1.5	2.2	1.4	1.4	1.7	1.6	1.7
F	1.4	- .9	- .3	.9	1.0	.6	.5	.4	.2	.0

The figures in the top part of tables 5.7. and 5.8. show that the term structure of expectations at the end of period 1 is quite complicated for each of the five simulations. Notice the many instances in which the growth of profits, $\hat{Z}$, continues to change from positive to negative and back, even near the end of the ten-year period that is depicted in the tables.

It follows that the outcomes of the simulations are incompatible with the investment equation of the model in two respects. First, it is not correct to model the expected rate of change of profits by the actual rate of change in the previous period:

$$\hat{z}^e_t \neq \hat{z}_t.$$

Second, the severe fluctuations in profits that occur in several simulations imply that rational economic agents will not simply predict profits one period ahead and make their investment plans according to these one-year forecasts. Rational agents will not invest heavily in years 2 and 5 of simulation (A), for example, although the model would predict large increases in profits for these two years.

In fact, whereas the model is built on the implicit assumption:

$$\hat{z}_{t-1} = {}_{t-1}E\hat{Z}_t = {}_{t-1}E\hat{Z}_{t+1} = {}_{t-1}E\hat{Z}_{t+2};$$

analysis of the simulations shows that none of these equalities holds.

Consider next the results in the other panels of tables 5.7. and 5.8. They show the same five simulations performed this time for each of the two proposed alterations embodied in the model. The amount of fluctuation in $\hat{Z}$ is greatly reduced, particularly when we compare the values for the second half of the ten-year period. In the first few years of the simulations, there are large swings in profits, irrespective of the version used, which is to some extent natural, for an unforeseen event

has occurred in year 1 and agents need to adjust their expectations. But, when we compare the absolute values of $\hat{Z}$,
beginning in, for example, year 4, for the three versions, then
the values are significantly smaller for the two altered
versions of the model. The number of times that $\hat{Z}$ changes sign
is reduced, and the value of the level of profits, Z, after,
say, five years, becomes more representative of the long-term
value of Z, in particular for version (1) of the model.

It must be noted, however, that the inconsistency between
the simulation results on the one hand and the theoretical
foundation of the model on the other is, though lessened,
not yet resolved. In the experiments with the original model,
the term structure of expectations for $\hat{Z}$ is so complicated,
that it can be doubted whether it is compatible with any
reasonable theory about the influence of expected profits on
the demand for investment. In the two other versions of the
model, the behaviour of future profits is less irregular, but
still inconsistent with the simple model

$$\hat{Z}_{t-1} = {}_{t-1}E\hat{Z}_t = {}_{t-1}E\hat{Z}_{t+1} = {}_{t-1}E\hat{Z}_{t+2} = \ldots .$$

that is implied by the maintained hypothesis of the original
Knoester model. The data in tables 5.7. and 5.8. suggest the
following tentative hypothesis, which, once again, would need
to be tested for other models:
Hypothesis 3: the dynamic characteristics of non-rational
models are very sensitive to the way in which expectations are
modelled. Complicated term structures of expectations are
generally incompatible with the simple specifications re-
garding expectations that have been assumed in the individual
equations of the model. In this event, simulations cannot be
offered as evidence for the hypothesis that the true economy
reacts to changes in economic policy with lags that are as
long and complicated as the lags found in simulations with
a non-rational econometric model.

The results in tables 5.7. and 5.8. show that the com-

plicated fluctuations in the original simulations are reduced
when some sources of systematic forecasting errors are removed.
Further work may show whether it is generally true that the
dynamic characteristics of large structural models are largely
caused by irrational assumptions about the way in which expectations are formed.

The importance of this issue for the potential scope of
economic policy is clear. It was stressed in a different
context at the end of section 5.3. If the short lags that are
found in simulations with rational models are judged to be
more reliable than the protracted fluctuations obtained with
non-rational structural models, then this means that the
possibilities for counter-cyclical economic policy are reduced
if not eliminated. For, assume that an unforeseen, external
shock hits the economy. If the repercussions of this disturbance are felt over a number of years, then the authorities
have an opportunity to cushion the shock and compensate for its
effects through some off-setting action. If, however, we have
to assume that rational behaviour implies that the private
sector reacts quickly and efficiently, then the government just
does not have the time to react to an unforeseen external shock
and -- considering that there is also a "recognition lag" and
an "action lag" in the political and bureaucratic process --
its reaction may well be too late and therefore counter-
productive and procyclical.

5.8. CONCLUSIONS

In this chapter we have discussed two potential criticisms of
the reduced form approach as used in chapters 2-4. First, it
can be argued that reduced forms are a poor alternative to
structural models of the economy, because a structural model,
although perhaps more difficult to specify and estimate, is
a more powerful tool for simulating the effects of changes in
economic policy. In the second place, objections may be made

to the outcomes of the experiments that can be made with reduced
forms such as those put forward in this study. They show that
the endogenous variables require one or two years only to reach
their new equilibrium path, whereas there is much evidence that
economies can easily require many more years before all the
temporary effects of an impulse have disappeared. Once one
realizes, however, that all this evidence is derived with the
help of large structural models, then both criticisms come down
to the assumption that (large) structural models are more trust-
worthy than (small) reduced-form models. Every economist will
accept the potential superiority of well-specified structural
models over reduced forms; a question that remains is whether
existing structural models are so deficient in regard to the
formation of expectations that a smaller reduced-form model in
which rational expectations can be implemented successfully has
to be preferred to a large non-rational model.

First we tried to show that results for many simulations
have to be rejected on logical grounds, irrespective of the
qualities of the model employed. Only admissible simulations, as
defined in section 5.2. make sense. Section 5.3. then deals with
the way in which existing structural models proxy expectations
about the endogenous variables.

Even a carefully specified model that gives an excellent
fit over the estimation period can easily produce simulations
that are implicitly based on irrational forecasts. It would be
convenient if one could just take an existing non-rational
model, impose rational expectations and analyse the results.
We have argued in sections 5.4. and 5.5. that this is generally
impossible. However, one can still try to remove some instances
of irrationality from these models.

In sections 5.6. and 5.7. empirical evidence is presented
for a recent structural model of the Dutch economy. This model
has been used for a number of simulations, all of which involve
a one-time change in government policy. In the original model,
it is assumed that agents never trouble to work out the consequences of changes in policy for the economy. A little effort

(reading the simulation results is sufficient!) would help
to avoid important forecasting errors in, for example, future
profits. Such effort would be profitable, so we should assume
that agents do not make forecasting errors that are avoidable.

In the alternative calculations, we do assume that agents
are aware of changes in policy. They will make prediction errors,
for each economy is subject every year to a number of unforeseen
shocks. However, some errors that can be easily avoided when
people realize that there has been a change in policy, are
eliminated in the alternative versions of the model.

When changes in economic policy are simulated with a less
irrational model, equilibrium is restored more quickly and there
are fewer fluctuations during the adjustment period. This is
an interesting result, in the first place because it suggests
that "reduced form" versus "structural" is not the real issue:
what matters more is whether agents are rational or whether
they should rather be assumed to make costly though avoidable
forecasting errors. The slow dynamic adjustment which many
structural models show may be not caused in the first place by
the wealth of structural detail in such models, but may be due
to irrationality in the way forecasts are formed in the model.
If this is so, then it has important implications for the
conduct of economic policy. The scope for fine-tuning the
economy is greatly reduced when one realizes that there is no
good reason to assume that the private sector requires more
time than the government to react to an external disturbance.

Chapter 6

CONCLUDING COMMENTS, 1979

Economic research can easily give a misleading impression
that outstanding issues have already been settled beyond doubt.
However, if a theoretical model is not rejected by the author's
own data, neither the author nor the reader should forget that
there may be alternative models that fit the data equally well.
Also, if the tradition in applied econometrics has shown one
thing, it is that extending the data by two or three additional
years is often sufficient to let impressively high values of $\bar{R}^2$
melt away. It may therefore be in order briefly to review some of
the main results of the preceding analysis, and to indicate some
unresolved questions that one should be aware of. First, some
issues that directly concern inflation will be discussed, and
after that a number of more general points will be made.

A first conclusion from the research is that there exists
an adequate economic explanation for the course of inflation in
the Netherlands. The residuals of our preferred inflation
regression are small and compare well with those of the price
equations in the models by Knoester and the Central Planning
Bureau. It seems unlikely that data revisions or superior
specifications of a cost-push price equation will ever reverse
that conclusion for the period 1953-1976. There is no need for
the power-theory of inflation to explain the rate of inflation.
This unambiguous result does not eliminate the possibility that,
for other countries or other periods, sudden large increases in
wages do have to be explained by more sociological factors or
that institutional arrangements make wages to an important extent

dependent on government decisions. In such cases, the expected growth rate of money may *temporarily* be a poor predictor of the rate of price change.

But this would not discredit the thesis that there can be no sustained inflation without excessive money growth, nor does it imply that the power-theory of inflation has a better predictive record. Malinvaud (1977), for example, in his discussion of the French wage explosion of 1968, admits that many firms could not have increased their prices sufficiently *if the Banque de France had not increased the money stock*. Even if wages are largely exogenous for institutional reasons (see Hagger, 1968, for Australia), this does not mean that unions and employers (including the government) *do not form expectations about the future growth of excess demand*.

The predictive power of the quantity theory may be weaker for other countries or periods than it happened to be for the U.S. and the Netherlands, but money growth remains a necessary and sufficient condition for inflation, unless there are drastic changes in the demand for money. Qualitative change in the technology of making payments, or the development of new close substitues for money may, of course, temporarily or permanently invalidate any association between money growth and inflation, that held in the past.

A RULE FOR STABLE GROWTH OF THE MONEY SUPPLY

Abstracting from such qualitative changes in the demand for money function, we may conclude that research on money and inflation is not only of theoretical interest, but has implications for policy, too. Basically, the best advice for policy-makers is still that contained in Friedman (1948): the monetary authorities should not attempt to act counter-cyclically, and money should grow in a stable and predictable way. As regards the optimal stable growth-rate of the money supply, Phelps (1978) has argued that a constant small positive rate of inflation is to be preferred to zero inflation, for why should money be exempt from taxation if all other goods and

services are subject to taxes in a world that does not rely
solely on lump-sum taxes? However, even a fully anticipated
inflation has its costs, and monetary expansion on any substantial scale leads to distortions in the tax system and
brings uncertainty about the likelihood of possible attempts by
the government to break the inflation through prices and incomes
policies or through a sudden monetary deceleration. Distortions
in relative prices and greater uncertainty lead to an increase
in the natural rate of unemployment, so that the optimal rate
of inflation should not be significantly different from zero
(Mundell, 1972, and Korteweg (1978, b).

The arguments for a money growth rule have shifted from
Friedman's emphasis on the long and variable lags in monetary
policy that make fine-tuning impossible, to the modern insight
that predictable shocks have no real effects on rational agents
(Barro, 1976). As recently as 1972, Fand wrote:

"Guidelines should be defined not on the grounds that
they incorporate all the necessary knowledge, but rather
that they will, in our current state of knowledge (or
ignorance) give us a reasonably good result on the average.
Rules and guidelines are therefore to be thought of as
temporary solutions, since the possibility always exists
that someone may find a better one."
(1972, p. 165).

Recently, the rational expectations school has provided
what appears to be a conclusive argument for preferring rules
to discretionary action. In chapter 1 we have attempted to set
forth the reasons why the economist has to assume that expectations are formed rationally, and the subsequent chapters
of this study have not shown any need to deviate from that
position.

In the mean time, there have also been some practical
experiments with money growth rules. The Swiss Central Bank
has shown that money stock control is possible, even in a small,
open economy (Schiltknecht, 1978). The German experience
indicates that money growth targets can indeed influence behaviour:

> "German trade unions had reacted (to the announced target
> for the growth in base money) by reducing their wage claims
> to about 6 per cent."
> (Giersch, 1977b, p. 38).

The effect of money growth rules in Germany and Switzerland on
the rate of inflation in these two countries in unequivocal, just
as in the case of some episodes in the past when only one reading
on the facts was possible. Evidence from the monetary squeeze in
the U.S. in 1966, and from the 1968 tax surcharge, for example,
was important at the time in winning converts to monetarism
(Gordon, 1976b).

However, progress towards a rational view of inflation will
be slow, because it is not in the short-term interest of the
inflation makers: governments, and Central Banks. Politicians
are bound to advocate income policies as a means to combat
inflation, in order to divert attention from the effects of
budget deficits on monetary growth, and as a response to public
clamour for quick and determined action against inflation. Any
subsequent failure of an income policy can be blamed on aggressive
unions or uncooperative employers. When on the other hand an
imcomes policy coincides with monetary and fiscal restraint and
thus has a more than purely temporary effect, the drop·in
inflation may well be credited to the more politically visible
incomes policy rather than to the accompanying lower growth in
the money stock.

One reason why those Central Banks that have not yet
switched to growth rules will be hesitant to engage in a systematic analysis of the links between money and prices and the
causes that underlie money growth, is that steps towards more
"cognitive rationality" (Brunner, 1972) would unavoidably
highlight their own responsibility and possible policy errors.
A traditional Central Bank prefers a complicated institutional
framework with numerous policy instruments and likes to rely on
informal and non-public methods of persuasion, so that the Bank
can write its own history (Chant and Acheson, 1972).
Visible success of money growth strategies remains the major

hope for a better understanding, but even governments and Central
Banks that do adhere to a money growth rule will be subject to
political pressure to become activist again if the natural rate
of unemployment is deemed too high. There have always been ups
and downs in the popularity of the quantity theory, and it would
be naive to assume that because the monetarists are winning the
current battle (cf. Johnson, 1971), there will be no more war.

Precisely because important political issues are at stake,
does it make sense that the economics profession has devoted so
much effort to investigating the precise links between money,
prices and output. Empirical tests of the influence of money
growth on output and prices tend to consist of the specification
and estimation of reduced form equations, and the present study
is no exception. Multivariate reduced forms are half-way between
statistical analyses of the relation between just two time series
on the one hand and full-fledged structural models on the other.
Now that the results of our reduced-form approach have been
presented, it should be explained why no bivariate analysis of
money and prices or income is reported here.

TESTS FOR CAUSALITY

In recent years, the well-known difficulties with the specification of structural equations have led some researchers to
concentrate on the statistical relations between just two
economic time series (Sims, 1972, Feige and Pearce, 1974, 1976,
Gebauer, 1975, Haugh, 1976). The investigation of the cross-
correlation functions of different pairs of series x and y is
certainly useful as a preliminary step towards the estimation
of a multivariate model. In Box and Jenkins (1970) the study of
the cross-correlation function is recommended for that purpose,
not as an aim in itself. The research strategy of estimating
a cross-correlation function only, or, equivalently, of
regressing y on a large number of past and/or future terms
of x, and vice versa, does not appear to be very informative
when taken by itself. The findings of such a purely statistical
analysis should be used for an *economic model* that connects

not only the two series in question, but also includes other
economically relevant variables. It seems likely that in almost
all cases, the parameters of such a model can be estimated with
greater precision than the cross-correlation coefficients that
are obtained from a bivariate analysis. Also, a multivariate
analysis permits multivariate "economic" models for the calculation of expectations, whereas in a bivariate model one has to
assume that the expectations about future x and y are based only
on the past of x and y, and not on any other information (cf.
Pierce, 1977, Pierce and Haugh, 1977).

   In the particular case of money growth and prices or
nominal income, it has become clear that the results which Sims
obtained for the U.S. cannot be replicated easily for other
countries. In small, open economies, with a currency that is not
the world's main reserve asset, monetary policy is less powerful
with the result that the effect of a domestic monetary shock is
less visible, and money and income can be influenced
simultaneously by developments abroad (Genberg and Swoboda,
1977a, b, Putnam and Wilford, 1978, and Mills and Wood, 1978).
Our finding of a high positive correlation between monetary
impulses in Holland and unanticipated changes in world trade in
chapter 4 pointed in the same direction. If a bivariate analysis
of money and nominal income or prices is not helpful in
distinghuishing between competing economic theories (Schwert,
1979), univariate studies of the velocity of money will be even
less informative. Gould and Nelson (1974) indicated correctly
that their results for velocity were compatible with many
different hypotheses about the links between money and nominal
income, and more recent work by Gould et al. (1978) shows again
the limitations of such a univariate approach.

GAPS IN THE ANALYSIS
Reduced forms have now been compared to the simpler bivariate
or univariate models, but what of the comparison with larger,
more structural models? To the general observations in chapter 5,
some remarks may be added about the modelling of the channels

between the monetary and the real sectors of the economy.

It is becoming clear from recent empirical work, that the links between expected money growth and inflation are suited best to investigation with annual data. Parkin and Swoboda rightly point out (1977, pp. 4-5), that monthly and quarterly data about the rate of price change contain too much noise to be useful as measures of inflation, which, by definition, has to do with longer-term trends. The use of annual data has the disadvantage of reducing the number of degrees of freedom available for estimation; it also means that the transmission of monetary shocks to the real sector can well take place within the period of observation, so that the transmission mechanism cannot be made explicit in our models. However,

"in general terms microeconomic theory already provides us with our transmission process and the charge of 'black box economics' that is so often levied at Friedman is totally unjustified".

(Mayer, 1978, p. 239).

It is only in disequilibrium models that the transmission mechanism has indeed to be spelled out in detail (Hayek, 1978). In equilibrium models, price theory can provide the answer to questions that cannot easily be solved empirically, and particularly not with annual data (cf. Lucas, 1972a, p. 51).

Perhaps, then, the rudimentary modelling of the transmission mechanism need not be too serious a defect of the present study. But there are at least two areas where the analysis should be made more structural. First, the supply of money. It appears very difficult to model the supply of base money, both for individual countries and on a world level. For the world as a whole, not only the total quantity of reserves, but also their distribution is important (Machlup, 1977, and Genberg and Swoboda, 1977b), and early attempts to estimate a world supply of money function (Parkin et al., 1976) are therefore not satisfactory. For individual countries, the modelling of the international component of the base has proved so hard, that economists have often left the base out of their

empirical models. If, instead, just a formula for money supplied
is given, as in Barro (1977, 1978) and in the present study,
then such an expression is often either a univariate statistical
model à la Box-Jenkins or an uneasy combination of supply and
demand elements, together with a reaction function for the
government. One hopes for progress in this field.

The second area where models such as ours are deficient and
where progress has to be made, is in the modelling of the supply
side of the real economy. Certainly, there remains a need for
short-term models that do not try to model the supply side, and
are used only for the preparation of unconditional forecasts.
Such models will be short-run in the double sense of being
estimated with monthly or quarterly data and being used to predict
only a few quarters in the future. They will concentrate on the
careful specification of distributed lags and will exploit
information contained in leading indicators and surveys of
consumer and business opinion. The emphasis will lie on statistical sophistication and not on the use of micro-economic
theory (Lucas, 1975). However, such models are useless for the
treatment of monetary and fiscal policy, particularly as regards
their longer-run effects on the stocks of financial assets and
productive capital (see Roberts, 1978, for a popular exposition).

There will be a need for a second category of models which
concentrate on the longer run; thus the supply side must receive
more attention, whereas much allocative detail can be discarded
(Brunner, 1973, Korteweg, 1978b).

One of the characteristics of monetarism has been an
interest in the longer-term (Gordon, 1976b, p. 55, and Modigliani,
1975, p. 181), and there certainly is a demand, theoretically as
well as empirically, for longer-run models. Important policy
problems, such as the influence of social security on savings,
the effects of taxes and social security on the labour market,
and the effects of government deficits on the economy cannot be
discussed within a Keynesian short-term frame-work, or with our
equation for the growth of output that concentrates on the
determinants of short-run fluctuations. Analysis of these issues

requires a model that pays adequate attention to the factors that
determine long-run economic growth. The absence of a structural
model for the supply of money and the lack of a long-term supply
function for output are two large gaps in the present analysis.
We have been concerned solely with the simpler issue of
revisiting the quantity theory under the assumption of rational
expectations, with particular emphasis on the term structure of
these expectations.

Appendix 1

NOTATIONS AND DATA

This Appendix contains all symbols that are used in more than
a single section of the text and lists the time series for the
Netherlands that have been utilized in the regressions, in as
far as they have not been included in the main text. All
variables refer to annual averages, and have been taken from
standard sources.

a, u, v, w   residual errors in ARIMA models or equations;

c, d   constant terms;

e   expected value: $\hat{x}_t^e$ equals the expected value of
$\hat{x}_t$, as held before the start of period t;

α, β, ...   fixed coefficients;

θ, ϕ coefficients in ARIMA models;

B   back-shift operator: $Bx_t = x_{t-1}$;

Δ $(1 - B)$

$\hat{}$ growth rate: $\hat{x}_t \equiv \ln x_t - \ln x_{t-1}$. In empirical work,
the growth rates are usually multiplied by a factor 100;

*   foreign variable.

VARIABLES IN THE THEORETICAL MODEL

g   index of real government expenditure;

i   representative, nominal rate of interest;

M   stock of money;

p   price level;

r   real rate of interest;

V   velocity of money, defined by $MV = py$;

y   rate of real output;

Z   vector of exogenous variables that influences demand.

VARIABLES USED IN THE EMPIRICAL WORK ON DUTCH INFLATION

B^r stock of re-defined base money, equal to currency outside banks plus bank reserves minus borrowed reserves plus net foreign assets of the banking sector;

$FP_{US/Ge}$ three-month forward premium of the dollar in terms of the German mark, with its sign such that an increase represents a weakening of the mark and a strengthening of the dollar (on an annual basis);

$FP_{US/NL}$ three-month forward premium of the dollar in terms of the Dutch guilder;

$FP_{Ge/NL}$ defined as $FP_{US/NL} - FP_{US/Ge}$;

gdp   real rate of gross domestic product;

glg   real rate of total direct government expenditure (transfers excluded);

gnp_{Ge}, gnp_{NL} real rate of gross national product in Germany and the Netherlands;

H labour productivity in enterprises;

m_w volume index of world trade;

M_{Ge}, M_{US}, M money stock, narrowly defined, in Germany, the U.S.A., and the Netherlands;

p^* price index for the O.E.C.D. area minus the Netherlands;

p_c implicit deflator of private consumption;

p_{gdp} implicit deflator of gdp;

p_{gdpb} implicit deflator of business output;

p_m price index of imported goods;

r_{S3} interest rate on three-month savings deposits;

r_{T3} interest rate of three-month time deposits, proxied by the rate on three-month loans to local authorities;

shift 68/69 dummy variable; see section 4.4.;

TRF/G government transfers as a proportion of total government expenditure;

TSP/Y total government receipts plus social security premiums as a proportion of net national income;

v real rate of business sales (inventory formation not included);

V   nominal rate of business sales (inventory formation
                    not included);

w   index of wages in enterprises;

y_{ag} volume index of agricultural production.

DATA USED

All the U.S. data, used in chapter 3, may be found in Barro
(1977, 1978). Table 4.1. contains the principal data on money
growth and inflation for the Netherlands. Forecasts by the
Dutch Central Planning Bureau are to be found in table 4.2.
The remaining time series used in the empirical analysis of
Dutch inflation are printed below in alphabetical order. All
growth rates are in the form 100 x Δln (variable)

jaar	Br-V	$FP_{US/Ge}$	$FP_{US/NL}$	gdp	glg	gnp_{Ge}	gnp_{NL}	m_w	r_{S3}	r_{T3}	TRF/G	w	y_{ag}
1953	4.5	- .19	- .32	8.3	13.8	--	8.5	3.0	.81	1.09	- 8.4	4.1	- 2.9
1954	5.4	- .10	- .37	6.4	2.5	6.8	6.4	9.3	.74	.95	4.7	8.8	2.0
1955	- 1.6	.10	- .58	6.4	4.0	11.2	6.5	11.3	.83	1.35	3.8	8.5	5.3
1956	- 4.5	.43	.73	4.7	4.3	6.7	4.2	7.3	2.04	2.94	1.4	8.3	- 6.4
1957	- 9.8	.26	2.15	2.6	1.3	5.5	2.5	6.5	3.47	5.47	7.9	10.3	6.4
1958	11.7	.33	.85	- 1.4	- 3.1	3.2	.9	1.5	2.72	3.80	4.3	4.3	6.2
1959	9.5	- .33	- .56	4.2	1.2	6.7	4.4	9.1	1.93	2.29	- 1.6	2.4	- 9.4
1960	8.8	- .35	- .72	8.1	4.8	8.5	7.7	13.2	2.42	2.58	.2	7.8	16.3
1961	- .8	- 1.47	- 1.76	3.0	4.0	5.3	3.3	5.1	2.17	1.72	- 2.5	7.0	- 9.4
1962	- 7.1	- .60	- .66	3.9	4.3	3.9	3.6	8.4	2.29	2.51	- 1.8	5.7	.6
1963	- 3.3	.06	.63	3.5	5.7	3.4	3.8	7.8	2.33	2.82	- 1.0	8.6	- 4.7
1964	-16.9	.63	.11	8.2	3.7	6.4	8.2	10.2	3.17	4.35	2.1	13.9	15.6
1965	- 5.6	- .29	- .35	5.2	1.7	5.4	5.0	8.9	3.87	4.73	2.6	10.5	- .1
1966	- 8.6	.08	- .12	2.8	2.1	2.9	2.6	6.4	4.10	6.44	4.0	10.4	- 1.2
1967	- 7.8	.93	- .18	5.2	4.0	.2	5.4	2.9	4.30	5.67	1.1	8.4	11.4
1968	- 6.7	- 2.85	- 1.36	6.5	4.9	7.1	6.1	12.8	4.49	5.19	.7	8.5	4.9
1969	- 4.7	- 4.29	- 1.61	6.6	2.4	7.9	6.6	14.1	4.74	7.76	- .0	12.6	3.1
1970	- 6.0	.16	- .82	6.6	5.2	5.6	6.4	9.8	5.21	7.96	1.0	12.4	5.3
1971	- .2	- .84	- 1.51	4.3	3.5	2.9	4.1	6.8	5.20	5.26	1.3	12.3	3.7
1972	6.0	- 2.43	- 2.60	3.8	.4	3.3	4.0	9.1	4.50	2.96	2.7	11.9	2.7
1973	- 5.1	- 3.80	- 2.40	5.7	- 1.6	5.0	6.1	10.7	4.85	6.89	2.6	14.3	8.1
1974	-11.8	- 1.55	- .66	4.1	1.5	.5	4.2	4.0	5.47	10.35	.4	14.7	8.6
1975	13.2	- 2.36	- 1.73	- 1.2	6.1	- 3.2	- 2.3	- 2.2	5.03	5.27	1.1	12.7	- .6
1976	.2	- 1.57	1.58	4.5	2.9	5.4	5.1	12.2	4.60	6.88	2.3	10.2	- 1.5

Appendix 2

UNIVARIATE MODELS FOR EXPECTATIONS

This Appendix describes those univariate Box-Jenkins models
that have not been discussed in the text. In no case have we
attempted to fit models of an order higher than 2, since
higher-order models would require longer time series. Moreover,
if a first-order or second-order univariate model for x^e proves
inadequate, then it would seem preferable first to extend the
information set on which the expectations are based with
current and one-year lagged values of other variables, before
including values of $\hat{x}$ from the more distant past. Multivariate models have in fact been used to model some expected
growth rates, notably those of $\hat{M}$ and $\hat{m}_w$ in chapter 4.

The different models are listed below, together with
details about the treatment of outliers, defined as all
observations more than 2.5 standard deviations away from the
sample mean. The models were estimated with a Box-Jenkins
program that incorporated the so-called back-forecasting
feature, so that no data were lost at the beginning of the
sample period. The series of residuals passed the Box-Pierce
(1970) test, but the power of this test is not great, because
of the limited amount of data.

BOX-JENKINS MODELS

If not indicated otherwise, the models have been estimated
over the period 1954-1976

$$(1) \qquad (1 - .27B)(\hat{Br} - \hat{v}) = a_t \qquad \sigma_a = 7.2 \qquad R^2 = .07$$
$$ (.20)$$

Estimated for the period 1952-1976, because of the early
starting-point of the Knoester model.

(2) $\hat{\Delta glg}_t = (1 - .05B - .88B^2)a_t \qquad \sigma_a = 1.9 \qquad R^2 = .48$

                        (.09)   (.09)

There are outliers in 1953, 1954, due to the floods in
February 1953. Therefore, the model is estimated for the
period 1955-1976. We assume that the decrease in $\hat{glg}$ after the
initial reaction to the floods was basically foreseen,
$(\hat{glg}-\hat{glg}^e)_{1954} = 0$, and set $\hat{glg}^e_{1953}$ equal to the previous
year's value, glg_{1952}.

(3) $\hat{\Delta p}_{gdp\ NL,t} = (1 - .44B)a_t \qquad \sigma_a = 1.6 \qquad R^2 = .14$

                        (.20)

Estimated over 1955-1976, due to an outlier in 1954.

(4) $\hat{\Delta p}_{gnp\ US,t} = a_t \qquad \sigma_a = .8$

The series is white noise for the period 1953-1973. There
are outliers, both during the Korean war period and in
1974, 1976.

(5) $\hat{\Delta (TRF/G)}_t = (1 - .42B - .55B^2)a_t \qquad \sigma_a = 2.1 \qquad R^2 = .35$

                        (.18)   (.18)

Large fluctuations in G, due to the floods of 1953, cause
outliers in 1954 and 1955. A model for the period 1956-1976
(estimated "backwards") is used to generate replacement
values for 1954 and 1955, which are inserted into the complete
series for the purpose of estimating the model parameters.
After that, we replace the calculated expectations for 1954
and 1955 by the realized values on the assumption that agents
could foresee the broad pattern of the changes in G in these
two years.

(6)
$$\Delta \hat{w}_t = (1 - .28B - .62B^2)a_t \qquad \sigma_a = 2.2 \qquad R^2 = .37$$
$$(.17) \quad (.17)$$

(7)
$$\Delta \hat{y}_{ag,t} = (1 - 1.49B + .74B^2)a_t \qquad \sigma_a = 5.8 \qquad R^2 = .72$$
$$(.14) \quad (.14)$$

REFERENCES

ABEL, A. et al. (1979): Money demand during hyperinflation;
    Journal of Monetary Economics 5 no. 1 (January), 97-104.
AGHEVLI, B.B. and M.S. KHAN (1977): Inflationary finance and the
    dynamics of inflation: Indonesia, 1951-72; American Eco-
    nomic Review 67 no. 3 (June), 390-403.
AIGNER, D. et al. (1977): Formulation and estimation of sto-
    chastic frontier production function models; Journal of
    Econometrics 6 no. 1 (July), 21-37.
ALCHIAN, A.A. (1950): Uncertainty, evolution, and economic theory;
    Journal of Political Economy 58 no. 3 (June), 211-221.
ALCHIAN, A.A. (1959): Costs and outputs; in: M. Abramowitz (ed.):
    The allocation of economic resources; Stanford: Stanford
    University Press, 23-40.
ALLISON, G.T. (1971): Essence of decision; explaining the Cuban
    missile crisis; Boston: Little, Brown, and Company.
ANDERSON, M. (1978): Power and inflation; in: F. Hirsch and
    J.H. Goldthorpe (eds.): The political economy of inflation;
    London: Martin Robertson, 240-262.
ANDERSON, P.A. (1979): Rational expectations forecasts from non-
    rational models; Journal of Monetary Economics 5 no. 1
    (January), 67-80.
ANDO, A. (1974): Some aspects of stabilization policies, the
    monetarist controversy, and the M.P.S. model; International
    Economic Review 15 no. 3 (October), 541-571.
ARGY, V. (1978): A comment on the Korteweg, Fratianni and Fourcans
    papers; in: K. Brunner and A.H. Meltzer (eds.): The problem
    of inflation; Journal of Monetary Economics, Supplement
    no. 8, 181-191.
ARROW, K.J. (1958): Tinbergen on economic policy; Journal of the
    American Statistical Association 53 no. 281 (March), 89-97.
BARRO, R.J. (1976): Rational expectations and the role of monetary
    policy; Journal of Monetary Economics 2 no. 1 (January),
    1-32.
BARRO, R.J. (1977): Unanticipated money growth and unemployment
    in the United States; American Economic Review 67 no. 2
    (March), 101-115.
BARRO, R.J. (1978): Unanticipated money, output, and the price
    level in the United States; Journal of Political Economy 86
    no. 4 (August), 549-580.
BARRO, R.J. and S. FISCHER (1976): Recent developments in mone-

tary theory; Journal of Monetary Economics 2 no. 2 (April),
133-167.

BARRY, B. (1976): Power: an economic analysis; in: B. Barry (ed.):
Power and political theory - some European perspectives;
London: John Wiley, 67-101.

BARTEN, A.P. et al. (1976): Comet - a medium-term macroeconomic
model for the European Economic Community; European Economic
Review 7, 63-115.

BELD, C.A. van den (1965): Forecasts and realization; Monograph
no. 10, Central Planning Bureau, The Hague.

BLACK, F. (1974): Uniqueness of the price level in monetary growth
models with rational expectations; Journal of Economic
Theory 7 no. 1 (January), 53-65.

BOSWORTH, B. (1978): quoted in "The Economist", July 29.

BOX, G.E.P. and G.M. JENKINS (1970): Time series analysis, forecasting and control; San Francisco: Holden-Day.

BOX, G.E.P. and D.A. PIERCE (1970): Distribution of residual autocorrelations in autoregressive-integrated moving average
time series models; Journal of the American Statistical
Association 65, 1509-1526.

BOX, G.E.P. and G.C. TIAO (1965): A change in level of a non-
stationary time series; Biometrika 52 (June), 181-192.

BRITTAN, S. (1978): Inflation and democracy; in F. Hirsch and
J.H. Goldthorpe (eds.): The political economy of inflation;
London: Martin Robertson, 161-185.

BROCK, W.A. (1972): On models of expectations that arise from
maximizing behaviour of economic agents over time; Journal
of Economic Theory 5 no. 3 (December), 348-376.

BROCK, W.A. (1974): Money and growth: the case of long run perfect foresight; International Economic Review 15 no. 3
(October), 750-777.

BRUNNER, K. (1972): The ambiguous rationality of economic policy;
Journal of Money, Credit, and Banking 4 no. 1, pt. 1
(February), 3-12.

BRUNNER, K. (1973): Discussion in: Controlling monetary aggregates
II: The implementation; Boston: Federal Reserve Bank of
Boston, 103-113.

BRUNNER, K. and A.H. MELTZER (1963): Predicting velocity: implications for theory and policy; Journal of Finance 18 no. 2
(May), 319-354.

BRYANT, R.C. (1975): Empirical research on financial capital
flows; in: P.B. Kenen (ed.): International trade and
finance-frontiers for research; Cambridge: Cambridge University Press, 321-362.

CAGAN, P. (1956): The monetary dynamics of hyperinflation; in:
M. Friedman (ed.): Studies in the quantity theory of money;
Chicago: University of Chicago Press.

CARLSON, J.A. (1975): Are price expectations normally distributed?;
Journal of the American Statistical Association 70 no. 352
(December), 749-754.

CARLSON, J.A. (1977): A study of price forecasts; Annals of Economic and Social Measurement 6 no. 1, 27-56.

CENTRAL PLANNING BUREAU (various years): Central Economic Plan,
The Hague (abreviated C.E.P.): Macro-Economische Ramingen,

The Hague; Macro-Economische Verkenning, The Hague
(abreviated M.E.V.).

CENTRAL PLANNING BUREAU (1954): Een vergelijking van de ramingen
van het C.P.B. met de feitelijke economische ontwikkeling
1949-1953, The Hague.

CHANT, J.F. and K. ACHESON (1972): The choice of monetary instruments and the theory of bureaucracy; Public choice 12
(Spring), 13-34.

CHIANG, A.C. (1963): Economic forecasting when the subject of the
forecast is influenced by the forecast: Comment; American
Economic Review 53 no. 4 (September), 730-734.

CORDEN, W.M. (1976): Inflation and the exchange rate regime;
Scandinavian Journal of Economics 78 no. 2, 370-383.

DEVLETOGLOU, E.A. (1961): Correct public prediction and the
stability of equilibrium; Journal of Political Economy 69
no. 2 (April), 142-161.

DREES Jr., W. (1957): Inflatiebestrijding, wenselijkheid en
mogelijkheid; in: Preadviezen 1957, Vereniging voor de
Staathuishoudkunde, The Hague: Martinus Nijhoff, 1-37.

EMMINGER, O. (1977): Discussion in: R.A. Mundell and J.J. Polak
(eds.): The new international monetary system; New York:
Columbia University Press, 48.

EVANS, P. (1978): Time-series analysis of the German hyperinflation; International Economic Review 19 no. 1
(February), 195-209.

FACKLER, J. and B. STANHOUSE (1977): Rationality of the Michigan
price expectations data; Journal of Money, Credit, and
Banking 9 no. 4 (November), 662-666.

FAND, D.I. (1972): Comment on a paper by Okun; Brookings Papers
on Economic Activity no. 1, 164-167.

FASE, M.M.G. (1975): Verruiming en verschraling; een poging het
liquiditeitsbegrip empirisch af te bakenen; Selecte Studies,
Utrecht: Rabobank, 7-32.

FASE, M.M.G. (1977): Spaargelden, termijndeposito's and rente-
verschillen; een econometrische analyse; Kwartaalbericht
De Nederlandsche Bank (1977) no. 1, 34-44 (English version:
Quarterly Statistics, De Nederlandsche Bank (1977) no. 2,
78-88.

FASE, M.M.G. (1978): Een verdeelmodel voor liquide activa; Economisch Statistische Berichten 63 no. 3144 (March 1),
215-218.

FAUSTEN, D.K. (1975): The consistency of British balance of
payments policies; London: Macmillan.

FEIGE, E.L. and D.K. PEARCE (1974): The causality between money
and income: a time series approach; Paper presented at
the Midwest Economic Association Meeting (April).

FEIGE, E.L. and D.K. PEARCE (1976): Economically rational expectations: are innovations in the rate of inflation independent of innovations in measures of monetary and
fiscal policy?; Journal of Political Economy 84 no. 3
(June), 499-522.

FISHER, I. (1930): The theory of interest; New York: Macmillan.

FOURCANS, A. (1978): Inflation and output growth: the French
experience, 1960-1975; in: K. Brunner and A.H. Meltzer (eds.):

The problem of inflation; Journal of Monetary Economics, Supplement no. 8, 81-140.

FRATIANNI, M. (1977): Italy at the crossroad of stagnation; Paper read at the May 1977 Conference of the Shadow European Economic Policy Committee, published by the Graduate School of Management, University of Rochester.

FRENKEL, J.A. (1975): Inflation and the formation of expectations; Journal of Monetary Economics 1 no. 4 (October), 403-421.

FRENKEL, J.A. (1977): The forward exchange rate, expectations, and the demand for money: The German hyperinflation; American Economic Review 67 no. 4 (September), 653-670.

FRIEDMAN, B.M. (1978): Stability and rationality in models of hyperinflation; International Economic Review 19 no. 1 (February), 45-64.

FRIEDMAN, M. (1948): A monetary and fiscal framework for economic stability; American Economic Review 38 no. 3 (June), 245-264.

FRIEDMAN, M. (1975): Comment on papers by Fisher and Brainard/ Cooper; American Economic Review 65 no. 2 (May), 176-179.

GALATIN, M. (1976): Optimal forecasting in models with uncertainty when the outcome is influenced by the forecast; Economic Journal 86 no. 2 (June), 278-295.

GEBAUER, W. (1975): Die Kausalitätsbeziehungen zwischen Geldmenge, Preisen und Produktion -- Eine empirische Untersuchung für die Bundesrepublik Deutschland; Zeitschrift für die gesamte Staatswissenschaft 131 no. 4, 603-626.

GENBERG, H. (1975): World inflation and the small open economy; Stockholm: Swedish Industrial Publications.

GENBERG, H. (1977): The concept and measurement of the world price level and rate of inflation; Journal of Monetary Economics 3 no. 2 (April), 231-252.

GENBERG, H. (1978): Purchasing power parity under fixed and flexible exchange rates; Journal of International Economics 8 no. 2 (May), 247-276.

GENBERG, H. and A.K. SWOBODA (1977a): Causes and origins of the current world-wide inflation; in: E. Lundberg (ed.): Inflation theory and anti-inflation policy; London: Macmillan, 72-93.

GENBERG, H. and A.K. SWOBODA (1977b): Worldwide inflation under the dollar standard; Discussion paper no. 12, Graduate School of International Studies, Geneva.

GIERSCH, H. (1977a): IMF surveillance over exchange rates; in: R.A. Mundell and J.J. Polak (eds.): The new international monetary system; New York: Columbia University Press, 53-68.

GIERSCH, H. (1977b): Comment on a paper by Parkin and Swoboda; in: E. Lundberg (ed.): Inflation theory and anti-inflation policy; London: Macmillan, 38.

GODELIER, M. (1966): Rationalité et irrationalité en économie; Paris: François Maspéro (English translation: Rationality and irrationality in economics, (1972); London: New Left Books).

GOLDSTEIN, H.N. (1977): Review of O.E.C.D. Economic Outlook 18;

Journal of Money, Credit, and Banking 9 no. 1 pt. 1 (February), 117-122.

GONEDES, N.J. and H.V. ROBERTS: Differencing of random walks and near random walks; Journal of Econometrics 6, 289-308.

GORDON, D.F. and A. HYNES (1970): On the theory of price dynamics; in: E.S. Phelps (ed.): Microeconomic foundations of employment and inflation theory; New York: W.W. Norton, 369-393.

GORDON, R.A. (1950): The treatment of government spending in income-velocity estimates; American Economic Review 40 no. 1 (March), 152-159.

GORDON, R.J. (1975): The demand for and supply of inflation; Journal of Law and Economics 18 no. 3 (December), 807-836.

GORDON, R.J. (1976a): Recent developments in the theory of inflation and unemployment; Journal of Monetary Economics 2 no. 2 (April), 185-219.

GORDON, R.J. (1976b): Comments on Modigliani and Ando; in: J.L. Stein (ed.): Monetarism; Amsterdam: North Holland, 52-66.

GORDON, R.J. (1978): Comment on a paper by Feldstein and Summers; Brookings Papers on Economic Activity 1, 102-107.

GORDON, R.J. (1979): A comment on the Perloff and Wachter paper; in: K. Brunner and A.H. Meltzer (eds.): Three aspects of policy and policy making: knowledge, data, and institutions; Journal of Monetary Economics, Supplement no. 10, 187-194.

GOULD, J.P. and C.R. NELSON (1974): The stochastic structure of the velocity of money; American Economic Review 64 no. 3 (June), 405-418.

GOULD, J.P. et al. (1978): The stochastic properties of velocity and the quantity theory of money; Journal of Monetary Economics 4 no. 2 (April), 229-248.

GRANGER, C.W.J. and P. NEWBOLD (1973): Some comments on the evaluation of economic forecasts; Applied Economics 5 no. 1 (March), 35-47.

GRANGER, C.W.J. and P. NEWBOLD (1977): Forecasting economic time series; New York: Academic Press.

GRAUWE, P. de (1975): The interaction of monetary policies in a group of European countries; Journal of International Economics 5 no. 2 (May), 207-228.

GRAVES, P.E. (1978): New evidence on income and the velocity of money; Economic Inquiry 16 no. 1 (January), 53-68.

GRAY, J.A. (1978): On indexation and contract length; Journal of Political Economy 86 no. 1 (February), 1-18.

GRIFFIN, J.M. and P.R. GREGORY (1976): An intercountry translog model of energy substitution responses; American Economic Review 66 no. 5 (December), 845-857.

GROSSMAN, H.I. (1978): Risk shifting, layoffs, and seniority; Journal of Monetary Economics 4 no. 4 (November), 661-686.

GRUNBERG, E. and F. MODIGLIANI (1954): The predictability of social events; Journal of Political Economy 62 no. 6 (December), 465-478.

HAGGER, A.J. (1968): Price stability growth and balance -- Australia's economic objectives; Melbourne: F.W. Cheshire.

HALL, R.E. (1978): The macroeconomic impact of changes in income taxes in the short and medium runs; Journal of Political

Economy 86 no. 2 pt. 2, S71–S85.

HAMBURGER, M.J. (1977a): The demand for money in an open economy; Journal of Monetary Economics 3 no. 1 (January), 25–40.

HAMBURGER, M.J. (1977b): Behaviour of the money stock: is there a puzzle?; Journal of Monetary Economics 3 no. 3 (July), 265–288.

HANSEN, L.P. and T.J. SARGENT (1978): Techniques for the application of rational expectations models to economic time series; Unpublished paper, Federal Reserve Bank of Minneapolis.

HARROD, R. (1972a): Discussion; in: R. Hinshaw (ed.): Inflation as a global problem; Baltimore: Johns Hopkins University Press, 43–45.

HARROD, R. (1972b): Options in therapy. Incomes policy as a remedy for cost-push inflation; in: R. Hinshaw (ed.): Inflation as a global problem; Baltimore: Johns Hopkins University Press, 98–111.

HARSANYI, J.C. (1976): Essays on ethics, social behaviour and scientific explanation; Dordrecht: D. Reidel Publishing Company.

HASSELMAN, B.H. (1976): De prijsvergelijkingen; Unpublished paper, The Hague: Central Planning Bureau.

HASSELMAN, B.H. et al. (1977): The fix-point estimation method and a revision of the 69-c annual model; in: C.A. van Bochove et al. (eds.): Modelling for government and business; essays in honor of P.J. Verdoorn, Leiden: Martinus Nijhoff, 79–112.

HAUGH, L.D. (1976): Checking the independence of two covariance-stationary time series: a univariate residual cross-correlation approach; Journal of the American Statistical Association 71 no. 354 (June), 378–385.

HAYEK, F.A. (1978): Personal recollections of Keynes and the "Keynesian revolution", chapter 18 in: New studies in philosophy, politics, economics, and the history of ideas; London: Routledge and Kegan Paul, 283–289.

HEIDE, H. ter (1970): Centraal Planbureau en vakbeweging; in: 25 Jaar Centraal Planbureau, The Hague: Staatsuitgeverij, 47–53.

HELD, V. (1977): Rationality and reasonable cooperation; Social Research 44 no. 4 (Winter), 708–744.

HIRSCH, F. (1978): The ideological underlay of inflation; in: F. Hirsch and J.H. Goldthorpe (eds.): The political economy of inflation, London: Martin Robertson, 263–284.

HOLTROP, M.W. (1972): On the effectiveness of monetary policy; Journal of Money, Credit, and Banking 4 no. 2 (May), 283–311.

JACOBS, R.L. (1977a): Hyperinflation and the supply of money; Journal of Money, Credit, and Banking 9 no. 2 (May), 287–303.

JACOBS, R.L. (1977b): Point and counter point: reply to Cagan and Kincaid; Economic Inquiry 15 no. 1 (January), 119–124.

JOHNSON, H.G. (1971): The Keynesian revolution and the monetarist counter-revolution; American Economic Review 61 no. 2 (May), 1–14.

JOHNSON, H.G. (1977a): A note on the dishonest government and the inflation tax; Journal of Monetary Economics 3 no. 3 (July), 375-377.

JOHNSON, H.G. (1977b): Comment on a paper by Salant; in: L.B. Krause and W.S. Salant (eds.):; Worldwide inflation; Washington: Brookings Institution, 650-652.

KARNOSKY, D.S. (1976): The link between money and prices, 1971-1976; Federal Reserve Bank of St. Louis Review 58 no. 6 (June), 17-23.

KEMP, M.C. (1962): Economic forecasting when the subject of the forecast is influenced by the forecast; American Economic Review 52 no. 3(June), 492-496.

KENEN, P.B. (1976): Assessing experience with floating exchange rates: a comment; in: K. Brunner and A.H. Meltzer (eds.): Institutional arrangements and the inflation problem; Journal of Monetary Economics Supplement no. 3, 115-122.

KINDLEBERGER, C.P. (1976): Lessons of floating exchange rates; in: K. Brunner and A.H. Meltzer (eds.): Institutional arrangements and the inflation problem; Journal of Monetary Economics Supplement no. 3, 51-78.

KLEIN, B. (1976): The social costs of the recent inflation: the mirage of steady "anticipated" inflation; in: K. Brunner and A.H. Meltzer (eds.): Institutional arrangements and the inflation problem; Journal of Monetary Economics Supplement no. 3, 185-212.

KLEIN, B. (1978): The measurement of long- and short-term un-certainty: A moving regression time series analysis; Economic Inquiry 16 no. 3 (July), 438-452.

KNIGHT, F.H. (1951): The role of principles in economics and politics; American Economic Review 41 no. 1 (March), 1-29.

KNOESTER, A. (1974): Een stelsel monetaire vergelijkingen ten behoeve van een empirisch macro-model voor Nederland; Maandschrift Economie 38 no. 10 (July), 473-530.

KNOESTER, A. (1975): De invloed van monetaire onevenwichtigheden op de reële sfeer; Unpublished paper, Rotterdam: Erasmus University.

KNOESTER, A. (1979): On monetary and fiscal policy in an open economy; De Economist 127 no. 1, 105-142.

KNOESTER, A. and P. BUITELAAR (1975): De interacties tussen de monetaire en reële sector in een empirisch macro-model voor Nederland; Maandschrift Economie 39 no. 10 (July), 493-548.

KOOT, R.S. (1975): A factor analytic approach to an empirical definition of money; Journal of Finance 30 no. 4 (September), 1081-1090.

KOOT, R.S. (1977): On the St. Louis equation and an alternative defintion of the money supply; Journal of Finance 32 no. 3 (June), 917-920.

KORTEWEG, P. (1978a): The economics of inflation and output fluctuations in the Netherlands, 1954-1975; in: K. Brunner and A.H. Meltzer (eds.): The problem of inflation; Journal of Monetary Economics Supplement no. 8, 17-79.

KORTEWEG, P. (1978b): The economics of stagflation: theory and Dutch evidence; forthcoming in Zeitschrift für die gesamte

Staatswissenschaft (originally published in Dutch as: De stagflatie van de jaren zeventig; feiten en verklaringen; in: Internationale stagflatie bij vaste en flexibele wissel-koersen, Preadviezen 1978 van de Vereniging voor de Staat-huishoudkunde).

KORTEWEG, P. and A.H. MELTZER (1978): Inflation and price changes: some preliminary estimates and tests of alternative theories; in K. Brunner and A.H. Meltzer (eds.): The problem of in-flation; Journal of Monetary Economics Supplement no. 8, 325-353.

KYDLAND, F.E. and E.C. PRESCOTT (1977): Rules rather than dis-cretion: the inconsistency of optimal plans; Journal of Political Economy 85 no. 3 (June), 473-491.

LAIDLER, D.E.W. (1976): Comment on Sjaastad; in: J.M. Parkin and G. Zis (eds.): Inflation in the world economy; Manchester: Manchester University Press, 86-87.

LAIDLER, D.E.W. (1977): Expectations and the behaviour of prices and output under flexible exchange rates; Economica 44 no. 176 (November), 327-336.

LEEUW, F. de (1977): Comments on Rasche and Tatom; in: G.L. Perry et al.: Productive capacity: Estimating the utilization gap; Working paper no. 23, St. Louis: Washington University.

LIU, T.C. (1960): Underidentification, structural estimation, and forecasting; Econometrica 28 no. 4 (October), 855-865.

LJUNG, G.M. and G.E.P. BOX (1978): On a measure of lack of fit in time series models; Biometrica 65 no. 2 (August), 297-303.

LUCAS, R.E. (1972a): Econometric testing of the natural rate hypothesis; in: O. Eckstein (ed.): The econometrics of price determination Conference; Washington: Board of Go-vernors of the Federal Reserve System and S.S.R.C., 50-59.

LUCAS, R.E. (1972b): Expectations and the neutrality of money; Journal of Economic Theory 4 no. 2 (April), 103-124.

LUCAS, R.E. (1975): Review of a volume by R.C. Fair; Journal of Economic Literature 13 no. 3 (September), 889-890.

LUCAS, R.E. (1976): Econometric policy evaluation: a critique; in K. Brunner and A.H. Meltzer (eds.): The Phillips curve and labor markets; Journal of Monetary Economics Supple-ment no. 1, 19-46.

LUCAS, R.E. (1977): Understanding business cycles; in: K. Brunner and A.H. Meltzer (eds.): Stabilization of the domestic and international economy; Journal of Monetary Economics Supple-ment no. 5, 7-29.

LUNDBERG, E. (1968): Instability and economic growth; New Haven: Yale University Press.

MACAULAY, T.B. (1829): Bentham's defence of Mill: Utilitarian system of philosophy; Edinburgh Review 98 (June).

McCALLUM, B.T. (1976): Rational expectations and the natural rate hypothesis: some consistent estimates; Econometrica 44 no. 1 (January), 43-52.

McCALLUM, B.T. (1978): Price level adjustments and the rational expectations approach to macroeconomic stabilization po-licy; Journal of Money, Credit, and Banking 10 no. 4 (November), 418-436.

McCRACKEN, P. et al. (1977): Towards full employment and price stability, A report to the O.E.C.D.; Paris.

MACHLUP, F. (1972): World inflation: factual background, in:
    R. Hinshaw (ed.): Inflation as a global problem; Baltimore:
    Johns Hopkins University Press, 26-38.

MACHLUP, F. (1977): Comments; in: R.A. Mundell and J.J. Polak
    (eds.): The new international monetary system; New York:
    Columbia University Press, 167-171.

McKINNON, R.I. (1976): Floating exchange rates 1973-1974: The
    emperor's new clothes; in: K. Brunner and A.H. Meltzer
    (eds.): Institutional arrangements and the inflation
    problem; Journal of Monetary Economics Supplement no. 3,
    79-114.

MAIER, C.S. (1978): The politics of inflation in the 20th cen-
    tury; in: F. Hirsch and J.H. Goldthorpe (eds.): The poli-
    tical economy of inflation; London: Martin Robertson,
    37-72.

MALINVAUD, E. (1977): Comment on papers by Parkin/Swoboda and
    Genberg/Swoboda; in: E. Lundberg (ed.): Inflation theory
    and anti-inflation policy; London: Macmillan, 96-98.

MAYER, T. (1978): Monetarism: economic analysis or Weltanschau-
    ung?; Banca Nazionale del Lavoro Quarterly Review 126
    (September), 233-250.

MELITZ, J. and H. CORREA (1970): International differences in
    income velocity; Review of Economics and Statistics 52
    no. 1 (February), 12-17.

MELTZER, A.H. (1977a): Anticipated inflation and unanticipated
    price change. A test of the price-specie flow theory and
    the Phillips-curve; Journal of Money, Credit, and Banking
    9 no. 1 pt. 2 (February), 182-205.

MELTZER, A.H. (1977b): Monetarist, Keynesian, and quantity
    theories; Kredit und Kapital 10 no. 2, 149-182.

MELTZER, A.H. (1978): The conduct of monetary policy under
    current monetary arrangements; Journal of Monetary Eco-
    nomics 4 no. 2 (April), 371-388.

MENIL, G. de (1977): Comments on a paper by Wachtel; in:
    J. Popkin (ed.): Analysis of inflation, 1965-1974; Cam-
    bridge, Massachusetts: Ballinger Publishing Company for
    the N.B.E.R., 396-402.

MILLER, P.J. (1976): On macroeconomic theories and models; in:
    A prescription for monetary policy -- proceedings from a
    seminar series; Minneapolis: Federal Reserve Bank of
    Minneapolis, 43-49.

MILLS, T.C. and G.E. WOOD (1978): Money income relationships
    and the exchange rate regime; St. Louis: Federal Reserve
    Bank of St. Louis Review 60 no. 8 (August), 22-27.

MODIGLIANI, F.M. (1975): Comment on papers by Fisher and
    Brainard/Cooper; American Economic Review 65 no. 2 (May),
    179-181.

MOORE, G.H. (1969): Forecasting short-term economic change;
    Journal of the American Statistical Association 64 no. 325
    (March), 1-22.

MOORE, G.H. (1972): Errors in GNP forecasts; American Statisti-
    cian 26 no. 4 (October), 52-53.

MORGAN GUARANTY: World Financial Markets (various issues).

MORTENSEN, D.T. (1978): Specific capital and labor turnover;
    Bell Journal of Economics 9 no. 2 (Autumn), 572-586.
MOTLEY, B. (1969): The consumer's demand for money: a neo-
    classical approach; Journal of Political Economy 77
    no. 5 (September/October), 817-826.
MULLINEAUX, D.J. (1978): On testing for rationality: another
    look at the Livingston price expectations data; Journal
    of Political Economy 86 no. 2 pt. 1 (April), 329-336.
MUNDELL, R.A. (1972): The role of fiscal and monetary policy;
    in: R. Hinshaw (ed.): Inflation as a global problem;
    Baltimore: Johns Hopkins University Press, 112-127.
MUSSA, M. (1975): Adaptive and regressive expectations in
    a rational model of the inflationary process; Journal of
    Monetary Economics 1 no. 4 (October), 423-442.
MUSSA, M. (1976a): A study in macro-economics; Amsterdam:
    North Holland.
MUSSA, M. (1976b): The exchange rate, the balance of payments,
    and monetary and fiscal policy under a regime of con-
    trolled floating; Scandinavian Journal of Economics 78
    no. 2, 229-248.
MUSSA, M. (1978): On the inherent stability of rationally
    adaptive expectations; Journal of Monetary Economics 4
    no. 2 (April), 307-313.
MUTH, J.F. (1960): Optimal properties of exponentially weighted
    forecasts; Journal of the American Statistical Association
    55 no. 290 (June), 299-306.
MUTH, J.F. (1961): Rational expectations and the theory of price
    movements; Econometrica 29 no. 3 (July), 315-335.
NEFTCI, S. and T.J. SARGENT (1978): A little bit of evidence on
    the natural rate hypothesis from the U.S.; Journal of
    Monetary Economics 4 no. 2 (April), 315-319.
NELSON, C.R. (1972): The prediction performance of the FRB-MIT-
    PENN model of the U.S. economy; American Economic Review
    62 no. 5 (December), 902-917.
NELSON, C.R. (1974): The first-order moving average process;
    Journal of Econometrics 2, 121-141.
NELSON, C.R. (1975): Rational expectations and the estimation of
    econometric models; International Economic Review 16 no. 3
    (October), 555-561.
NELSON, C.R. (1976): The interpretation of R^2 in autoregressive-
    moving average time series models; American Statistician 30
    no. 4 (November), 175-180.
NERLOVE, M. (1967): Distributed lags and unobserved components
    in economic time-series; in: W. Fellner et al.: Ten studies
    in the tradition of I. Fisher; New York: Wiley, 127-169.
PANNE, C. van de (1959): De voorspellingskwaliteit van de Cen-
    trale Economische Plannen, 1949-1956; De Economist 197,
    91-123.
PARKIN, J.M. (1975): The politics of inflation; Government and
    Opposition 10 no. 2 (Spring), 189-202.
PARKIN, J.M. (1977a): The transition from fixed exchange rates
    to money supply targets; Journal of Money, Credit, and
    Banking 9 no. 1 pt. 2 (February), 228-242.
PARKIN, J.M. (1977b): The economy of the United Kingdom; Paper

    read at the May 1977 Conference of the Shadow European
    Economic Policy Committee, published by the Graduate
    School of Management, University of Rochester.

PARKIN, J.M. and A.K. SWOBODA (1977): Inflation: a review of the
    issues; in: E. Lundberg (ed.): Inflation theory and anti-
    inflation policy; London: Macmillan, 3-29.

PARKIN, J.M. et al. (1976): The determination and control of the
    world money supply under fixed exchange rates, 1961-1971;
    in: J.M. Parkin and G. Zis (eds.): Inflation in open eco-
    monies; Manchester: Manchester University Press, 24-47.

PATINKIN, D. (1965): Money, interest, and prices; New York/
    London: Harper and Row. Second edition.

PERLOFF, J.M. and M.L. Wachter (1979): A production function --
    nonaccelerating inflation approach to potential output: is
    measured potential output too high?; in: K. Brunner and
    A.H. Meltzer (eds.): Three aspects of policy and policy-
    making: knowledge, data, and institutions; Journal of
    Monetary Economics Supplement no. 10, 113-164.

PESANDO, J.E. (1976): Rational expectations and distributed lag
    expectations proxies; Journal of the American Statistical
    Association 71 no. 353 (March), 36-42.

PHELPS, E.S. (1978): Inflation planning reconsidered; Economica
    45 no. 178 (May), 109-123.

PIERCE, D.A. (1977): Relationships -- and the lack thereof --
    between economic time series, with special reference to
    money and interest rates -- with discussion; Journal of
    the American Statistical Association 72 no. 357 (March),
    11-26.

PIERCE, D.A. and L.D. HAUGH (1977): Causality in temporal systems;
    Journal of Econometrics 5 no. 3 (May), 265-293.

PIERCE, D.A. and J.M. MASON (1978): On estimating the fundamental
    dynamic equations of structural econometric models;
    Washington: Federal Reserve Board, Division of Research
    and Statistics, Special studies paper no. 111.

PLOSSER, C.I. and G.W. SCHWERT (1977): Estimation of a non-
    invertible moving average process; the case of over-
    differencing; Journal of Econometrics 6 no. 2 (September),
    199-224.

PLOSSER, C.I. and G.W. SCHWERT (1978): Money, income, and sun-
    spots: measuring economic relationships and the effects of
    differencing; Journal of Monetary Economics 4 no. 4
    (November), 637-660.

PRESCOTT, E.C. (1977): Should control theory be used for economic
    stabilization?; in: K. Brunner and A.H. Meltzer (eds.):
    Optimal policies, control theory and technology exports;
    Journal of Monetary Economics Supplement no. 7, 13-38.

PUTNAM, B.H. and D.S. WILFORD (1978): Money, income, and cau-
    sality in the United States and the United Kingdom: a
    theoretical explanation of different findings; American
    Economic Review 68 no. 3 (June), 423-427.

RASCHE, R.H. and J.A. TATOM (1977a): The effects of the new
    energy regime on economic capacity, production, and
    prices; Federal Reserve Bank of St. Louis Review 59 no. 5
    (May), 2-12.

RASCHE, R.H. and J.A. TATOM (1977b): Energy resources and po-
       tential GNP; Federal Reserve Bank of St. Louis Review 59
       no. 6 (June), 10-24.
ROBERTS, P.C. (1978): The breakdown of the Keynesian model; The
       Public Interest 52 (Summer), 20-33.
RUTTEN, F.W. (1978): Bijsturen van de economie; Economisch
       Statistische Berichten 63 no. 3136 (January 4), 4-7.
SAHLINS, M.D. (1976): Culture and practical reason; Chicago:
       University of Chicago Press.
SARGENT, T.J. (1976a): The observational equivalence of natural
       and unnatural rate theories of macroeconomics; Journal of
       Political Economy 84 no. 3 (June), 631-640.
SARGENT, T.J. (1976b): Testing for neutrality and rationality;
       in: A prescription for monetary policy: proceedings from
       a seminar series; Minneapolis: Federal Reserve Bank of
       Minneapolis, 65-85.
SARGENT, T.J. (1976c): Econometric exogeneity and alternative
       estimators of portfolio balance schedules for hyper-
       inflations: a note; Journal of Monetary Economics 2 no. 4
       (November), 511-522.
SARGENT, T.J. (1977a): The demand for money during hyperinfla-
       tions under rational expectations: I; International Eco-
       nomic Review 18 no. 1 (February), 59-82.
SARGENT, T.J. (1977b): Observations on improper methods of
       simulating and teaching Friedman's time series consumption
       model; International Economic Review 18 no. 2 (June),
       445-462.
SARGENT, T.J. (1979): A note on maximum likelihood estimation of
       the rational expectations model of the term structure;
       Journal of Monetary Economics 5 no. 1 (January), 133-143.
SARGENT, T.J. and C.A. SIMS (1977): Business cycle modelling
       without pretending to have too much a priori economic
       theory; in: New methods in business cycle research --
       proceedings from a conference; Minneapolis: Federal Re-
       serve Bank of Minneapolis, 45-109.
SARGENT, T.J. and N. WALLACE (1973a): Rational expectations and
       the dynamics of hyperinflation; International Economic
       Review 14 no. 2 (June), 328-350.
SARGENT, T.J. and N. WALLACE (1973b): The stability of models
       of money and growth with perfect foresight; Econometrica 41
       no. 6 (November), 1043-1048.
SCHILTKNECHT, K. (1978): Von der Kreditpolitik zur Geldmengen-
       politik. Die Geldpolitik der Schweizerischen Nationalbank
       in den letzten zehn Jahren; Kredit und Kapital 11 no. 3,
       287-307.
SCHLESINGER, H. (1978): Die Geldpolitik der Deutschen Bundes-
       bank 1967-1977; Kredit und Kapital 11 no. 1, 3-29.
SCHWERT, G.W. (1979): Tests of causality: the message in the
       innovations; in: K. Brunner and A.H. Meltzer (eds.): Three
       aspects of policy and policy-making: knowledge, data, and
       institutions; Journal of Monetary Economics Supplement
       no. 10, 55-96.
SELDEN, R.T. (1975): A critique of Dutch monetarism; Journal of
       Monetary Economics 1 no. 2 (April), 221-232.

SHILLER, R.J. (1973): Rational expectations and term structure
of interest rates, a comment; Journal of Money, Credit, and
Banking 5 no. 3 (August), 856-860.

SIMON, H.A. (1978a): Rationality as process and as product of
thought; American Economic Review 68 no. 2 (May), 1-16.

SIMON, H.A. (1978b): On how to decide what to do; Bell Journal of
Economics 9 no. 2 (Autumn), 494-507.

SIMS, C.A. (1972): Money, income, and causality; American Economic Review 62 no. 4 (September), 540-552.

SIMS, C.A. (1979): Macro-economics and reality; Econometrica,
forthcoming.

SJAASTAD, L.A. (1976): Why stable inflations fail: an essay in
political economy; in: J.M. Parkin and G. Zis (eds.):
Inflation in the world economy; Manchester: Manchester
University Press, 73-86.

SMYTH, D.J. and J.C.K. ASH (1975): Forecasting gross national
product, the rate of inflation, and the balance of trade:
the O.E.C.D. performance; Economic Journal 85 no. 2 (June),
361-364.

STEIN, J.L. (1978): Inflation, employment and stagflation;
Journal of Monetary Economics 4 no. 2 (April), 193-228.

SWEENEY, R.J. (1978): Efficient information processing in output
markets: tests and implications; Economic Inquiry 16
no. 3 (July), 313-331.

TINBERGEN, J. (1956): Economic policy: principles and design;
Amsterdam: North Holland.

TITMUSS, R.M. (1971): The gift relationship; New York: Pantheon
Books.

VERDOORN, P.J. (1964): The short-term model of the Central Plan-
ning Bureau and its forecasting performance (1953-1963); in:
Macro-economic models for planning and policy-making; New
York: United Nations, no. 67.II.E.3.

VERDOORN, P.J. and J.J. POST (1976): Herschatting jaarmodel - 12;
Unpublished research paper; The Hague: Central Planning
Bureau.

VERDOORN, P.J., J.J. POST and S.S. GOSLINGA (1970): The 1969 re-
estimation of the annual model; The Hague: Central
Planning Bureau.

VICKREY, W. (1977): Economic rationality and social choice; Social
Research 44 no. 4 (Winter), 691-707.

WACHTEL, P. (1977): Survey measures of exptected inflation and
their potential usefulness; in: J. Popkin (ed.): Analysis
of inflation, 1965-1974; Cambridge, Massachusetts: Ballinger
Publishing Company for the N.B.E.R., 361-395.

WALLICH, H.C. (1971): Income velocity; Review of Economics and
Statistics 53 no. 2 (May), 200-201.

WANNISKI, J. (1978): The way the world works; New York: Basic
Books.

WILES, P. (1973): Cost inflation and the state of economic theory;
Economic Journal 83 no. 2 (June), 377-398.

ZARNOWITZ, V. (1978): On the accuracy and properties of recent
macroeconomic forecasts; American Economic Review 68 no. 2
(May), 313-319.

INDEX